The Power of
INTENTION

Other Hay House Products by Dr. Wayne W. Dyer

BOOKS

A New Way of Thinking, A New Way of Being
Being in Balance
Change Your Thoughts—Change Your Life
Everyday Wisdom
Everyday Wisdom for Success
Excuses Begone!
Getting in the Gap (book-with-CD)
Incredible You!
(children's book with Kristina Tracy)
Inspiration
The Invisible Force
It's Not What You've Got!
(children's book with Kristina Tracy)
Living the Wisdom of the Tao
No Excuses!
(children's book with Kristina Tracy)
The Power of Intention
A Promise Is a Promise
The Shift
Staying on the Path
10 Secrets for Success and Inner Peace
Unstoppable Me!
(children's book with Kristina Tracy)
Your Ultimate Calling

AUDIO/CD PROGRAMS

Advancing Your Spirit
(with Marianne Williamson)
*Applying the 10 Secrets for Success
and Inner Peace*
Change Your Thoughts—Change Your Life
(unabridged audio book)
Change Your Thoughts Meditation
Everyday Wisdom (audio book)
Excuses Begone!
(available as an audio book and a lecture)
*How to Get What You Really,
Really, Really, Really Want*
Inspiration (abridged 4-CD set)
Inspirational Thoughts
Making Your Thoughts Work for You
(with Byron Katie)
Meditations for Manifesting

101 Ways to Transform Your Life
(audio book)
The Power of Intention (abridged 4-CD set)
A Promise Is a Promise (audio book)
The Secrets of the Power of Intention
(6-CD set)
10 Secrets for Success and Inner Peace
There Is a Spiritual Solution to Every Problem
*The Wayne Dyer Audio Collection/
CD Collection*
Your Journey to Enlightenment (6-tape program)

DVDs

Change Your Thoughts—Change Your Life
Excuses Begone! (the audio version is also available
as a CD program)
Inspiration
The Power of Intention
The Shift, the movie (available as a 1-DVD program
and an expanded 2-DVD set)
10 Secrets for Success and Inner Peace
There's a Spiritual Solution to Every Problem

MISCELLANEOUS

*Change Your Thoughts—Change Your Life
Perpetual Flip Calendar*
Everyday Wisdom Perpetual Flip Calendar
Inner Peace Cards
Inspiration Cards
Inspiration Perpetual Flip Calendar
The Power of Intention Cards
The Power of Intention Perpetual Flip Calendar
10 Secrets for Success and Inner Peace Cards
10 Secrets for Success and Inner Peace gift
products: *Notecards, Candle,* and *Journal*

All of the above are available at your local bookstore, or may be ordered by visiting:

Hay House USA: **www.hayhouse.com**
Hay House Australia: **www.hayhouse.com.au**
Hay House UK: **www.hayhouse.co.uk**
Hay House South Africa: **www.hayhouse.co.za**
Hay House India: **www.hayhouse.co.in**

The Power of
INTENTION

Learning to Co-create Your World Your Way

Dr. Wayne W. Dyer

LIFE
Styles

HAY HOUSE, INC.
Carlsbad, California • New York City
London • Sydney • Johannesburg
Vancouver • Hong Kong • New Delhi

Published and distributed in the United States by: Hay House, Inc.: www.hayhouse.com •
Published and distributed in Australia by: Hay House Australia Pty. Ltd.: www.hayhouse.com.au •
Published and distributed in the United Kingdom by: Hay House UK, Ltd.: www.hayhouse.co.uk
• *Published and distributed in the Republic of South Africa by:* Hay House SA (Pty), Ltd.:
www.hayhouse.co.za • *Distributed in Canada by:* Raincoast: www.raincoast.com • *Published
in India by:* Hay House Publishers India: www.hayhouse.co.in

Wayne Dyer's editor: Joanna Pyle • *Editorial supervision:* Jill Kramer • *Design:* Amy Gingery
Illustrated by: Jui Ishida

The poems on pages 96 and 102 are from the Penguin publication *I Heard God Laughing, Rendering of Hafiz,* copyright 1996 & 2006 by Daniel Ladinsky and used with his permission.

Library of Congress Control Number: 2008944378

ISBN: 978-1-4019-2596-3

13 12 11 10   4   3   2   1
1st edition, October 2010

Printed in China

"Every beauty which is seen here below by persons of perception resembles more than anything else that celestial source from which we all come..."
— Michelangelo

"Self-realization means that we have been consciously connected with our source of being. Once we have made this connection, then nothing can go wrong...."
— Swami Paramananda

...

For my daughter Skye Dyer.
Your singing voice is a perfect vibrational
match to your angelic soul.
I love you!

...

Contents

Preface

The book that you're now holding in your hands, and all of the information it contains, was once a formless idea residing in the invisible domain of the field of intention. This book, *The Power of Intention,* was intended into the material world by applying all of the principles written about here. I managed to make my own vibrational energy match up to the all-creating Source, and allowed these words and ideas to flow through me directly to you. You're holding in your hands evidence that anything we can conceive of in our minds—while staying in harmony with the universal all-creating Source—can and must come to pass.

If you'd like to know how this book might impact you and how you might think, feel, and co-create after reading and applying its messages, I encourage you to read the final chapter, *A Portrait of a Person Connected to the Field of Intention,* before beginning this journey. You and everyone else, as well as all of life, emanated from the universal all-creating field of intention. Live from that perspective, and you will come to know and apply the power of intention. You have an endless stream of green lights before you!

— Dr. Wayne W. Dyer
Maui, Hawaii

❖❖❖

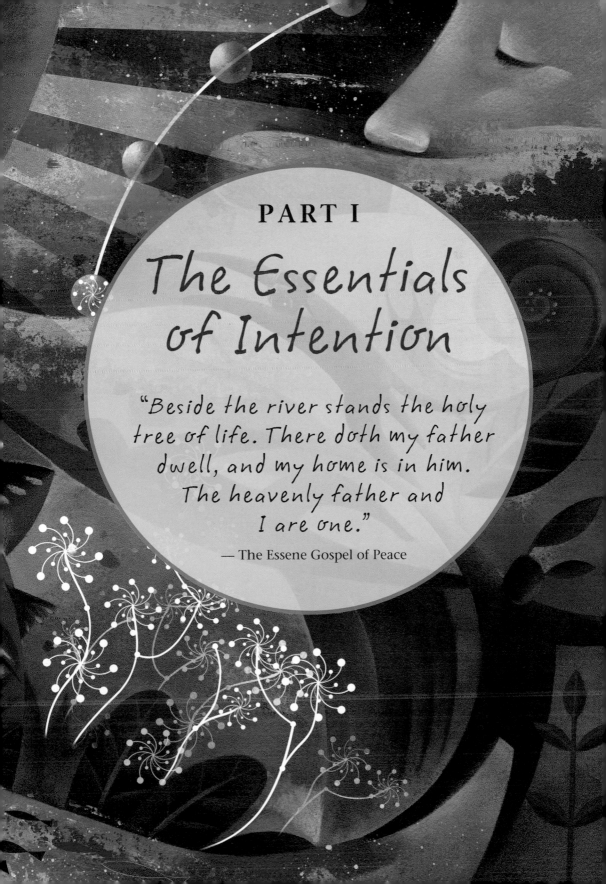

PART I

The Essentials of Intention

"Beside the river stands the holy tree of life. There doth my father dwell, and my home is in him. The heavenly father and I are one."

— The Essene Gospel of Peace

Viewing Intention from a New Perspective

"In the universe there is an immeasurable, indescribable force which shamans call intent, and absolutely everything that exists in the entire cosmos is attached to intent by a connecting link."

— Carlos Castaneda

During the past several years, I've been so strongly attracted to studying *intention* that I've read hundreds of books by psychological, sociological, and spiritual writers; ancient and modern scholars; and academic researchers. My research reveals a fairly common definition of *intention* as a strong purpose or aim, accompanied by a determination to produce a desired result. People driven by intention are described as having a strong will that won't permit anything to interfere with achieving their inner desire. I imagine a sort of pit-bull kind of resolve or determination. If you're one of those people with a never-give-up attitude combined with an internal picture that propels you toward fulfilling your dreams, you fit this description of someone with intention. You are, most likely, a super-achiever and probably proud of your ability to recognize and take advantage of opportunities that arise.

For many years I've held a similar belief about intention. In fact, I've written and spoken often about the power of intention being just what I've described above. Over the past quarter of a century, however, I've felt a shift in my thinking from a purely psychological or personal-growth emphasis, toward a spiritual orientation where healing, creating miracles, manifesting, and making a connection to divine intelligence are genuine possibilities.

This hasn't been a deliberate attempt to disengage from my academic and professional background, but rather a natural evolution that's been unfolding as I began to make more conscious contact with Spirit. My writing now emphasizes a belief that we can find spiritual solutions to problems by living at higher levels and calling upon faster energies. In my mind, intention is now something much greater than a determined ego or individual will. It's something almost totally opposite. Perhaps this comes from shedding many levels of ego in my own life, but I also feel the strong influence of two sentences I read in a book by Carlos Castaneda. In my writing life, I've often come across something in a book that starts a thought germinating in me that ultimately compels me to write a new book. At any rate, I read these two sentences in Castaneda's final book, *The Active Side of Infinity,* while I was waiting to have a cardiac procedure to open one clogged artery leading into my heart that had caused a mild heart attack.

Castaneda's words were: "Intent is a force that exists in the universe. When sorcerers (those who live of the Source) beckon intent, it comes to them and sets up the path for attainment, which means that sorcerers always accomplish what they set out to do."

When I read those two sentences, I was stunned by the insight and clarity it gave me about the power of intention. Imagine that intention is not something *you do,* but rather a force that exists in the universe as an invisible field of energy! I had never considered intention in this way before reading Castaneda's words.

I wrote those two sentences down, and then I had them printed on a card and laminated. I carried the laminated card with me into the catheter lab for my minor surgical procedure, and as soon as I could, I began talking about the power of intention to everyone who would listen. I made intention a part of every speech I gave. I immersed myself in this idea to use it, not only for my own healing, but to help others use the power of intention to carry them where they're fully equipped to go. I had experienced *satori,* or instant awakening, and was intent on offering this insight to others. It had become clear to me that accessing the power of intention relieved so much of the seemingly impossible work of striving to fulfill desires by sheer force of will.

Since that defining moment, I've thought of the power of intention in virtually all of my waking hours—and books, articles, conversations, telephone calls, items arriving in my mailbox, and arbitrary works I might be looking at in a bookstore all seemed to conspire to keep me on this path. So here it is: *The Power of Intention.* I hope this book will help you view intention in a new way and make use of it in a manner that leads you to define yourself as Patanjali suggested more than 20 centuries ago: "Dormant forces, faculties, and talents come alive, and you discover yourself to be a greater person by far than you ever dreamed yourself to be."

Patanjali's two words, "dormant forces," kick-started me in the direction of writing about intention. Patanjali was referring to forces that *appear to be* either nonexistent or dead, *and* he was referring to the powerful energy a person feels when inspired. If you've ever felt inspired by a purpose or calling, you know the feeling of Spirit working through you. *Inspired* is our word for *in-spirited.* I've thought long and hard about the idea of being able to access seemingly dormant forces to assist me at key times in my life to achieve an inner burning desire. What are these forces? Where are they located? Who gets to use them? Who is denied access? And why? Questions like these have propelled me to research and write this book and subsequently arrive at a totally new perspective of intention.

At this point, as I'm writing about my excitement of realizing a long-obscured truth, I *know* that intention is a force that we all have within us. Intention is a field of energy that flows invisibly beyond the reach of our normal, everyday habitual patterns. It's there even before our actual conception. We have the means to attract this energy to us and experience life in an exciting new way.

Where Is This Field Called Intention?

Some prominent researchers believe that our intelligence, creativity, and imagination interact with the energy field of intention rather than being thoughts or elements in our brain. The brilliant scientist David Bohm, writing in *Wholeness and the Implicate Order,* suggested that all ordering influence and information is present in an invisible domain or higher reality and can be called upon in times of need. I found thousands of examples of these kinds of conclusions in the research and reading I did. If scientific evidence appeals to you, I suggest that you read *The Field: The Quest for the Secret Force of the Universe* by Lynne McTaggart. Her book is filled with studies supporting the existence of a higher, faster energy dimension or field of intention that can be tapped in to and used by everyone.

The answer to *Where is this field?* is: *There's no place that it's not,* because everything in the universe has intention built into it. This is true for all life forms, whether it be a wildebeest, a rosebush, or a mountain. A mosquito has intent built into its creation and life experience. A tiny acorn with no apparent power to think or make plans for its future contains intention from the invisible field. If you cut the acorn open, you won't see a giant oak tree, but you know it's there. An apple blossom in the springtime appears to be a pretty little flower, yet it has intent built into it and will manifest in the summer as an apple. Intention doesn't err. The acorn never turns into a pumpkin, or the apple blossom into an orange. Every aspect of nature, without exception, has intention built into it, and as far as we can tell, nothing in nature questions its path of intent. Nature simply progresses in harmony from the field of intention. We, too, are *intended* from the energy of this field. There is what some call a *future-pull* in the DNA that's present at conception in each of us. In the moment of our conception, when an infinitely tiny drop of human protoplasm combines with an egg, life in physical form begins, and intention directs the growth process. Our body structure, the shape of our physical features, our development, including our aging, are intended in that one moment of conception. The sagging skin, the wrinkles, and even our death are all there. But wait, what exactly happens at the moment of conception? Where did this life, born of intention, begin?

As we examine that seed/egg dance attempting to discover its origin, moving backwards toward Creation, we first find molecules, then atoms, then electrons, then subatomic particles, and then sub-subatomic particles. Ultimately, were we to put these tiny quantum subatomic particles into a particle accelerator and collide them, trying to put our finger on the source of life, we'd discover what Einstein and his scientific compatriots discovered: There's no particle at the source; particles do not create more particles. The Source, which is intention, is pure, unbounded energy vibrating so fast that it defies measurement and observation. It's invisible, without form or boundaries. So, at our Source, we are formless energy, and in that formless vibrating spiritual field of energy, intention resides. On a lighter note, *I know* it's there, since somehow it managed to get into a drop of sperm and an ovarian egg and determine that my hair will no longer grow on my head after 25 years . . . and in 50 years, it will grow in my nose and ears, and all I (the observer) can do is watch it and snip it away!

This field of intent can't be described with words, for the words emanate from the field, just as do the questions. That placeless place is intention, and it handles everything for us. It grows my fingernails, it beats my heart, it digests my food, it writes my books, and it does this for everyone and everything in the universe. This reminds me of an ancient Chinese story I love, told by Chuang Tzu:

There once was a one-legged dragon called Hui. "How on earth do you manage those legs?" he asked a centipede. "I can hardly manage one!"

"Matter of fact," said the centipede, "I do not manage my legs."

There's a field, invisible and formless, that manages it all. The intention of this universe is manifested in zillions of ways in the physical world, and every part of you, including your soul, your thoughts, your emotions, and of course the physical body that you occupy, are a part of this intent. So, if intention determines everything in the universe and is omnipresent, meaning there's no place that it's not, then why do so many of us feel disconnected from it so frequently? And even more important, if intention determines everything, then why do so many of us lack so much of what we'd like to have?

The Meaning of Omnipresent Intention

Try imagining a force that's everywhere. There's no place that you can go where it isn't. It can't be divided and is present in everything you see or touch. Now extend your awareness of this infinite field of energy beyond the world of form and boundaries. This infinite invisible force is everywhere, so it's in both the physical and the non-physical. Your physical body is one part of your totality emanating from this energy. At the instant of conception, *intention* sets in motion how your physical form will appear and how your growing and aging process will unfold. It also sets in motion your nonphysical aspects, including your emotions, thoughts, and disposition. In this instance, *intention is infinite potential activating your physical and nonphysical appearance on Earth.* You've formed out of the omnipresent to become present in time and space. Because it's omnipresent, this energy field of intent is accessible to you after your physical arrival here on Earth! The only way you deactivate this *dormant force* is by believing that you're separate from it.

Activating intention means rejoining your Source and becoming a modern-day sorcerer. Being a sorcerer means attaining the level of awareness where previously inconceivable things are available. As Carlos Castaneda explained, "The task of sorcerers was to face infinity" *(intention),* "and they plunged into it daily, as a fisherman plunges into the sea." Intention is a power that's present everywhere as a field of energy; it isn't limited to physical development. It's the source of nonphysical development, too. This field of intention is here, now, and available to you. When you activate it, you'll begin to feel purpose in your life, and you'll be guided by your infinite self. Here's how a poet and a spiritual teacher describes what I'm calling intention:

> *O Lord, thou art on the sandbanks*
> *As well as in the midst of the current;*
> *I bow to thee.*
> *Thou art in the little pebbles*
> *As well as in the calm expanse of the sea;*
> *I bow to thee.*
> *O all-pervading Lord,*
> *Thou art in the barren soil*
> *And in the crowded places;*
> *I bow to thee.*

— from *Veda XVI* by Sukla Yajur

As *you* make your metaphorical bow to this power, recognize that you're bowing to yourself. The all-pervading energy of intention pulses through you toward your potential for a purposeful life.

How You Came to Experience Yourself as Disconnected from Intention

If there's an omnipresent power of intention that's not only within me, but in everything and everyone, then we're connected by this all-pervading Source to everything and everyone, and to what we'd like to be, what we'd like to have, what we want to achieve, and to everything in the universe that will assist us. All that's required is realigning ourselves and activating intention. But how did we get disconnected in the first place? How did we lose our natural ability to connect? Lions, fish, and birds don't get disconnected. The animal, vegetable, and mineral worlds are always connected to their Source. They don't question their intention. We humans, however, with our capability for presumably higher brain functions, have something we refer to as *ego,* which is an idea that we construct about who and what we are.

Ego is made of six primary ingredients that account for how we experience ourselves as disconnected. By allowing ego to determine your life path, you deactivate the power of intention. Briefly, here are the six ego beliefs. I've written more extensively about them in several of my previous books, most notably *Your Sacred Self.*

1. *I am what I have.* My possessions define me.

2. *I am what I do.* My achievements define me.

3. *I am what others think of me.* My reputation defines me.

4. *I am separate from everyone. My body defines me as alone.*

5. *I am separate from all that is missing in my life.* My life space is disconnected from my desires.

6. *I am separate from God.* My life depends on God's assessment of my worthiness.

No matter how hard you try, intention can't be accessed through ego, so take some time to recognize and readjust any or all of these six beliefs. When the supremacy of ego is weakened in your life, you can seek intention and maximize your potential.

Holding on to the Trolley Strap

This is a practice I find exceedingly helpful when I want to activate intention. You may find that it works for you, too. (See Chapter 3 for an entire chapter describing ways to access intention.)

One of my earliest memories is my mother taking her three boys on the streetcar on the east side of Detroit to Waterworks Park. I was two or three years old, and I recall looking up from the seat and seeing the hand straps hanging down. The grown-ups were able to hold on to the straps, but all I could do was imagine what it would be like to be so tall as to grab those straps way above my head. I actually pretended that I was light enough to float up to the hanging handles. I then imagined feeling safe and the trolley taking me where it was destined to go, at whatever speed it chose, picking up other passengers to go along on this glorious adventure of streetcar riding.

In my adult life, I use the image of the trolley strap to remind myself to get back to intention. I imagine a strap hanging down about three to four feet above my head, higher than I'm capable of reaching or jumping up to grab. The strap is attached to the trolley, only now the trolley symbolizes a flowing power of intention. I've either let go of it or it's just out of my reach temporarily. In moments of stress, anxiety, worry, or even physical discomfort, I close my eyes and imagine my arm reaching up, and then I see myself float up to the trolley strap. As I grab the strap, I have an enormous feeling of relief and comfort. What I've done is eliminate ego thoughts and allow myself to reach intention, and I trust this power to take me to my destination, stopping when necessary, and picking up companions along the way.

In some of my earlier works, I've called this process the *pathway to mastery*. The four pathways may be helpful to you here as steps toward activating intention.

Four Steps to Intention

Activating your power of intention is a process of connecting with your natural self and letting go of total ego identification. The process takes place in four stages:

1. **Discipline** is the first stage. Learning a new task requires training your body to perform as your thoughts desire. So, eliminating ego identification doesn't mean disconnecting from your relationship with your body, but rather, training your body to activate those desires. You do that with practice, exercise, nontoxic habits, healthy foods, and so on.

2. **Wisdom** is the second stage. Wisdom combined with discipline fosters your ability to focus and be patient as you harmonize your thoughts, your intellect, and your feelings with the work of your body. We send children off to school telling them: *Be disciplined* and *Use your head,* and call this education, but it falls short of mastery.

3. **Love** is the third stage. After disciplining the body with wisdom, and intellectually studying a task, this process of mastery involves loving what you do and doing what you love. In the world of sales, I call it falling in love with what you're offering, and then selling your love or enthusiasm to potential customers. When learning to play tennis, it involves practicing all of the strokes while studying strategies for playing the game. It also involves enjoying the feeling of hitting the ball and of being on the tennis court—and everything else about the game.

4. **Surrender** is the fourth stage. This is the place of intention. This is where your body and your mind aren't running the show and you move into intent. "In the universe there is an immeasurable, indescribable force which shamans call intent, and absolutely everything that exists

in the entire cosmos is attached to intent by a connecting link," is the way Carlos Castaneda describes it. You relax, grab the trolley strap, and allow yourself to be carried by the same power that turns acorns into trees, blossoms into apples, and microscopic dots into humans. So grab that trolley strap and create your own unique connecting link. *Absolutely everything in the entire cosmos* includes you and your disciplined, wise, loving self, and all of your thoughts and feelings. When you surrender, you lighten up and can consult with your infinite soul. Then the power of intention becomes available to take you wherever you feel destined to go.

All of this talk of intention and surrender may cause you to question where your free will fits in. You might be inclined to conclude that free will is nonexistent or that you become whatever your program dictates. So, let's take a look at your will and how it fits into this new view of intention. As you read the next two sections, please keep an open mind, even if what you read conflicts with what you've believed all your life!

Intention and Your Free Will Are Paradoxical

A paradox is a seemingly absurd or contradictory statement, even if well founded. *Intention* and *free will* certainly qualify as being paradoxical. They conflict with many a preconceived notion of what's reasonable or possible. How can you possess free will and also have intention shaping your body and your potential? You can fuse this dichotomy by choosing to believe in the infinity of intention *and* in your capacity to exercise free will. You know how to think rationally about the rules of cause and effect, so try your intellect on this.

Obviously, it's impossible to have two infinites, for then neither would be infinite; each would be limited by the other. You can't divide *infinite* into parts. Essentially, infinite is unity, continuity, or oneness, like the air in your home. Where does the air in your kitchen stop and the air in your living room begin? Where does the air inside your home stop and the air outside start? How about the air you breathe in and out? Air may be the closest we can come to understanding the infinite, universal, omnipresent Spirit. Somehow, you must travel in thought beyond the idea of your individual existence to the idea of a unity of universal being, and then beyond this to the idea of a universal energy. When you think of part of a whole being in one place and part in another, you've lost the idea of unity. And (keeping an open mind as I beseeched you earlier), get this! At any moment in time, all Spirit is concentrated at the point where you focus your attention. Therefore, *you* can consolidate all creative energy at a given moment in time. *This is your free will at work.*

Your mind and your thoughts are also thoughts of the divine mind. Universal Spirit is in your thoughts *and* in your free will. When you shift your thoughts from Spirit to ego, you seem to lose contact with the power of intention. Your free will can either move *with* Universal Spirit and its unfolding, or *away* from it toward ego dominance. As it moves away from Spirit, life appears to be a struggle. Slower energies flow through you, and you may feel hopeless, helpless, and lost. You can use your free will to rejoin higher, faster energies. The truth is that *we* do not create anything alone; we are all creatures with God. Our free will combines and redistributes what's already created. *You choose!* Free will means that you have the choice to connect to Spirit or not!

So, the answer to the questions, *Do I have a free will?* and *Is intention working with me as an all-pervasive universal force?* is *Yes*. Can you live with this paradox? If you think about it, you live with paradox in every moment of your existence. At the exact same instant that you're a body with beginnings and ends, with boundaries, and a definition in time and space, you're also an invisible, formless, unlimited, thinking and feeling being. A ghost in the machine, if you will. Which are you? Matter or essence? Physical or metaphysical? Form or spirit? The answer is *both*, even though they appear to be opposites. Do you have a free will, and are you a part of the destiny of intention? *Yes*. Fuse the dichotomy. Blend the opposites, and live with both of these beliefs. Begin the process of allowing Spirit to work with you, and link up to the field of intention.

At Intention, Spirit Will Work for You!

With your free will consciously deciding to reconnect to the power of intention, you're altering its direction. You'll begin to feel pleasant recognition and reverence for the unity of Spirit and yourself as an individual concentration of it. I silently repeat the word *intent* or *intention* to help me get my ego and my self-absorption out of the picture. I think often of this quote from Castaneda's *Power of Silence:* "Having lost hope of ever returning to the source of everything, the average man seeks solace in his selfishness." For me, personally, I attempt to return to the source of everything on a daily basis, and I refuse to be the "average man" that Castaneda describes.

Many years ago I decided to give up drinking alcohol. I wanted to experience continuous sobriety to improve my ability to do the work that I felt was burning inside of me. I felt called upon to teach self-reliance through my writing and speaking. Several teachers had told me that complete sobriety was a prerequisite for the work I was called to do. In the early stages of this dramatic life change, a power seemed to help me when I was tempted to return to my old habits of having a few beers each evening. On one occasion, in my state of wavering, I actually went out to purchase a six-pack but forgot to bring money with me. I *never* forget to take cash with me!

In the few minutes it took me to return home and retrieve the cash, I reevaluated the free will that would allow me to buy beer, and chose to stay with my intention. I found, as the first weeks passed, that these kinds of events started occurring with regularity. I'd be guided by circumstances that led me away from situations where drinking was a temptation. A telephone call might distract me from a tempting situation; a family minicrisis would erupt and deter me from a potential slip. Today, a couple of decades later, it's clear to me that a firm handle on that trolley strap I described earlier allows me to be whisked along my path to destinations invoked eons ago by intention. And I also see that my free will is a paradoxical partner of the power of intention.

My awareness of intention as a power for me to reconnect to, rather than something my ego must accomplish, has made a huge difference in my life's work. The simple awareness that my writing and speaking are manifested from the field of intention has been of immeasurable benefit to me. I'm awed by the creative energy when I get my self-importance and ego identification out of the way. Before taking the microphone, I send ego to the lobby or tell it to have a seat in the audience. I repeat the word *intent* to myself and feel myself floating up to this energy field of intention. I surrender and allow, and I find myself completely at ease, remembering tiny details in the midst of my speech, never losing my way, and experiencing the unique connection that's occurring with the audience. Fatigue dissolves, hunger disappears—even the need to pee vanishes! Everything that's necessary for delivering the message seems almost effortlessly available.

Combining Free Will with Intention

In mathematics, two angles that are said to *coincide* fit together perfectly. The word *coincidence* does not describe luck or mistakes. It describes that which *fits together perfectly*. By combining free will with intention, you harmonize with the universal mind. Rather than operating in your own mind outside of this force called intention, your goal may very well be, as you read this book, to work at being in harmony at all times with intention. When life appears to be working against you, when your luck is down, when the supposedly wrong people show up, or when you slip up and return to old, self-defeating habits, recognize the signs that you're out of harmony with intention. You can and will reconnect in a way that will bring you into alignment with your own purpose.

For example, when I write, I open myself to the possibilities of universal Spirit and my own individual thoughts collaborating with fate to produce a helpful, insightful book. But as I reconsidered my account of leaving alcohol behind me, I wanted *another* example to put in this chapter of how intention collaborates with life circumstances to produce what we need.

Recently my 19-year-old daughter, Sommer, told me that she'd quit her temporary job as a restaurant hostess and wasn't sure what she wanted to do before resuming her college studies. I asked her what made her feel most purposeful and happy, and she said it was teaching horseback riding to young children, but she refused to return to the old barn where she'd worked a year before because she felt unappreciated, overworked, and underpaid.

I was in Maui writing this first chapter on a new perspective on intention when we had this telephone conversation. I launched into my intention-as-a-force-in-the-universe spiel and told my daughter that she needed to realign her thoughts, and so on. "Open up to receiving the assistance you desire," I told her. "Trust in intention. It exists for you. Stay alert, and be willing to accept any guidance that comes your way. Stay in vibrational harmony with the all-providing Source."

The next day, at the very moment I was searching for that additional example of intention to put into this chapter, the telephone rang, and it was Sommer, bubbling with enthusiasm. "You're not going to believe this, Dad. On second thought, I'm sure you'll believe it. Remember yesterday how you told me to be open to intention? I was skeptical, even thinking, *That's my weird dad,* but I decided to try it. Then I saw a sign on a telephone pole that said *Horseback-Riding Lessons* and there was a telephone number. I wrote the number down and just called it. The woman who answered told me that she needed to hire someone she could trust to do trail rides with young kids. She pays exactly double what I was making at the restaurant. I'm going out to see her tomorrow. Isn't that cool?!"

Cool? Hell yes, it's cool! Here I am writing a book, looking for a good example, and it arrives in the form of help I was attempting to offer the day before to my daughter. Two for the price of one!

*Merging Your Individual Thoughts
with the Universal Mind*

Our individual thoughts create a prototype in the universal mind of intention. You and your power of intention are not separate. So, when you form a thought within you that's commensurate with Spirit, you form a spiritual prototype that connects you to intention and sets into motion the manifestation of your desires. Whatever you wish to accomplish is an existing fact, already present in Spirit. Eliminate from your mind thoughts of conditions, limitations, or the possibility of it not manifesting. If left undisturbed in your mind and in the mind of intention simultaneously, it will germinate into reality in the physical world.

In simpler words, "All things whatsoever ye pray and ask for, believe that ye have received them, and ye shall receive them" [Mark 11:24]. In this scriptural quotation, you are told to believe that your desire has already been fulfilled, and then it will be accomplished. Know that your thought or prayer is already here. Remove all doubt so that you create a harmonious thought with universal mind or intention. When you know this beyond doubt, it will be realized in the future. This is the power of intention at work.

I'll close this section with words from Aldous Huxley, one of my favorite authors: "The spiritual journey does not consist in arriving at a new destination where a person gains what he did not have, or becomes what he is not. It consists in the dissipation of one's own ignorance concerning one's self and life, and the gradual growth of that understanding which begins the spiritual awakening. The finding of God is a coming to one's self."

❖ ❖ ❖

In this first chapter, I've asked you to stop doubting the existence of a universal, omnipresent force I've called intention, and told you that you can link to and be carried to your destination on the energy of intention. Here are my suggestions for putting this to work in your life.

Five Suggestions for Implementing the Ideas in This Chapter

1. *Whenever you feel out of sorts, lost, or even in a sour mood, visualize the trolley strap hanging down from the field of intention three or four feet above your head.* Imagine floating up and allowing the trolley to carry you to your built-in intention. This is a tool for implementing surrender in your life.

2. *Say the word* intent *or* intention *repeatedly when you're in a state of anxiety or when everything around you seems to have conspired to keep you from your mission.* This is a reminder to be peaceful and calm. Intention is spirit, and spirit is silently blissful.

3. *Tell yourself that you have a life mission and a silent partner who's accessible at any moment you choose.* When ego defines you by what you have or do, or compares you to others, use your power of free will to terminate those thoughts. Say to yourself, "I'm here on purpose, I can accomplish anything I desire, and I do it by being in harmony with the all-pervading creative force in the universe." This will become an automatic way of responding to life. Synchronistic results will begin to happen.

4. *Act as if anything you desire is already here.* Believe that all that you seek you've already received, that it exists in spirit, and know you shall have your desires filled. One of my ten secrets for success and inner peace is to *treat yourself as if you already are what you'd like to become.*

5. *Copy this ancient Hasidic saying and carry it with you for a year.* It's a reminder of the power of intention and how it can work for you every day in every way.

> *When you walk across the fields with your mind pure and holy,*
> *then from all the stones, and all growing things, and all animals,*
> *the sparks of their soul come out and cling to you, and then*
> *they are purified and become a holy fire in you.*

In the next chapter, I describe how this field of intention might look were you able to see it, and what the *faces of intention* look like. I'll close this chapter with another quotation from Carlos Castaneda's teacher, don Juan Matus: " . . . the spirit reveals itself to everyone with the same intensity and consistency, but only warriors are consistently attuned to such revelations."

Readers and warriors alike, proceed in the spirit of free will to access the power of intention.

The Seven Faces of Intention

"Four thousand volumes of metaphysics
will not teach us what the soul is."

— Voltaire

Moving from Thinking about
Intention to Knowing Intention

Yesterday, while writing this book here on Maui, I experienced a *knowing* that I'll attempt to explain to you. A woman from Japan was pulled from the surf, her body bloated from an excessive intake of seawater. I knelt over her, with others, attempting to get her heartbeat going with CPR, while many of her friends from Japan cried out in anguish as the futile attempts at resuscitation proceeded. Suddenly I felt a quiet awareness of this woman's spirit hovering above our lifesaving attempts. As I watched the rescue scene on the beach, I felt the presence of blissfully peaceful energy, and in some unfathomable way I knew that she wasn't going to be revived and that she was no longer connected to the body that so many well-meaning people, including myself, were trying to bring back to life.

This quiet knowing led me to stand up, put my hands together, and say a silent prayer for her. We were from different parts of this world and didn't even share a common language, yet I felt connected to her. I felt peaceful, with a knowing that her spirit and mine were somehow connected in the mystery of the transient/ephemeral nature of our physical lives.

As I walked away, the pain of death wasn't dominating my thoughts. Instead, I knew and felt that the departure of this woman's spirit from what was now a lifeless, bloated body was inexplicably all a part of perfect divine order. I couldn't prove it. I had no scientific evidence. I didn't think it—I *knew* it. This is an example of what I mean by *silent knowledge*. I still feel her presence as I write this, 24 hours later. In *Power of Silence,* Carlos Castaneda describes silent knowledge as "something that all of us have. Something that has complete mastery, complete knowledge of everything. But it cannot think, therefore it cannot speak of what it knows. . . . Man has given up silent knowledge for the world of reason. The more he clings to the world of reason, the more ephemeral intent becomes."

Since intention is being presented in this book as an invisible energy field that is inherent in all physical form, intention, then, is a part of the inexplicable, nonmaterial world of Spirit. Spirit eludes our attempts to explain and define it because it's a dimension beyond beginnings and ends, beyond boundaries, beyond symbols, and beyond form itself. Consequently, written and spoken words, our symbols for communicating our experiences in this world, can't really explain Spirit the way they do the physical world.

I agree with Voltaire's statement at the beginning of this chapter and readily admit that I can't definitively teach anyone what Spirit is or use words that give a precise picture of what it looks like. What I *can* do is describe a way that I conceptualize intention—if it were somehow possible to remove the veil that keeps the field of intention from our sensory perception and reasoning mind. I'll give you my concept of what I refer to as the *seven faces of intention.* These points represent my imagined picture of what the power of intention looks like.

Intention is something that I believe we can feel, connect with, know, and trust. It's an inner awareness that we explicitly feel, and yet at the same time cannot truly describe with words. I use this concept to help guide me toward the power of intention that's the source of creation, and activate it in my daily life. It's my hope that you too will begin to recognize what you personally need to do to begin activating intention in your life. The descriptions that follow are distilled from my experience with master teachers, my professional work with others over the past 30 years, the veritable library of metaphysical books I've read and studied, and my personal evolution. I'm attempting to convey my personal knowing of the extraordinary benefits of linking to intention. Hopefully *you* will feel inspired by the *silent knowing* of the power of intention and go on to create an increasingly enchanted experience for yourself and everyone else in your life.

Silent knowledge starts when you invite the power of intention to play an active part in your life. This is a private and very personal choice that needn't be explained or defended. When you make this inner choice, silent knowledge will gradually become a part of your normal, everyday awareness. Opening to the power of intention, you begin *knowing* that conception, birth, and death are all natural aspects of the energy field of creation. Clinging to attempts to think or reason your way to intention is futile. By banishing doubt and trusting your intuitive feelings, you clear a space for the power of intention to flow through. This may sound like hocus-pocus, but I prefer to think of it as emptying my mind and entering the heart of mystery. Here, I set aside rational thoughts and open to the magic and excitement of an illuminating new awareness.

A great teacher in my life named J. Krishnamurti once observed: "To be empty, completely empty, is not a fearsome thing; it is absolutely essential for the mind to be unoccupied; to be empty, unenforced, for then only can it move into unknown depths."

Take a moment right now to put this book down and allow yourself to trust and gently experience an awareness of your non-physical self. First, close your eyes and empty your mind of rational thoughts and the multitudinous ever-changing chatter that goes on. Next, hit the delete button every time doubt appears. Finally, open to the emptiness. Then you can begin to discover how to silently know the power of intention. (In the following chapter, I'll discuss in more depth other ways to access and reconnect to intention.)

But now, I'll describe what I think our view might be if we could be outside of ourselves, floating above our body, like the spirit of the Japanese lady on the beach yesterday. From this perspective, I imagine myself looking at the faces of intention through eyes that are capable of seeing higher vibrations.

The Seven Faces of Intention

1. The face of creativity. The first of the seven faces of intention is the creative expression of the power of intention that designed us, got us here, and created an environment that's compatible with our needs. The power of intention has to be creative or nothing would come into existence. It seems to me that this is an irrefutable truth about intention/spirit, because its purpose is to bring life into existence in a suitable environment. Why do I conclude that the life-giving power of intention *intends* us to have life, and have it in increasing abundance? Because, if the opposite were true, life as we know it couldn't come into form.

The very fact that we can breathe and experience life is proof to me that the nature of the life-giving Spirit is creative at its core. This may seem obvious to you, or in fact it may appear confusing, or even irrelevant. But what *is* clear is: You are here in your physical body; there was a time when you were an embryo, before that a seed, and before that formless energy. That formless energy contained intention, which brought you from *no where* to *now here*. At the very highest levels of awareness, intention started you on a path toward your destiny. The face of creativity intends you toward continued creativity to create and co-create anything

26

that you direct your power of intention toward. Creative energy is a part of you; it originates in the life-giving Spirit that *intends* you.

2.   **The face of kindness.** Any power that has, as its inherent nature, the need to create and convert energy into physical form must also be a kindly power. Again, I'm deducing this from the opposite. If the all-giving power of intention had at its core the desire to be unkind, malevolent, or hurtful, then creation itself would be impossible. The moment unkind energy became form, the life-giving Spirit would be destroyed. Instead, the power of intention has a face of kindness. It is kind energy intending what it's creating to flourish and grow, and to be happy and fulfilled. Our existence is proof to me of the kindness of intention. Choosing to be kind is a choice to have the power of intention active in your life.

The positive effect of kindness on the immune system and on the increased production of serotonin in the brain has been proven in research studies. Serotonin is a naturally occurring substance in the body that makes us feel more comfortable, peaceful, and even blissful. In fact, the role of most antidepressants is to stimulate the production of serotonin chemically, helping to ease depression. Research has shown that a simple act of kindness directed toward another improves the functioning of the immune system and stimulates the production of serotonin in both the recipient of the kindness and the person extending the kindness. Even more amazing is that persons observing the act of kindness have similar beneficial results. Imagine this! Kindness extended, received, or observed beneficially impacts the physical health and feelings of everyone involved! Both the face of kindness and the face of creativity are smiling here.

When you're unkind, you're blocking the face of kindness. You're moving away from the power of intention. No matter whether you call it God, Spirit, Source, or intention, be aware that unkind thoughts weaken, and kind thoughts strengthen, your connection. Creativity and kindness are two of the seven faces of intention.

3. The face of love. The third of the seven faces of intention is the face of love. That there's a life-giving nature inherent in the power of intention is an irrefutable conclusion. What would we name this quality that encourages, enhances, and supports all of life, if not love? It's the prime moving power of the Universal Spirit of intent. As Ralph Waldo Emerson put it: "Love is our highest word and the synonym for God."

The energy field of intention is pure love resulting in a nurturing and totally cooperative environment. Judgment, anger, hate, fear, or prejudice won't thrive here. So, were we able to actually see this field, we'd see creativity and kindness in an endless field of love. We entered the physical world of boundaries and beginnings through the universal force field of pure love. This face of intention that is an expression of love wishes only for us to flourish and grow, and become all that we're capable of becoming. When we're not in harmony with the energy of love, we've moved away from intention and weakened our ability to activate intention through the expression of love. For example, if you aren't doing what you love and loving what you do, your power of intention is weakened. You attract into your life more of the dissatisfaction that isn't the face of love. Consequently, more of what you don't love will appear in your life.

Thoughts and emotions are pure energy; some higher and faster than others. When higher energies occupy the same field as lower energies, the lower energies convert to higher energies. A simple example of this is a darkened room that has lower energy than a room bathed in light. Since light moves faster than non-light, when a candle is brought into a dark room, the darkness not only dissolves and disappears, but it seems magically converted into light. The same is true of love, which is a higher/faster energy than the energy of hate.

St. Francis, in his famous prayer, beseeches God: "Where there is hatred, let me sow love." What he is seeking is the power to dissolve and ultimately convert hate to the energy of love. Hate converts to love when the energy of love is in its presence. This is true for you, too. Hate, directed toward yourself

28

or others, can be converted to the life-giving, love-granting life force of intention. Pierre Teilhard de Chardin put it this way: "The conclusion is always the same: Love is the most powerful and still the most unknown energy of the world."

4. The face of beauty. The fourth of my seven faces of intention is the face of beauty. What else could a creative, kind, and loving expression be, other than beautiful? Why would the organizing intelligence of intention ever elect to manifest into form anything that's repugnant to itself? Obviously, it wouldn't. So we can conclude that the nature of intention has an eternal interaction of love and beauty, and add the expression of beauty to the face of a creative, kind, loving power of intention.

John Keats, the brilliant young romantic poet, concludes his *Ode on a Grecian Urn* with: "'Beauty is truth, truth beauty,' that is all/ Ye know on earth, and all ye need to know." Obviously truth exists in the creation of everything. It's true that it shows up here in form. It's now here in a form that's an expression of the invisible creative power. So, I agree with Keats that we need to *silently know* that truth and beauty are one and the same. Out of the truth of the originating spirit in an expression of the power of intention comes truth as beauty. This *knowing* leads to valuable insights in relation to exercising your individual will, imagination, and intuition.

In order to grasp the significance of beauty as one of the faces of intention, remember this: *Beautiful thoughts build a beautiful soul.* As you become receptive to seeing and feeling beauty around you, you're becoming attuned to the creative power of intention within everything in the natural world, including yourself. By choosing to see beauty in everything, even a person who was born into poverty and ignorance will be able to experience the power of intention. Seeking beauty in the worst of circumstances with individual intent connects one to the power of intention. It works. It has to work. The face of beauty is always present, even where others see non-beauty.

I was deeply honored to be on a panel with Viktor Frankl in 1978 in Vienna, Austria. I strongly recollect that he shared with me and the audience his assertion that it's the ability to see beauty in all of life's circumstances that gives our lives meaning. In his book *Man's Search for Meaning,* he describes a bowl of filthy water with a fish head floating in it, given to him by his Nazi captors in a concentration camp during WWII. He trained himself to see beauty in this meal, rather than focus on the horror of it. He attributed his ability to see beauty anywhere as a vital factor in surviving those horrific camps. He reminds us that if we focus on what's ugly, we attract more ugliness into our thoughts, and then into our emotions, and ultimately into our lives. By choosing to hang on to one's corner of freedom even in the worst situations, we can process our world with the energy of appreciation and beauty, and create an opportunity to transcend our circumstances.

I love the way Mother Teresa described this quality when she was asked, "What do you do every day in the streets of Calcutta at your mission?" She responded, "Every day I see Jesus Christ in all of his distressing disguises."

5. The face of expansion. The elemental nature of life is to increase and seek more and more expression. If we could sharply focus on the faces of intention, we'd be startled. I imagine that one of the faces we'd see is a continuously expanding expression of the power of intention. The nature of this creative spirit is always operating so as to expand. Spirit is a forming power. It has the principle of increase, meaning that life continues to expand toward more life. Life as we know it originates from formless intention. Therefore, one of the faces of intention looks like something that's eternally evolving. It might look like a tiny speck in a continuous state of duplicating itself, and then enlarging itself, and then moving forward, all the while continuing its expansion and expression.

This is precisely what's happening in our physical world. This fifth face of intention takes the form of what is expressing it. It can be no other way, for if this ever-expanding force disliked itself or felt unconnected, it could only destroy itself. But it doesn't work that way. The power of intention manifests as an expression of expanding creativity, kindness, love, and beauty. By establishing your personal relation to this face of intention, you expand your life through the power of intention, which was, is, and always will be, a component of this originating intention.

The power of intention is the power to expand and increase all aspects of your life. No exceptions! It's the nature of intention to be in a state of increased expression, so it's true for you, too.

The only proviso to this forward movement of intention is to cooperate with it everywhere and allow this spirit of increase to express itself through you and for you, and for everyone you encounter. Then you will have no worry or anxiety. Trust the face of expansion and do what you do because you're loving what you do and doing what you love. Know that expansive, beneficial results are the only possibilities.

6. **The face of unlimited abundance.** This sixth face of intention is an expression of something that has no boundaries, is everywhere at once, and is endlessly abundant. It's not just huge, it never stops. This marvelous gift of abundance is what you were created from. Thus you too share this in the expression of your life. You're actually fulfilling the law of abundance. These gifts are given freely and fully to you just as the air, the sun, the water, and the atmosphere are provided in unlimited abundance for you.

From the time of your earliest memories, you probably were taught to think in terms of limitations. *My property starts here. Yours over there.* So we build fences to mark our boundaries. But ancient explorers gave us an awareness of the world as potentially endless. Even more ancient astronomers pushed back our beliefs about an immense dome-shaped ceiling covering the earth. We've learned about galaxies that are measured in the distance light travels in a year. Science books that are only two years old are outdated. Athletic records that supposedly demonstrated the limits of our physical prowess are shattered with amazing regularity.

What all this means is that there are no limits to our potential as people, as collective entities, and as individuals. This is largely true because we emanate from the unlimited abundance of intention. If the face of the power of intention is unlimited abundance, then we can know that our potential for manifestation and attracting anything into our lives is the same. The face of abundance has absolutely no limits. Imagine the vastness of the resources from which all objects are created. Then consider the one resource that stands above all others. This would be your mind and the collective mind of humankind. Where does your mind begin and end? What are its boundaries? Where is it located? More important, where is it not located? Is it born with you, or is it present before your conception? Does it die with you? What color is it? What shape? The answers are in the phrase *unlimited abundance*. You were created from this very same unlimited abundance. The power of intention is everywhere. It is what allows everything to manifest, to increase, and to supply infinitely.

Know that you're connected to this life force and that you share it with everyone and all that you perceive to be missing. Open to the expression of the face of unlimited abundance, and you'll be co-creating your life as you'd like it to be. As is so often true, the poets can express in a few short words what seems so difficult for us to grasp. Here is Walt Whitman speaking to us in *Song of Myself*. As you read these lines, substitute *the face of endless abundance* for *God* to gain a flavor of what the power of intention is.

> I hear and behold God in every object, yet understand
>   God not in the least . . .
> I see something of God each hour of the twenty-four,
>   and each moment then,
> In the faces of men and women I see God, and
>   in my own face in the glass;
> I find letters from God dropt in the street,
>   and every one is signed by God's name,
> And I leave them where they are, for I know
>   that whereso'er I go
> Others will punctually come forever and ever.

You don't have to have an intellectual understanding. It's enough to *silently know* and proceed to live with your awareness of this face of endless abundance.

7. The face of receptivity. This is how I imagine the seventh face, the receptive face of intention. It's simply receptive to all. No one and no thing is rejected by the receptive face of intention. It welcomes everyone and every living thing, without judgment—never granting the power of intention to some and withholding it from others. The receptive face of intention means to me that all of nature is waiting to be called into action. We only need to be willing to recognize and receive. Intention can't respond to you if you fail to recognize it. If you see chance and coincidence governing your life and the world, then the universal mind of intention will appear to you as nothing but an amalgamation of forces devoid of any order or power.

Simply put, to be unreceptive is to deny yourself access to the power of intention. In order to utilize the all-inclusive receptivity of intention, you must produce within yourself an intelligence equal in affinity to the universal mind itself. You must not only become receptive to having guidance available to you to manifest your human intentions, but you must be receptive to giving this energy back to the world. As I've said many times in speeches and earlier writings, your job is not to say *how,* it's to say *yes! Yes, I'm willing. Yes, I know that the power of intention is universal. It's denied to no one.*

The face of receptivity smiles on me, as what I need flows to me from the Source, and the Source is receptive to my tapping in to it to co-create books, speeches, videos, audios, and anything else that I've been fortunate enough to have on my résumé. By being receptive, I'm in harmony with the power of intention of the universal creative force. This works in so many different ways. You'll see the right people magically appearing in your life; your body healing; and if it's something that you want, you'll even discover yourself becoming a better dancer, card player, or athlete! The field of intention allows everything to emanate into form, and its unlimited potential is built into all that has manifested even before its initial birth pangs were being expressed.

* * *

33

In this chapter, you've read about my concept of the seven faces of intention. They're creative, kind, loving, beautiful, ever-expanding, endlessly abundant, and receptive to all, and you can connect to this alluring field of intention. Here are five suggestions you can implement now to put into practice the essential messages in this chapter.

Five Suggestions for Implementing the Ideas in this Chapter

1. *Visualize the power of intention.* Invite *your* visualization of the field of energy, which is the power of intention, to appear in your mind. Be receptive to what appears as you visualize your concept of this field of energy. Even though you know it's invisible, close your eyes and see what images you receive. Recite the seven words that represent the seven faces of intention: *creative, kind, loving, beautiful, expanding, abundant,* and *receptive.* Memorize these seven words and use them to bring you to harmony with the power of intention as you visualize it. Remind yourself that when you feel or behave inconsistently with these seven faces of intention, you've disconnected from the power of intention. Allow the seven words to decorate your visualization of the power of intention, and notice the shift in your perspective as you regain your connection to it.

2. *Be reflective.* A mirror reflects without distortion or judgment. Consider being like a mirror, and reflect what comes into your life without judgment or opinions. Be unattached to all who come into your life by not demanding that they stay, go, or appear, at your whim. Discontinue judging yourself or others for being too fat, too tall, too ugly—too anything! Just as the power of intention accepts and reflects you without judgment or attachment, try to be the same with what appears in your life. Be like a mirror!

3. *Expect beauty.* This suggestion includes expecting kindness and love along with beauty to be in your life by deeply loving yourself, your surroundings, and by showing reverence for all of life. There's always something beautiful to be experienced wherever you are. Right now, look around you and select beauty as your focus. This is so different from habitually being alert for ways to feel hurt, angry, or offended. Expecting beauty helps you perceive the power of intention in your life.

4. *Meditate on appreciation.* Cherish the energy that you share with all living beings now and in the future, and even those that have lived before you. Feel the surge of that life force that allows you to think, sleep, move about, digest, and even meditate. The power of intention responds to your appreciation of it. The life force that's in your body is key to what you desire. As you appreciate your life force as representative of the power of intention, a wave of determination and knowing surges through you. The wisdom of your soul as it responds to your meditation on appreciation assumes command and knows every step that must be taken.

5. *Banish doubt.* When doubt is banished, abundance flourishes and anything is possible. We all tend to use our thoughts to create the world we choose. If you doubt your ability to create the life you intend, then you're refusing the power of intention. Even when nothing seems to indicate that you're accomplishing what you desire in your life, refuse to entertain doubt. Remember, the trolley strap of intention is waiting for you to float up and be carried along.

   Shakespeare declared, "Our doubts are traitors, and make us lose the good we oft might win by fearing to attempt." And Ramana Maharshi observed, "Doubts arise because of an absence of surrender."

You may well choose to doubt what others say to you or what you experience with your senses, but banish doubt when it comes to knowing that a universal force of intention designed you and got you here! Don't doubt your creation from a field of energy that's always available to you.

❖ ❖ ❖

In the following chapter, I offer what may seem to you to be unusual methods for polishing the connecting link between you and this enthralling energy field we're calling intention.

❖ ❖ ❖ ❖ ❖

Connecting to Intention

*"The law of floatation was not discovered by contem-
plating the sinking of things, but by contemplating
the floating of things which floated naturally, and then
intelligently asking why they did so."*

— Thomas Troward

Examine this observation by the great mental-science practitioner
of the early 20th century, Thomas Troward. In the early days of
shipbuilding, ships were made of wood, and the reasoning was
that wood floats in water and iron sinks. Yet today, ships all over the
world are built of iron. As people began studying the law of flotation, it
was discovered that *anything* could float if it's lighter than the mass of
liquid it displaces. So today, we're able to make iron float by the very
same law that makes it sink. Keep this example in mind as you read
and apply the contents of this chapter on connecting to all that you're
intended to become.

The key word here is *contemplating*, or what you're placing your
thoughts on, as you begin utilizing the enormous potential and power

of intention. You must be able to connect to intention, and you can't access and work with intention if you're contemplating the impossibility of being able to intend and manifest. You can't discover the law of co-creation if you're contemplating what's missing. You can't discover the power of awakening if you're contemplating things that are still asleep. The secret to manifesting anything that you desire is your willingness and ability to realign yourself so that your inner world is in harmony with the power of intention. Every single modern advance that you see and take for granted was created (and creating is what we're doing here in this book) by someone contemplating what they intended to manifest.

The way to establish a relationship with Spirit and access the power of this creating principle is to continuously contemplate yourself as being surrounded by the conditions you wish to produce. I encourage you to emphasize this idea by underlining the previous sentence both in this book and in your mind. Dwell on the idea of a supreme infinite power producing the results that you desire. This power is the creative power of the universe. It's responsible for everything coming into focus. By trusting it to provide the form and the conditions for its manifestation, you establish a relationship to intention that allows you to be connected for as long as you practice this kind of personal intent.

The Wright brothers didn't contemplate the *staying on the ground of things*. Alexander Graham Bell didn't contemplate the *noncommunication of things*, Thomas Edison didn't contemplate the *darkness of things*. In order to float an idea into your reality, you must be willing to do a somersault into the inconceivable and land on your feet, contemplating what you want instead of what you don't have. You'll then start floating your desires instead of sinking them. The law of manifestation is like the law of flotation, and you must contemplate it working *for you* instead of contemplating it not working. This is accomplished by establishing a strong connecting link between you and the invisible, formless field of energy—the power of intention.

Entering into the Spirit of Intention

Whatever you intend to create in your life involves generating the same life-giving quality that brings everything into existence. The spirit of anything, the quality that allows it to come into the world of form, is true as a general principle, so why not activate it within you? The power of intention simply awaits your ability to make the connection.

We've already established that intention isn't a material substance with measurable physical qualities. As an example of this, think of artists. Their creations aren't merely a function of the quality of the paint, brush, canvas, or any other combination of materials they use. To understand and grasp the creation of a masterpiece, we have to take into account the thoughts and feelings of the artist. We must know and enter into the movement of the creative mind of the artist in order to understand the creation process. The artist creates something out of nothing! Without the thoughts and feelings of the artist, there would be no art. It's their particular creative mind in contemplation that links to intention to give birth to what we call an artistic creation. This is how the power of intention worked in creating you, someone new, entirely unique, someone out of nothing. Reproducing this in yourself means encountering the creative impulse and knowing that the power of intention is reaching for the realization of all that it *feels,* and that it is expressing itself as you.

What you're feeling is a function of how you're thinking, what you're contemplating, and how your inner speech is being formulated. If you could tap in to the *feeling* of the power of intention, you'd sense that it is ever-increasing, and confident in itself because it's a formative power so infallible that it never misses its mark. It's always increasing and creating. The forward movement of spirit is a given. The power of intention yearns toward fuller expressions of life, just as the artist's feelings pour out in a fuller expression of his or her ideas and thoughts. Feelings are clues about your destiny and potential, and they're seeking the full expression of life through you.

How do you enter into the spirit of intention, which is all about feelings expressing life? You can nurture it by your continual ongoing expectation of

41

the infallible spiritual law of increase being a part of your life. We saw it through our imaginary capacity to see higher vibrations, and we heard it in the voice given to it by spiritual masters through-out the ages. It's everywhere. It wants to express life. It's pure love in action. It's confident. And guess what? You are it, but you've forgotten. You need to simply trust your ability to cheerfully rely upon Spirit to express itself through and for you. Your task is to contemplate the energies of life, love, beauty, and kindness. Every action that's in harmony with this originating principle of intention gives expression to your own power of intention.

Your Will and Your Imagination

There's no disputing the existence of your free will. You're a being with a mind capable of making choices. Indeed, you're in a continuous state of deliberate choice-making during your life. This isn't about free will versus predetermined destiny, but look carefully at how you've chosen to rely on your ability to will yourself toward whatever you desire. Intention, in this book, isn't about having a strong desire and backing it up with a pit-bull kind of determination. Having a strong will and being filled with resolve to accomplish inner goals is asking ego to be the guiding force in your life. *I will do this thing, I will never be stupid, I will never give up.* These are admirable traits, but they won't reconnect you to intention. Your willpower is so much less effective than your imagination, which is your link to the power of intention. Imagination is the movement of the universal mind within you. Your imagination creates the inner picture that allows you to *participate* in the act of creation. It's the invisible connecting link to manifesting your own destiny.

Try to imagine willing yourself to do something that your imagination doesn't want you to do. Your will is the ego part of you that believes you're separate from others, separate from what you'd like to accomplish or have, and separate from God. It also believes that you are your acquisitions, achievements, and accolades. This *ego will* wants you to constantly acquire evidence of your importance. It pushes you toward proving your superiority and acquiring things you're willing to chase after with hyperdedication and resolve. On the other hand, your imagination is the concept of Spirit within you. It's the God within you. Read William Blake's description of imagination. Blake believed that with imagination, we have the power to be anything we desire to be.

> *I rest not from my great task!*
> *To open the Eternal Worlds,*
> *   to open the immortal Eyes of Man*
> *Inwards into the Worlds of Thought;*
> *Into eternity, ever expanding*
> *In the Bosom of God,*
> *The Human Imagination*

— from *Jerusalem* by William Blake

Now go back to the idea of willing yourself to do something when your imagination says no. An example of a fire walk comes to my mind. You can stare at those hot coals and will yourself to walk across them, and if you rely exclusively on your willpower, you'll end up with severe burns and blisters. But if you imagine yourself divinely protected—in Blake's words, *in the Bosom of God,* and can see yourself in your imagination able to be something beyond your body, you can accomplish the fire walk unscathed. As you imagine yourself impervious to the heat of the red-hot coals, you begin to feel yourself as something beyond your body. You visualize yourself as stronger than the fire. Your inner picture of purity and protection lets you will yourself to walk across the coals. It's your imagination that allows you to be safe. Without it, you'd be scorched!

I recall imagining myself being able to complete my first marathon run of 26-plus miles. It wasn't my will that got me through those three and a half hours of continuous running. It was my inner imagination. I tuned in to it and then allowed my body to be pushed to its limit through my will. Without that image, no amount of will would have been sufficient for me to complete that endeavor.

And so it is with everything. Willing yourself to be happy, successful, wealthy, number one, famous, the top salesperson, or the richest person in your community are ideas born of the ego and its obsessive self-absorption. In the name of this willpower, people run roughshod over anyone who gets in their way; cheating, stealing, and deceiving to accomplish their personal intention. Yet these kinds of practices will ultimately lead to disaster. You may achieve the physical goal of your individual intention. However, your imagination, that inner place where you do all of your living, won't allow you to feel peaceful.

I've used this power of imagination over my will in the production of all of my life's work. For instance, I see myself as having already completed this book. This *thinking from the end* causes me to behave as if all that I'd like to create is already here. My credo is: *Imagine myself to be and I shall be,* and it's an image that I keep with me at all times. I don't complete a book because I have a strong will to do so. That would mean I believe that it's me, the body named Wayne Dyer, that's doing all of this, whereas my imagination has no physical boundaries and no name called Wayne Dyer. My imagination is my very own "chip off of the old block" of intention. It provides what I need, it allows me to sit here and write, it guides my pen in my hand, and fills in all the blanks. I, Wayne Dyer, am not willing this book into reality. My picture of it is so clear and precise that it manifests itself. In ancient times, a divine being named Hermes wrote:

> *That which* IS *is manifested;*
> *That which has been or shall be, is unmanifested,*
>   *but not dead;*
> *For soul, the eternal activity of God, animates all things.*

These are significant words to ponder as you think about reconnecting to intention and gaining the power to create anything that's in your imagination. You, your body, and your ego do not intend, do not create, do not animate anything into life. Set your ego aside. By all means, have an aim in life and be full of determination, but rid yourself of the illusion that you're the one who's going to manifest your heart's desire through your will. It's your *imagination* that I want you to focus on throughout the reading of this book, and view all of your determined goals and activities as functions of your imagination working, guiding, encouraging, and even pushing you in the direction that intention had for you while you were still in an *unmanifested* state. You're looking for a vibrational match-up of your imagination and the Source of all Creation.

Your imagination allows you the fabulous luxury of *thinking from the end.* There's no stopping anyone who can think from the end. You create the means and surmount limitations in connection with your desires. In imagination, dwell on the end, fully confident that it's there in the material world and that you can use the ingredients of the all-creative Source to make it tangible. Since the Source of everything proceeds with grace, and its alluring seven faces, then you too shall use this method and only this method, to co-create all that you were intended to be. Become indifferent to doubt and to the call of your will. Remain confident that through continued reliance on your imagination, your assumptions are materializing into reality. Reconnecting to intention involves expressing the same seven faces that the all-creating Source uses to bring the unmanifest into the manifest. If imagination works for God, then surely it works for you, too. Through imagination, God imagines everything into reality. This is your new strategy as well.

Applying the Seven Faces for Connecting to Intention

Having been in the business of human development for most of my life, the question I most frequently hear is: "How do I go about getting what I want?" At this juncture of my life, as I sit here writing this book, my response is: "If you become what you think about, and what you think about is getting what

45

you want, then you'll stay in a state of wanting. So, the answer to how to get what you want is to reframe the question to: *How do I go about getting what I intend to create?"* My answer to that question is in the remaining pages of this chapter, but my short answer is this: "You get what you intend to create by being in harmony with the power of intention, which is responsible for all of creation." Become just like intention and you'll co-create all that you contemplate. When you become one with intention, you're transcending the ego-mind and becoming the universal all-creative mind. John Randolph Price writes in *A Spiritual Philosophy for the New World:* "Until you transcend the ego, you can do nothing but add to the insanity of the world. That statement should delight you rather than create despair, for it removes the burden from your shoulders."

Begin to remove that ego burden from your shoulders and reconnect to intention. When you lay your ego aside and return to that from which you originally emanated, you'll begin to immediately see the power of intention working with, for, and through you in a multitude of ways. Here are those seven faces revisited to help you to begin to make them a part of your life.

1. **Be creative.** Being creative means trusting your own purpose and having an attitude of unbending intent in your daily thoughts and activities. Staying creative means giving form to your personal intentions. A way to start giving them form is to literally put them in writing. For instance, in my writing space here on Maui, I've written out my intentions, and here are a few of them that stare at me each day as I write:

- *My intention is for all of my activities to be directed by Spirit.*

- *My intention is to love and radiate my love to my writing and any who might read these words.*

- *My intention is to trust in what comes through me and to be a vehicle of Spirit, judging none of it.*

- *My intention is to recognize the Spirit as my Source and to detach from my ego.*

- *My intention is to do all that I can to elevate the collective consciousness to be more closely in rapport with the Spirit of the originating supreme power of intention.*

To express your creativity and put your own intentions into the world of the manifest, I recommend that you practice *Japa*, a technique first offered by the ancient Vedas. Japa meditation is the repetition of the sound of the names of God while simultaneously focusing on what you intend to manifest. Repeating the sound within the name of God while asking for what you want generates creative energy to manifest your desires. And your desires are the movement of the universal mind within you. Now, you may be skeptical about the feasibility of such an undertaking. Well, I ask you to open yourself to this idea of Japa as an expression of your creative link to intention. I won't describe the method in depth here because I've written about it in a small book with an accompanying CD by Hay House called *Getting in the Gap: Making Conscious Contact with God Through Meditation.* For now, just know that I consider meditating and practicing Japa essential in the quest to realign yourself with the power of intention. That power is Creation, and you need to be in your own unique state of creativity to collaborate with the power of intention. Meditation and Japa are surefire ways to do so.

2. **Be kind.** A fundamental attribute of the supreme originating power is kindness. All that's manifested is brought here to thrive. It takes a kindly power to want what it creates to thrive and multiply. Were this not the case, then all that's created would be destroyed by the same power that created it. In order to reconnect to intention, you must be on the same kindness wavelength as intention itself. Make an effort to live in cheerful

kindness. It's a much higher energy than sadness or malevolence, and it makes the manifestation of your desires possible. *It's through giving that we receive;* it's through acts of kindness directed toward others that our immune systems are strengthened and even our serotonin levels increased!

Low energy thoughts that weaken us fall in the realm of shame, anger, hatred, judgment, and fear. Each of these inner thoughts weakens us and inhibits us from attracting into our lives what we desire. If we become what we think about, and what we think about is what's wrong with the world and how angry and ashamed and fearful we are, it stands to reason that we'll act on those unkind thoughts and become what we're thinking about. When you think, feel, and act kindly, you give yourself the opportunity to be like the power of intention. When you're thinking and acting otherwise, you've left the field of intention, and you've assured yourself of feeling cheated by the all-creative Spirit of intent.

— *Kindness toward yourself.* Think of yourself like this: There's a universal intelligence subsisting throughout nature inherent in every one of its manifestations. You are one of those manifestations. You are a piece of this universal intelligence—a slice of God, if you will. Be good to God, since all that God created was good. Be good to yourself. You are God manifested, and that's reason enough to treat yourself kindly. Remind yourself that you want to be kind to yourself in all the choices that you make about your daily life. Treat yourself with kindness when you eat, exercise, play, work, love, and everything else. Treating yourself kindly will hasten your ability to connect to intention.

— *Kindness toward others.* A basic tenet of getting along and being happy, as well as enlisting the assistance of others toward achieving all that you want to attract, is that people want to help you and do things for you. When you're kind to others, you receive kindness in return. A boss who's unkind gets very little cooperation from his employees. Being unkind with children makes them want to get even rather than help you out. Kindness given is kindness returned. If you wish to connect to intention and become someone who achieves all of your objectives in life, you're going to need the assistance of a multitude of folks. By practicing extending kindness everywhere, you'll find support showing up in ways that you could never have predicted.

This idea of extending kindness is particularly relevant in how you deal with people who are helpless, elderly, mentally challenged, poor, disabled, and so on. These people are all part of God's perfection. They, too, have a divine purpose, and since all of us are connected to each other through Spirit, their purpose and intent is also connected to you. Here's a brief story that will touch you at the heart level. It suggests that those whom we meet who are less than able to care for themselves may have come here to teach us something about the perfection of intention. Read it and know that this kind of thinking, feeling, and behavior empowers you to connect to intention through matching its kindness with your own.

In Brooklyn, New York, Chush is a school that caters to learning-disabled children. Some children remain in Chush for their entire school career, while others can be mainstreamed into conventional schools. At a Chush fundraiser dinner, the father of a Chush child delivered a speech that would never be forgotten by all who attended. After extolling the school and its dedicated staff, he cried out, "Where is the perfection in my son, Shaya? Everything God does is done with perfection. But my child cannot understand things as other children do. My child cannot remember facts and figures as other children do. Where is God's perfection?" The audience was shocked by the question, pained by the father's anguish, and stilled by the piercing query.

"I believe," the father answered, "that when God brings a child like this into the world, the perfection that he seeks is in the way people react to this child." He then told the following story about his son, Shaya.

One afternoon Shaya and his father walked past a park where some boys Shaya knew were playing baseball. Shaya asked, "Do you think they'll let me play?" Shaya's father knew that his son was not at all athletic and that most boys would not want him on their team. But

Shaya's father understood that if his son was chosen to play, it would give him a sense of belonging. Shaya's father approached one of the boys on the field and asked if Shaya could play. The boy looked around for guidance from his teammates. Getting none, he took matters into his own hands and said, "We're losing by six runs, and the game is in the eighth inning. I guess he can be on our team, and we'll try to put him up to bat in the ninth inning."

Shaya's father was ecstatic as Shaya smiled broadly. Shaya was told to put on a glove and go out to play in center field. In the bottom of the eighth inning, Shaya's team scored a few runs but was still behind by three. In the bottom of the ninth inning, Shaya's team scored again, and now had two outs and the bases loaded, with the potential winning run on base, Shaya was scheduled to be up. Would the team actually let Shaya bat at this juncture and give away their chance to win the game?

Surprisingly, Shaya was given the bat. Everyone knew that it was all but impossible because Shaya didn't even know how to hold the bat properly, let alone hit with it. However, as Shaya stepped up to the plate, the pitcher moved a few steps to lob the ball in softly so Shaya could at least be able to make contact. The first pitch came in, and Shaya swung clumsily and missed. One of Shaya's teammates came up to Shaya, and together they held the bat and faced the pitcher waiting for the next pitch. The pitcher again took a few steps forward to toss the ball softly toward Shaya. As the pitch came in, Shaya and his teammate swung the bat, and together they hit a slow ground ball to the pitcher. The pitcher picked up the soft grounder and could easily have thrown the ball to the first baseman. Shaya would have been out and that would have ended the game. Instead, the pitcher took the ball and threw it on a high arc to right field far beyond the reach of the first baseman. Everyone started yelling, "Shaya, run to first. Run to first." Never in his life had Shaya run to first. He scampered down the baseline wide-eyed and startled. By *the time he reached first base, the right-fielder had the ball. He could have thrown the ball to the second baseman who would tag out Shaya, who was still running.*

But the right-fielder understood what the pitcher's intentions were, so he threw the ball high and far over the third baseman's head. Everyone yelled, "Run to second, run to second." Shaya ran toward second base as the runners ahead of him deliriously circled the bases toward home. As Shaya reached second base, the opposing shortstop ran to him, turned him in the direction of third base, and shouted, "Run to third." As Shaya rounded third, the boys from both teams ran behind him screaming, "Shaya, run home." Shaya ran home, stepped on home plate, and all 18 boys lifted him on their shoulders and made him the hero, as he had just hit a "grand slam" and won the game for his team.

"That day," said the father softly with tears now rolling down his face, "those 18 boys reached their level of God's perfection."

If you don't feel a tug in your heart and a tear in your eye after reading this story, then it's unlikely that you'll ever know the magic of connecting back to the kindness of the supreme all-originating Source.

— *Kindness toward all of life.* In the ancient teachings of Patanjali, we're reminded that all living creatures are impacted dramatically by those who remain steadfast in the absence of thoughts of harm directed outward. Practice kindness toward all animals, tiny and huge, the entire kingdom of life on Earth such as the forests, the deserts, the beaches, and all that has the essence of life pulsating within it. You can't reconnect to your Source and know the power of intention in your life without the assistance of the environment. You're connected to this environment. Without gravity, you can't walk. Without the water, you can't live a day. Without the forests, the sky, the atmosphere, the vegetation, the minerals —all of it—your desire to manifest and reach intention is meaningless.

Extend thoughts of kindness everywhere. Practice kindness toward Earth by picking up a piece of litter that's on your path, or saying a silent prayer of gratitude for the existence of rain, the color of flowers, or even the paper you hold in your hand that was donated by a tree. The universe responds in kind to what you elect to radiate outward. If you say with kindness in your voice and in your heart, "How may I serve you?" the universe's response will be, "How may I serve you as well?" It's attractor energy. It's this spirit of cooperation with all of life that emerges from the essence of intention. And this spirit of kindness is one that you must learn to match if connecting back to intention is your desire. My daughter Sommer has written from her experience about how small acts of kindness go a long way:

I was getting off the turnpike one rainy afternoon and pulled up to the tollbooth while fumbling through my purse. The woman smiled at me and said, "The car before you has paid your toll." I told her I was traveling alone and extended my money. She replied, "Yes, the man instructed me to tell the next person who came to my booth to have a brighter day." That small act of kindness did give me a brighter day. I felt so moved by someone I would never know. I began to wonder how I could brighten someone else's day. I called my best friend and told her about my paid toll. She said she'd never thought of doing that, but it was a great idea. She goes to the University of Kentucky and decided to pay for the person behind her every day on her way to school as she exits the toll road. I laughed at her sincerity. "You think I'm kidding," she said, "but like you said, it's only 50 cents." As we hung up, I wondered if the man who paid my toll even fathomed that his thoughtfulness would travel to Kentucky.

I had an opportunity to extend kindness at the supermarket one day when I had my cart filled to the top with food that my roommate and I would share over the next two weeks. The woman behind me had an antsy toddler and not nearly as much in her cart as I had. I said to her, "Why don't you go first? You don't have as much as I do." The woman looked at me as if I'd just sprouted extra limbs or something. She replied, "Thank you so much. I haven't seen many people around here be thoughtful of another person. We've moved here from Virginia and are considering moving back because we're questioning whether this is the right place to raise our three children." Then she told me that she was about ready to give up and move back home, even though it would create a huge financial strain on her family. She said, "I'd promised myself if I didn't see a sign by the end of today, I was going to demand that we move back to Virginia. You are my sign."

She thanked me again, smiling as she left the store. I was flabbergasted, realizing that such a small gesture had impacted a whole family. The clerk said as she was checking me out, "You know what, girl? You just made my day." I walked out smiling, wondering how many people my act of kindness would affect.

The other day I was getting a breakfast sandwich and coffee and thought my co-workers might like some doughnuts. The four guys I work with at the stables live in the little apartments at the front of the barns. None of them has a car, but they share a bike. I explained to them that the doughnuts were for them. The look of gratitude on each of their faces was rewarding in an immeasurable way. I haven't worked there all that long, and I think that those 12 small doughnuts helped break the ice a little bit. My small act of kindness turned into something huge as the week went on. We started looking out for one another more carefully and working as a team.

3. Be love. Ponder these words thoughtfully: *God is love,* "and he that dwelleth in love dwelleth in me, and I in him." That is God talking, so to speak. Keeping in mind the central theme of this chapter, and in fact, this entire book, that you must learn to be like the energy that allowed you to be in the first place, then being in a state of love is absolutely necessary for you to reconnect to intention. You were intended out of love, you must be love in order to intend. Volumes have been written about love, and still we have as many definitions for this word as we have people to offer them. For the purposes of this chapter, I'd like you to think about love in the following two ways.

— *Love is cooperation rather than competition.* What I'd like you to be able to experience right here in physical form on planet Earth is the essence of the spiritual plane. If this were possible, it would mean that your very life is a manifestation of love. Were this to be true for you, you'd see all of life living together in harmony and cooperating with each other.

You'd sense that the power of intention that originates all life cooperates with all other life forms to ensure growth and survival. You'd note that we all share the same life force, and the same invisible intelligence that beats my heart and your heart, beats the heart of everyone on the planet.

— *Love is the force behind the will of God.* I'm not suggesting the kind of love that we define as affection or sentiment. Nor is this kind of love a feeling that seeks to please and press favors on others. Imagine a kind of love that is the power of intention, the very energy that is the cause behind all of creation. It's the spiritual vibration that carries divine intentions from formless to concrete expression. It creates new form, changes matter, vivifies all things, and holds the cosmos together beyond time and space. It's in every one of us. It is what God is.

I recommend that you pour your love into your immediate environment and hold to this practice on an hourly basis if possible. Remove all unloving thoughts from your mind, and practice kindness in all of your thoughts, words, and actions. Cultivate this love in your immediate circle of acquaintances and family, and ultimately it will expand to your community and globally as well. Extend this love deliberately to those you feel have harmed you in any way or caused you to experience suffering. The more you can extend this love, the closer you come to being love, and it's in the beingness of love that intention is reached and manifestation flourishes.

4. **Be beauty.** Emily Dickinson wrote: "Beauty is not caused. It is . . . " As you awaken to your divine nature, you'll begin to appreciate beauty in everything you see, touch, and experience. Beauty and truth are synonymous as you read earlier in John Keats's famous observation in *Ode on a Grecian Urn:* "Beauty is truth, truth beauty." This means, of course, that the creative Spirit brings things into the world of boundaries to thrive and flourish and expand. And it wouldn't do so were it not infatuated with the beauty of every manifested creature, including you. Thus, to come back into conscious contact with your Source so as to regain the power of your

Source is to look for and
experience beauty in
all of your under-
takings. Life, truth,
beauty. These are all symbols for
the same thing, an aspect of the God-force.

When you lose this awareness, you lose the
possibility of connecting to intention. You were brought
into this world from that which perceived you as an expression of beauty. It couldn't have done so if it thought you to be
otherwise, for if it has the power to create; it also possesses the power
not to do so. The choice to do so is predicated on the supposition that
you're an expression of loving beauty. This is true for everything and
everyone that emanates from the power of intention.

Here's a favorite story of mine that illustrates appreciating beauty
where once you didn't. It was told by Swami Chidvilasananda, better
known as Gurumayi, in her beautiful book, *Kindle My Heart*.

> "There was a man who did not like his in-laws because he felt they
> took up more space in the house than they should. He went to a teacher
> who lived nearby, as he had heard a lot about him, and he said, 'Please
> do something! I cannot bear my in-laws anymore. I love my wife, but
> my in-laws—never! They take up so much space in the house; somehow
> I feel they are always in my way.'
>
> The teacher asked him, 'Do you have some chickens?'
> 'Yes, I do,' he said.
> 'Then put all your chickens inside the house.'
> He did what the teacher said and then went back to him.
> The teacher asked, 'Problem solved?'
> He said, 'No! It's worse.'
> 'Do you have any sheep?'
> 'Yes.'
> 'Bring all the sheep inside.' He did so and returned to the teacher.
> 'Problem solved?'
> 'No! It's getting worse.'
> 'Do you have a dog?'
> 'Yes, I have several.'

55

'Take all those dogs into the house.'

Finally, the man ran back to the teacher and said, 'I came to you for help, but you are making my life worse than ever!'

The teacher said to him, 'Now send all the chickens, sheep, and dogs back outside.'

The man went home and emptied the house of all the animals. There was so much space! He went back to the teacher. 'Thank you! Thank you!' he said. 'You have solved all my problems.'"

5. Be ever-expansive. The next time you see a garden full of flowers, observe the flowers that are alive, and compare them to the flowers that you believe are dead. What's the difference? The dried-up, *dead* flowers are no longer growing, while the alive flowers are indeed still growing. The all-emerging universal force that intended you into beingness and commences all life is always growing, and perpetually expanding. As with all seven of these faces of intention, by reason of its universality, it must have a common nature with yours. By being in an ever-expanding state and growing intellectually, emotionally, and spiritually, you're identifying with the universal mind.

By staying in a state of readiness in which you're not attached to what you used to think or be, and by thinking from the end and staying open to receiving divine guidance, you abide by the law of growth and are receptive to the power of intention.

6. Be abundant. Intention is endlessly abundant. There's no scarcity in the universal invisible world of Spirit. The cosmos itself is without end. How could there be an end to the universe? What would be at the end? A wall? So how thick is the wall? And what's on the other side of it? As you contemplate connecting to intention, know in your heart that any attitude you have that reflects a scarcity consciousness will hold you back. A reminder here is in order. You must match intention's attributes with your own in order to capitalize on those powers in your life.

Abundance is what God's kingdom is about. Imagine God thinking, *I can't produce any more oxygen today, I'm just too tired; this universe is big enough already, I think I'll erect that wall and bring this expansion thing to a halt.* Impossible! You emerged from a consciousness that was and is unlimited. So what's to prevent you from rejoining that limitless awareness in your mind and holding on to these pictures regardless of what goes before you? What prevents you is the conditioning you've been exposed to during your life, which you can change today—in the next few minutes if you so desire.

When you shift to an abundance mind-set, you repeat to yourself over and over again that you're unlimited because you emanated from the inexhaustible supply of intention. As this picture solidifies, you begin to act on this attitude of unbending intent. There's no other possibility. We become what we think about, and as Emerson reminded us: "The ancestor to every action is a thought." As these thoughts of plentitude and excessive sufficiency become your way of thinking, the all-creating force to which you're always connected will begin to work with you, in harmony with your thoughts, just as it worked with you in harmony with your thoughts of scarcity. If you think you can't manifest abundance into your life, you'll see intention agreeing with you, and *assisting* you in the fulfillment of meager expectations!

* * *

I seem to have arrived into this world fully connected to the abundance attributes of the spiritual world from which I emanated. As a child growing up in foster homes, with poverty consciousness all around me, I was the "richest" kid in the orphanage, so to speak. I always thought I could have money jingling in my pocket. I pictured it there, and I consequently acted on that picture. I'd collect soda-pop bottles, shovel snow, bag groceries, cut lawns, carry out people's ashes from their coal furnaces, clean up yards, paint fences, babysit, deliver newspapers, and on and on. And always, the universal force of abundance worked *with* me in providing opportunities. A snowstorm was a giant blessing for me. So too were discarded bottles by the side of the road, and little old ladies who needed help carrying their groceries to their automobiles.

Today, over a half century later, I still have that abundance mentality. I've never been without several jobs at one time throughout many economic slumps over my lifetime. I made large amounts of money as a schoolteacher by starting a driver-education business after school hours. I began a lecture series in Port Washington, New York, on Monday evenings for 30 or so local residents to supplement my income as a professor at St. John's University, and that Monday-night series became an audience of over a thousand people in the high school auditorium. Each lecture was tape-recorded by a staff member, and those tapes led to the outline for my first book to the public, which was called *Your Erroneous Zones*.

One of the attendees was the wife of a literary agent in New York City who encouraged him to contact me about writing a book. That man, Arthur Pine, became like a father to me and helped me meet key publishing people in New York. And the same story of unlimited thinking goes on and on. I saw the book *from the end* becoming a tool for everyone in the country, and proceeded to go to every large city in America to tell people about it.

The universal Spirit has always worked with me in bringing my thoughts of unlimited abundance into my life. The right people would magically appear. The right break would come along. The help I needed would seemingly manifest out of nowhere. And in a sense, I'm still collecting pop bottles, shoveling snow, and carrying out groceries for little old ladies today. My vision hasn't changed, although the playing field is enlarged. It's all about having an inner picture of abundance, thinking in unlimited ways, being open to the guidance that intention provides when you're in a state of rapport with it—and then being in a state of ecstatic gratitude and awe for how this whole thing works. Every time I see a coin on the street, I stop, pick it up, put it into my pocket, and say out loud, "Thank you, God, for this symbol of abundance that keeps flowing into my life." Never once have I asked, "Why only a penny, God? You know I need a lot more than that."

Today, I arise at 4 A.M. with a knowing that my writing will complete what I've already envisioned in the contemplations of my imagination. The writing flows, and letters arrive from intention's manifest abundance urging me to read a particular book, or to talk to a unique individual, and I know that it's all working in perfect, abundant unity. The phone rings, and just what I need to hear is resonating in my ear. I get up to get a glass of water, and my eyes fall on a book that's been on my shelf for 20 years, but this time I'm compelled to pick it up. I open it, and I'm once again being directed by spirit's willingness to assist and guide me as long as I stay in harmony with it. It goes on and on, and I'm reminded of Jelaluddin Rumi's poetic words from 800 years ago: "Sell your clever-ness, and purchase bewilderment."

7. **Be receptive.** The universal mind is ready to respond to anyone who recognizes their true relationship to it. It will reproduce whatever conception of itself you impress upon it. In other words, it's receptive to all who remain in harmony with it and stay in a relationship of reverence for it. The issue becomes a question of your receptivity to the power of intention. Stay connected and know you'll receive all that this power is capable of offering. Take it on by yourself as separate from the universal mind (an impossibility, but nevertheless, a strong belief of the ego), and you remain eternally disconnected.

The nature of the universal mind is peaceful. It isn't receptive to force or violence. It works in its own time and rhythm, allowing everything to emanate by and by. It's in no hurry because it's outside of time. It's always in the eternal now. Try getting down on your hands and knees and hurrying along a tiny tomato plant sprout. Universal Spirit is at work peacefully, and your attempts to rush it or tug new life into full creative flower will destroy the entire process. Being receptive means allowing your "senior partner" to handle your life for you. *I accept the guidance and assistance of the same force that created me, I let go of my ego, and I trust in this wisdom to move at its own peaceful pace. I make no demands on it.* This is how the all-creating field of intention creates. This is how you must think in order to reconnect to your Source. You practice meditation because it allows you to receive the inner knowing of making conscious contact with God. By being peaceful, quiet, and receptive, you pattern yourself in the image of God, and you regain the power of your Source.

That is what this chapter, and indeed this entire book, is all about. That is, tapping in to the essence of originating Spirit, emulating the attributes of the creative force of intention, and manifesting into your life anything that you desire that's consistent with the universal mind—which is creativity, kindness, love, beauty, expansion, abundance, and peaceful receptivity.

* * *

A beautiful woman born in India in 1923 named Shri Mataji Nirmala Devi arrived here on Earth in a fully realized state and lived in the ashram of Mahatma Gandhi, who often consulted her on spiritual questions. She's spent her life working for peace, and discovered a simple method through which all people can receive their self-realization. She teaches Sahaja Yoga, and has never charged for this instruction. She emphasizes the following points, which are a perfect summary on this chapter on connecting to intention:

- *You cannot know the meaning of your life until you are connected to the power that created you.*

- *You are not this body, you are not this mind, you are the Spirit . . . this is the greatest truth.*

- *You have to know your Spirit . . . for without knowing your Spirit, you cannot know the truth.*

- *Meditation is the only way you can grow. There is no other way out. Because when you meditate, you are in silence. You are in thoughtless awareness. Then the growth of awareness takes place.*

Connect to the power that created you, know that you are that power, commune with that power intimately, and meditate to allow that *growth of awareness* to take place. A great summary indeed, from a fully realized being, no less.

Five Suggestions for Implementing the Ideas of this Chapter

1. *To realize your desires, match them with your inner speech.* Keep all inner talk focused on good reports and good results. Your inner speech mirrors your imagination, and your imagination is your connecting link to Spirit. If your inner speech is in conflict with your desires, your inner voice will win. So, if you match desires with inner speech, those desires will ultimately be realized.

2. *Think from the end.* That is, assume within yourself the feeling of the wish being fulfilled, and keep this vision regardless of the obstacles that emerge. Eventually you'll act on this *end thinking,* and the Spirit of Creation will collaborate with you.

3. *To reach a state of impeccability, you need to practice unbending intent.* This will match you up with the unbending intent of the all-creative universal mind. For example, if I set out to write a book, I keep a solid picture of the completed book in my mind, and I refuse to let that intention disappear. There's nothing that can keep me from that intention being fulfilled. Some say that I have great discipline, but I

know otherwise. My unbending intent won't allow for anything but its completion to be expressed. I'm pushed, prodded, and propelled, and finally almost mystically attracted to my writing space. All waking and sleeping thoughts are focused on this picture, and I never lack for being in a state of awe at how it all comes together.

4. *Copy the seven faces of intention on three-by-five cards.* Have them laminated and place them in crucial locations that you must look at each day. They'll serve as reminders for you to stay in fellowship with the originating Spirit. You want a relationship of camaraderie to exist with intention. The seven reminders strategically placed around your living and working environment will do just that for you.

5. *Always keep the thought of God's abundance in mind. If any other thought comes, replace it with that of God's abundance.* Remind yourself every day that the universe can't be miserly; it can't be wanting. It holds nothing but abundance, or as St. Paul stated so perfectly, "God is able to provide you with every blessing in abundance." Repeat these ideas on abundance until they radiate as your inner truth.

This concludes the steps for connecting to intention. But before you make this somersault into the inconceivable, I urge you to examine any and all self-imposed obstacles that need to be challenged and eradicated as you work anew at living and breathing this power of intention that was placed in your heart before a heart was even formed. As William Penn put it: "Those people who are not governed by God will be ruled by tyrants." Remember as you read on, that those tyrants are often the self-imposed roadblocks of your lower self at work.

❀ ❀ ❀ ❀ ❀

Obstacles to Connecting to Intention

*". . . does a firm persuasion that a thing is so, make it so?
He replied, 'All poets believe that it does. And in ages of
imagination, this firm persuasion removed mountains; But
many are not capable of a firm persuasion of anything.'"*

— from *The Marriage of Heaven and Hell* by William Blake

William Blake's passage from *The Marriage of Heaven and Hell* is the basis of this chapter about overcoming obstacles to the unlimited power of intention. Blake is telling us that poets have an inexhaustible imagination and consequently an unlimited ability to make something so. He also reminds us that many aren't capable of such a firm persuasion.

In the previous chapter, I gave you suggestions for making positive connections to intention. I deliberately arranged the chapters this way so that you'd read about what you're capable of before examining barriers you've erected that keep you from the bliss of your intention. In the past, as a practicing counselor and therapist, I've encouraged clients to first consider what they want to manifest in their lives and hold that thought firmly in their imagination. Only after this was solidified would I have them examine and consider the obstacles. Often my clients were unaware of the obstructions even when they were self-imposed. Learning to iden-tify ways in which you're creating your own obstacles is tremendously enlightening if you're willing to explore this area of your life. You may discover the obstacles that keep you from *a firm persuasion of anything.*

I'm devoting this chapter to three areas that may be unrecognized obstacles to your connection to the power of intention. You'll be exam-ining *your inner speech, your level of energy,* and *your self-importance.* These three categories can create almost insurmountable blocks to connecting to intention when they're mismatched. Taken one at a time, you'll have the opportunity to become aware of these blockages and explore ways of overcoming them.

There's a game show that has aired on television for several decades now (in syndication). It's called *The Match Game.* The object of this game is to match up your thoughts and potential responses with that of someone on your team, usually a partner or family member. A question or statement is given to one partner, and several possible responses are offered. The more matches made, in competition with two other couples, the more points received. The winner is the one with the most matches.

I'd like to play the match game with you. In my version, I'm asking you to match up with the universal Spirit of intention. As we go through the three categories of obstacles that hinder your connection to intention, I'll describe the areas that don't match, and offer suggestions for creating a match. Remember that your ability to activate the power of intention in *your* life depends on your matching up with the creative Source of *all* life. Match up with that Source, and you win the prize of being like the Source—and the power of intention. Fail to match up . . . and the power of intention eludes you.

Your Inner Speech—Match or No Match?

We can go all the way back to the Old Testament to find a reminder about our inner dialogue. For instance, *as a man thinketh, so is he.* Generally, we apply this idea of becoming what we think to our positive thoughts—that is, think positively and you'll produce positive results. But thinking also creates stumbling blocks that produce negative results. Below are four ways of thinking that can prevent you from reaching for and connecting to the universal, creative Spirit of intention.

1. **Thinking about what's missing in your life.** To match up with intention, you first have to catch yourself in that moment you're thinking about *what's missing.* Then shift to intention. Not *what I find missing in my life,* but to *what I absolutely intend to manifest and attract into my life*—with no doubts, no waffling, and no explaining! Here are some suggestions to help you break the habit of focusing your thoughts on what's missing. Play a version of the match game, and match up with the *all-creating force:*

No match: I don't have enough money.
Match: I intend to attract unlimited abundance into my life.

No match: My partner is grouchy and boring.
Match: I intend to focus my thoughts on what I love about my partner.

No match: I'm not as attractive as I'd like to be.
Match: I'm perfect in the eyes of God, a divine manifestation of the process of creation.

No match: I don't have enough vitality and energy.
Match: I'm a part of the ebb and flow of the limitless Source of all life.

This isn't a game of empty affirmations. It's a way of *matching* yourself to the power of intention and recognizing that what you think about, expands. If you spend your time thinking about what's missing, then that's what expands in your life. Monitor your inner dialogue, and match your thoughts to what you want and intend to create.

2. **Thinking about the circumstances of your life.** If you don't like some of the circumstances of your life, by all means don't think about them. This may sound like a paradox to you, in this match game, you want to match up with the Spirit of creation. You must train your imagination (which is the universal mind running through you) to shift from what you don't want to what you do want. All of that mental energy you spend complaining about *what is*—to anyone who will listen—is a magnet for attracting *more of what is* into your life. You, and only you, can overcome this impediment because you've put it on your path to intention. Simply change your inner speech to what you intend the new circumstances of your life to be. Practice *thinking from the end* by playing the match game, and by realigning yourself with the field of intention.

Here are some examples of a **no match** versus a **match** for the inner dialogue relating to the circumstances of your life:

No match: I hate this place we're living in; it gives me the creeps.

Match: I can see our new home in my mind, and I intend to be living in it within six months.

No match: When I see myself in the mirror, I despise the fact that I'm nearsighted and out of shape.

Match: I'm placing this drawing of how I intend to look right here on my mirror.

No match: I dislike the work I'm doing and the fact that I'm not appreciated.

Match: I'll act upon my inner intuitive impulses to create the work or job of my dreams.

No match: I hate the fact that I'm sick so often and always seem to be getting colds.

Match: I am divine health. I intend to act in healthy ways and attract the power to strengthen my immune system in every way I can.

You must learn to assume responsibility for the circumstances of your life without any accompanying guilt. The circumstances of your life aren't the way they are because of karmic debt or because you're being punished. The circumstances of your life, including your health, are yours. Somehow they showed up in your life, so just assume that you participated in all of it. Your inner speech is uniquely your own creation, and it's responsible for attracting more of the circumstances that you don't want. Link up with intention, use your inner speech to stay focused on what you intend to create, and you'll find yourself regaining the power of your Source.

3. **Thinking about what has always been.** When your inner speech focuses on the way things have always been, you act upon your thoughts of what has always been, and the universal all-creating force continues to deliver what has always been. Why? Because your imagination is a part of that which imagined you into existence. It's the force of creation, and you're using it to work against you with your inner speech.

Imagine the absolute Spirit thinking like this: *I can't create life anymore because things haven't worked for me in the past. There have been so many mistakes in the past, and I can't stop thinking about them!* How much creating do you think would occur if Spirit imagined in this way? How can you possibly connect to the power of intention if your thoughts, which are responsible for your intending, focus on all that's gone before, which you abhor? The answer is obvious, and so is the solution. Make a shift and catch yourself when you're focusing on *what always has been,* and move your inner speech to *what you intend to manifest.* You'll get points in this match game by being on the same team as the absolute Spirit.

No match: I've always been poor; I was raised on shortages and scarcity.
Match: I intend to attract wealth and prosperity in unlimited abundance.

No match: We've always fought in this relationship.
Match: I'll work at being peaceful and not allowing anyone to bring me down.

No match: My children have never shown me any respect.
Match: I intend to teach my children to respect all of life, and I'll treat them in the same way.

No match: I can't help feeling this way; it's my nature. I've always been this way.
Match: I'm a divine creation, capable of thinking like my Creator. I intend to substitute love and kindness for feelings of inadequacy. It's my choice.

The **match** items reflect a rapport with the originating Spirit. The **no match** statements represent interference that you've constructed to keep you from matching up with intention. Any thought that takes you backward is an impediment to manifesting desires. The highest functioning people understand that if you don't have a story, you don't have to live up to it. Get rid of any parts of your story that keep you focused on *what has always been.*

4. **Thinking about what "they" want for you.** There's probably a long list of people, most of them relatives, who have strong ideas about what you should be doing, how you should be thinking and worshiping, where you should be living, how you should be scheduling your life, and how much of your time you should be spending with them—especially

on special occasions and holidays! Our definition of friendship thankfully excludes the manipulation and guilt that we so often put up with in our families.

Inner dialogue that commiserates about the manipulative expectations of others ensures that this kind of conduct continues to flow into your life. If your thoughts are on what others expect of you—even though you despise their expectations—you'll continue to act on and attract more of what they want and expect for you. Removing the obstacle means that you decide to shift your inner speech to what you intend to create and attract into your life. You must do this with unswerving intent, and a commitment to not giving mental energy to what others feel about how you live your life. This can be a tough assignment at first, but you'll welcome the shift when you do it.

Practice catching yourself when you have a thought of what others want for you, and ask yourself, *Does this expectation match up with my own?* If not, simply laugh at the absurdity of being upset or frustrated over the expectations of others about how you should be running your life. This is a way to match up and become impervious to the criticisms of others, and simultaneously put a stop to the insidious practice of continuing to attract into your life something you don't want. But the big payoff is that these critics realize that their judgments and critiques are pointless, so they simply desist. A three-for-one bonus, achieved by shifting your attention *away* from what others want or expect for you *to* how you want to live your life.

Here are a few examples of how to win at the match game:

> **No match:** I'm so annoyed with my family. They just don't understand me and they never have.
> **Match:** I love my family; they don't see things my way, but I don't expect them to. I'm totally focused on my own intentions, and I send them love.

No match: I make myself sick trying to please everyone else.

Match: I'm on purpose and doing what I signed up to do in this lifetime.

No match: I feel so unappreciated by those I serve that it sometimes makes me cry.

Match: I do what I do because it's my purpose and my destiny to do so.

No match: No matter what I do or say, it seems as if I can't win.

Match: I do what my heart tells me to do with love, kindness, and beauty.

Your Level of Energy—Match or No Match?

A scientist will tell you that energy is measured by speed and the size of the wave being created. The size of the wave is measured from low to high, and slow to fast. Anything else that we attribute to the conditions we see in our world is a judgment imposed upon those pulsating frequencies. That being said, I'd like to introduce a judgment of my own here: *Higher energy is better than lower energy.* Why? Because this is a book written by a man who stands for healing, love, kindness, health, abundance, beauty, compassion, and similar expressions; and these expressions are associated with higher and faster energies.

The impact of higher and faster frequencies on lower and slower frequencies can be measured, and it's in this regard that you can make a huge impact on eradicating the energy factors in your life that are obstructing your connection to intention. The purpose of moving up the frequency ladder is to change your vibratory level of energy so that you're at the higher and faster frequencies where your energy level matches up with the highest frequencies of all: the energy of the all-creating Spirit of intention itself. It was Albert Einstein who observed, "Nothing happens until something moves."

Everything in this universe is a movement of energy. Higher/faster energy dissolves and converts lower/slower energy. With this in mind,

I'd like you to consider yourself and all of your thoughts in the context of being an *energy* system. That's right—you're an *energy* system, not just a system of bones, fluids, and cells, but actually a multitude of energy systems encapsulating an inner energy system of thoughts, feelings, and emotions. This energy system that you are can be measured and calibrated. Every thought you have can be energetically calibrated, along with its impact on your body and your environment. The higher your energy, the more capable you are of nullifying and converting lower energies, which weaken you, and impacting in a positive way everyone in your immediate and even distant surroundings.

The objective in this section is to become aware of your own energy level and the actual frequencies of thought that you regularly employ in daily life. You can become proficient at raising your energy level and permanently obliterate energetic expressions that weaken or inhibit your connection to intention. Ultimately, your goal is to have a perfect match with the highest frequency of all. Here's a simple explanation of the five levels of energy that you work with, moving from the lowest and slowest frequencies to the highest and fastest.

1. **The material world.** Solid form is energy slowed down so that it's approximately commensurate with your sense perception of the world of boundaries. Everything that you see and touch is energy slowed down so that it appears to be coalesced mass. Your eyes and your fingers agree, and there you have the physical world.

2. **The sound world.** You seldom perceive sound waves with your eyes, but they can actually be felt. These invisible waves are also high/low and fast/slow. This *sound* level of energy is where you connect to the highest frequencies of Spirit through the practice of Japa meditation, or the repetition of the sound of God, as I've written about extensively in *Getting in the Gap.*

73

3. **The light world.** Light moves faster than the material world and faster than sound, yet there are no actual particles to form a substance called light. What you see as red is what your eye perceives a certain pulsating frequency to be, and what you perceive as violet is an even faster and higher frequency. When light is brought to darkness, darkness becomes light. The implications for this are startling. Low energy when faced with high energy experiences an automatic conversion.

4. **The thought world.** Your thoughts are an extremely high frequency of pulsation that moves beyond the speed of sound and even light. The frequency of thoughts can be measured, and the impact that they have on your body and your environment can be calculated. Once again, the same rules apply. Higher frequencies nullify lower; faster energies convert slower. A colleague I admire enormously, David Hawkins, M.D., has written a work, which I've referenced often, called *Power vs. Force.* In this remarkable book, Dr. Hawkins elaborates on the lower frequencies of thought and their accompanying emotions, and how they can be impacted and converted by exposure to higher and faster frequencies. I urge you to read his book, and I'll present some of those findings in the section on raising your energy levels. Every thought you have can be calculated to determine if it's strengthening or weakening your ability to reconnect to the highest and fastest energy in the universe.

5. **The Spirit world.** Here is the ultimate in energy. These frequencies are so supersonically rapid that the presence of disorder, disharmony, and even disease is impossible. These measurable energies consist of the seven faces of intention, written about throughout the pages of this book. They are the energies of creation. When you reproduce them in yourself, you reproduce the same creative quality of life that called you into existence. They are the qualities of creativity, kindness, love, beauty, expansion, peaceful abundance, and receptivity. These are the

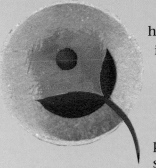

highest energies of the universal Spirit itself. You came into existence from this energy, and you can match up with it energetically as you remove the low-energy pulsations from your thoughts and feelings.

Consider these words of the Nobel Prize–winning physicist Max Planck as he accepted his award for his study of the atom: "As a man who has devoted his whole life to the most clear-headed science, to the study of matter, I can tell you as the result of my research about atoms this much: There is no matter as such! All matter originates and exists only by virtue of a force which brings the particles of an atom to vibration and holds this most minute solar system of the atom together. . . . We must assume behind this force the existence of a conscious and intelligent mind. This mind is the matrix of all matter." It is to this mind that I urge you to match up.

Raising Your Energy Level

Every thought you have has an energy that will either strengthen or weaken you. It's obviously a good idea to eliminate the thoughts that weaken you, since these thoughts are obstacles to creating a winning *match* with the universal, supreme Source of intention. Take a moment to ponder the meaning behind Anthony de Mello's observation in *One Minute Wisdom*:

> *Why is everyone here so happy except me?*
> "Because they have learned to see goodness
> and beauty everywhere," said the Master.
>
> *Why don't I see goodness and beauty everywhere?*
> "Because you cannot see outside of you what
> you fail to see inside."

What you may fail to see inside is a result of how you choose to process everything and everyone in your world. You project onto the world what you see inside, and you fail to project into the world what you fail to see inside. If you knew that you were an expression of the universal Spirit of intention, that's what you'd see. You'd raise your energy level beyond any possibility of encumbrances to your connection to the power of intention. *It is only discord acting within your own feelings that will ever deprive you of every good thing that life holds for you!* If you understand this simple observation, you'll curb interferences to intention.

There's a vibratory action to your thoughts, your feelings, and your body. I'm asking you to increase those frequencies so they're high enough to allow you to connect to the power of intention. This may sound like an oversimplification, but I hope you'll try raising your energy level as a way to remove the obstacles that prevent you from experiencing the perfection you're a part of. *You cannot remedy anything by condemning it.* You only add to the destructive energy that's already permeating the atmosphere of your life. When you react to the lower energies you encounter with your own low energies, you're actually setting up a situation that attracts more of that lower energy. For example, if someone behaves in a hateful manner toward you and you respond by *hating them for hating you,* you're participating in a lower energy field, and impacting all who enter that field. If you're angry at those around you for being angry people, you're attempting to remedy the situation through condemnation.

Don't use weakening energies employed by those around you. Other people can't bring you down if you're operating at the higher energies. Why? Because higher and faster energies nullify and convert lower/slower energies, not the reverse. If you feel that the lower energies of those around you are bringing you down, it's because you're joining them at their energy levels.

Your unbending intention may be to be slim and healthy. You know that the universal all-creative Spirit brought you into existence in that microscopic dot of human cellular tissue not to be sickly, overweight,

or unattractive . . . but to create
love, be kind, and express beauty.
This is what the power of intention
intended for you to become. Now get this:
You cannot attract attractiveness into your life by
hating anything about what you've allowed yourself to
become. Why? Because hatred creates a counter-force
of hatred that disempowers your efforts. Here is how
Dr. Hawkins describes it in *Power vs. Force:*

> Simple kindness to one's self and all that lives is the
> most powerful transformational force of all. It produces no
> backlash, has no downside, and never leads to loss or despair.
> It increases one's own true power without exacting any toll.
> But to reach maximum power such kindness can permit no
> exceptions, nor can it be practiced with the expectation of
> some selfish reward. And its effect is as far reaching as it is subtle."
> [Note that *kindness* is one of the seven faces of intention.]

He adds further:

> That which is injurious loses its capacity to harm when it is brought
> into the light, and we attract to us that which we emanate.

The lesson is clear in terms of removing lower energy obstacles. We
must raise ourselves to the levels of energy where we *are* the light we seek,
where we *are* the happiness we desire, where we *are* the love we feel is
missing, where we *are* the unlimited abundance we crave. By being it, we
attract it to us. By condemning its absence, we ensure that condemnation
and discord will continue to flow into our lives.

If you're experiencing scarcity, anguish, depression, an absence of
love, or any inability to attract what you desire, seriously look at how
you've been attracting these circumstances into your life. Low energy
is an attractor pattern. It shows up because you've sent for it, even if
on a subconscious level. It's still yours and you own it. However, if you
practice deliberately raising your energy level by being cognizant of your
immediate environment, you'll move rather rapidly toward intention and

remove all of those self-imposed roadblocks. The obstacles are in the low-energy spectrum.

A Mini-Program for Raising Your Energy Vibrations

Here's a short list of suggestions for moving your energy field to a higher faster vibration. This will help you accomplish the twofold objective of removing the barriers and allowing the power of intention to work with and through you.

Become conscious of your thoughts. Every thought you have impacts you. By shifting in the middle of a weakening thought to one that strengthens, you raise your energy vibration and strengthen yourself and the immediate energy field. For example, in the midst of saying something to one of my teenage children that was intended to make her feel ashamed of her conduct, I stopped and reminded myself that there's no remedy in condemnation. I proceeded to extend love and understanding by asking her how she felt about her self-defeating behavior and what she'd like to do to correct it. The shift raised the energy level and led to a productive conversation.

Raising the energy level to a place where my daughter and I connected to the power of intention took place in a split second of my becoming aware of my low-energy thinking and making a decision to raise it. We all have the ability to call this presence and power of intention into action when we become conscious of our thoughts.

Make meditation a regular practice in your life. Even if it's only for a few moments each day while sitting at a stoplight, this practice is vital. Take some time to be silent, and repeat the sound of God as an inner mantra. Meditation allows you to make conscious contact with your Source and regain the power of intention by assisting you in cultivating a receptivity that matches up with the force of creation.

Become conscious of the foods you eat. There are foods that calibrate low, and there are high-energy foods as well. Foods with toxic chemicals sprayed on them will make you weak even if you have no idea that the toxins are present. Artificial foods such as sweeteners are low-energy products. In general, foods high in alkalinity such as fruits, vegetables, nuts, soy, non-yeast breads, and virgin olive oil calibrate at the high end and will strengthen you on muscle testing, while highly acidic foods such as flour-based cereals, meats, dairy, and sugars calibrate at the lower energies, which will weaken you. This is not an absolute for everyone; however, you can detect how you feel after consuming certain foods, and if you feel weak, lethargic, and fatigued, you can be pretty sure you've allowed yourself to become a low-energy system, which will attract more of the same low energy into your life.

Retreat from low-energy substances. I discussed in Chapter 1 how I learned that total sobriety was absolutely essential for me to achieve the level of consciousness I craved and was destined to achieve. Alcohol, and virtually all artificial drugs, legal and otherwise, lower your body's energy level and weaken you. Furthermore, they put you in a position to continue to attract more disempowering energy into your life. Simply by consuming low-energy substances, you'll find people with similar low energy showing up regularly in your life. They'll want to buy those substances for you, party with you as you get high, and urge you to do it again after your body recovers from the devastation of these low-energy substances.

Become conscious of the energy level of the music you listen to. Harsh, pounding, musical vibrations with repetitive, loud sounds lower your energy level and weaken you and your ability to make conscious contact with intention. Similarly, the lyrics of hate, pain, anguish, fear, and violence are low energies sending weakening messages to your subconscious and infiltrating your life with similar attractor energies. If you want to attract violence, then listen to the lyrics of violence and make violent music a part of your life. If you want to attract peace and love, then listen to the higher musical vibrations and lyrics that reflect your desires.

Become aware of the energy levels of your home environment. Prayers, paintings, crystals, statues, spiritual passages, books, magazines, the colors on your walls, and even the arrangement of your furniture all create energy into which you're catapulted for at least half of your waking life. While this may seem silly or absurd, I urge you to transcend your conditioned thinking and have a mind that's open to everything. The ancient Chinese art of *feng shui* has been with us for thousands of years and is a gift from our ancestors. It describes ways to increase the energy field of our home and workplace. Become aware of how being in high-energy surroundings impacts us in ways that strengthen our lives and remove barriers to our connection to intention.

Reduce your exposure to the very low energy of commercial and cable television. Children in America see 12,000 simulated murders in their living room before their 14th birthday! Television news programming puts a heavy emphasis on bringing the bad and the ugly into your home, and in large part, leaving out the good. It's a constant stream of negativity that invades your living space and attracts more of the same into your life. Violence is the main ingredient of television entertainment, interspersed with commercial breaks sponsored by the huge drug cartels telling us that happiness is found in their pills! The viewing public is told that it needs all sorts of low-energy medicines to overcome every mental and physical malady known to humankind.

My conclusion is that the majority of television shows provide a steady stream of low energy most of the time. This is one of the reasons I've elected to devote a significant portion of my time and efforts in support of noncommercial public television and help replace messages of negativity, hopelessness, violence, profanity, and disrespect with the higher principles that match up with the principle of intention.

Enhance your energy field with photographs. You may find it difficult to believe that photography is a form of energy reproduction and that every photograph contains energy. See for yourself by strategically placing photographs taken in moments of happiness, love, and receptivity to spiritual help around your living quarters, in your workplace, in your automobile, and even on your clothing or in a pocket or wallet. Arrange photographs of nature, animals, and expressions of joy and love in your environment, and let their energy radiate into your heart and provide you with their higher frequency.

Become conscious of the energy levels of your acquaintances, friends, and extended family. You can raise your own energy levels by being in the energy field of others who resonate closely to spiritual consciousness. Choose to be in close proximity to people who are empowering, who appeal to your sense of connection to intention, who see the greatness in you, who feel connected to God, and who live a life that gives evidence that Spirit has found celebration through them. Recall that higher energy nullifies and converts lower energy, so be conscious of being in the presence of, and interacting with, higher-energy people who are connected to Spirit and living the life they were intended to. Stay in the energy field of higher-energy people and your anger, hate, fear, and depression will melt—magically converting to the higher expressions of intention.

Monitor your activities and where they take place. Avoid low-energy fields where there's excessive alcohol, drug consumption, or violent behavior, and gatherings where religious or ethnic exclusion and vitriolic prejudice or judgment are the focus. All of these kinds of venues discourage you from raising your energy and encourage you to match up with lower, debilitating energy. Immerse yourself in nature, appreciating its beauty, spending time camping, hiking, swimming, taking nature walks, and reveling in the natural world. Attend lectures on spirituality, take a yoga class, give or receive a massage, visit monasteries or meditation centers, and commit to helping others in need with visits to the elderly in geriatric centers or sick children in hospitals. Every activity has an energy field. Choose to be in places where the energy fields reflect the seven faces of intention.

Extend acts of kindness, asking for nothing in return. Anonymously extend financial aid to those less fortunate, and do it from the kindness of your heart, expecting not even a thank you. Activate your *magnificent obsession* by learning to be kind while keeping your ego—which expects to be told how wonderful you are—out of the picture completely. This is an essential activity for connecting to intention because the universal all-creating Spirit returns acts of kindness with the response: *How may I be kind to you?*

Pick up some litter and place it in a proper receptacle and tell no one about your actions. In fact, spend several hours doing nothing but cleaning and clearing out messes that you didn't create. Any act of kindness extended toward yourself, others, or your environment matches you up with the kindness inherent in the universal power of intention. It's an energizer for you, and causes this kind of energy to flow back into your life.

82

This poignant story "The Valentine," by Ruth McDonald, illustrates the kind of giving I'm suggesting here. The little boy symbolizes the magnificent obsession I just referred to.

He was a shy little boy, not very popular with the other children in Grade One. As Valentine's Day approached, his mother was delighted when he asked her one evening to sit down and write the names of all the children in his class so that he could make a Valentine for each. Slowly he remembered each name aloud, and his mother recorded them on a piece of paper. He worried endlessly for fear he would forget someone.

Armed with a book of Valentines to cut out, with scissors and crayons and paste, he plodded his conscientious way down the list. When each one was finished, his mother printed the name on a piece of paper and watched him laboriously copy it. As the pile of finished Valentines grew, so did his satisfaction.

About this time, his mother began to worry whether the other children would make Valentines for him. He hurried home so fast each afternoon to get on with his task, that it seemed likely the other children playing along the street would forget his existence altogether. How absolutely horrible if he went off to the party armed with 37 tokens of love—and no one had remembered him! She wondered if there were some way she could sneak a few Valentines among those he was making so that he would be sure of receiving at least a few. But he watched his hoard so jealously, and counted them over so lovingly, that there was no chance to slip in an extra. She assumed a mother's most normal role, that of patient waiting.

The day of the Valentine box finally arrived, and she watched him trudge off down the snowy street, a box of heart-shaped cookies in one hand, a shopping-bag clutched in the other with 37 neat tokens of his labor. She watched him with a burning heart. "Please, God," she prayed, "let him get at least a few!"

All afternoon her hands were busy here and there, but her heart was at the school. At half-past three she took her knitting and sat with studied coincidence in a chair that gave a full view of the street.

Finally, he appeared, alone. Her heart sank. Up the street he came, turning every once in a while to back up a few steps into the wind. She strained her eyes to see his face. At that distance it was just a rosy blur.

It was not until he turned in at the walk that she saw it—the one lone Valentine clutched in his little red mitt. Only one. After all his work. And from the teacher probably. The knitting blurred before her eyes. If only you could stand between your child and life! She laid down her work and walked to meet him at the door.

"What rosy cheeks!" she said. "Here, let me untie your scarf. Were the cookies good?"

He turned toward her a face shining with happiness and complete fulfillment. "Do you know what?" he said. "I didn't forget a one. Not a single one!"

Be specific when you affirm your intentions to raise your energy level and create your desires. Place your affirmations in strategic places where you'll notice and read them throughout the day. For example: *I intend to attract the job I desire into my life. I intend to be able to afford the specific automobile I envision myself driving by the 30th of next month. I intend to donate two hours of my time this week to the underprivileged. I intend to heal myself of this persistent fatigue.*

Written affirmations have an energy of their own and will guide you in raising your energy level. I practice this myself. A woman named Lynn Hall who lives in Toronto sent me a beautiful plaque that I look at each day. In her letter she stated: "Here is a gift for you, written solely for you in an effort to convey heartfelt gratitude for the blessing of your presence in my life. That said, I am sure that the sentiment is a universal one speaking for every other soul on the planet who has experienced the same good fortune. May the light and love that you emit forever reflect back to you in joyful abundance, Dr. Dyer." The beautiful etched-in-soul plaque reads like this:

Spirit
Has found
Great voice
In you.
In vibrant truths,
And joyful splendor.

Spirit
Has found
Revelation
Through you,
In resonant
And reflective ways.

Spirit
Has found
Celebration
Through you,
In infinite expanses
And endless reach.

To
All those
Awakened
To the
Grace of
Your gifts—

Spirit
Has found
Both
Wings
And
Light.

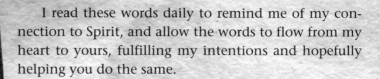

I read these words daily to remind me of my connection to Spirit, and allow the words to flow from my heart to yours, fulfilling my intentions and hopefully helping you do the same.

As frequently as possible, hold thoughts of forgiveness in your mind. In muscle testing, when you hold a thought of revenge, you'll go weak, while a thought of forgiveness keeps you strong. Revenge, anger, and hatred are exceedingly low energies that keep you from matching up with the attributes of the universal force. A simple thought of forgiveness toward anyone who may have angered you in the past—without any action taken on your part—will raise you to the level of Spirit and aid you in your individual intentions.

You can either serve Spirit with your mind or use that same mind to divorce yourself from Spirit. Married to the seven faces of spiritual intention, you connect to that power. Divorced, your self-importance, your ego, takes over.

Here's the final obstacle to making your connection to intention.

❖ ❖ ❖

Your Self-Importance

In *The Fire from Within,* Carlos Castaneda hears these words from his sorcerer teacher: "Self-importance is man's greatest enemy. What weakens him is feeling offended by the deeds and misdeeds of his fellow man. Self-importance requires that one spend most of one's life offended by something or someone." This is a major impediment to connecting to intention; you can all too easily create a *no match* here.

Basically, your feelings of self-importance are what make you feel special, so let's deal with this concept of being special. It's essential that you have a strong self-concept and that you feel unique. The problem is when you misidentify who you truly are by identifying yourself as your body, your achievements, and your possessions. Then you identify people who have accomplished less as inferior, and your self-important superiority causes you to be constantly offended in one way or another.

This misidentification is the source of most of your problems, as well as most of the problems of humankind. Feeling *special* leads us to our self-importance. Castaneda writes later in his life, many years after his initial emergence into the world of sorcery, about the futility of self-importance. "The more I thought about it, and the more I talked to and observed myself and my fellow men, the more intense the conviction that something was rendering us incapable of any activity or any interaction or any thought that didn't have the self as its focal point."

With the self as a focal point, you sustain the illusion that you are your body, which is a completely separate entity from all others. This sense of separateness leads you to compete rather than cooperate with everyone else. Ultimately, it's a no match with Spirit, and becomes a huge obstacle to your connection to the power of intention. In order to relinquish your self-importance, you'll have to become aware of how entrenched it is in your life. Ego is simply an *idea of who you are* that you carry around with you. As such, it can't be surgically removed by having an egoectomy! This *idea* of who you think you are will persistently erode any possibility you have of connecting to intention.

Seven Steps for Overcoming Ego's Hold on You

Here are seven suggestions to help you transcend ingrained ideas of self-importance. All of these are designed to help prevent you from falsely identifying with the self-important ego.

1. Stop being offended. The behavior of others isn't a reason to be immobilized. That which offends you only weakens you. If you're looking for occasions to be offended, you'll find them at every turn. This is your ego at work convincing you that the world shouldn't be the way it is. But you can become an appreciator of life and match up with the universal Spirit of Creation. You can't reach the power of intention by being offended. By all means, act to eradicate the horrors of the world, which emanate from massive ego identification, but stay in peace. As *A Course in Miracles* reminds us: *Peace is of God, you who are part of God are not at home except in his peace.* Being offended creates the same destructive energy that offended you in the first place and leads to attack, counterattack, and war.

2. Let go of your need to win. Ego loves to divide us up into winners and losers. The pursuit of winning is a surefire means to avoid conscious contact with intention. Why? Because ultimately, winning is impossible all of the time. Someone out there will be faster, luckier, younger, stronger, and smarter—and back you'll go to feeling worthless and insignificant.

You're not your winnings or your victories. You may enjoy competing, and have fun in a world where winning is everything, but you don't have to be there in your thoughts. There are no losers in a world where we all share the same energy source. All you can say on a given day is that you performed at a certain level in comparison to the levels of others on that day. But today is another day, with other competitors and new circumstances to consider. You're still the infinite presence in a body that's another day (or decade) older. Let go of *needing* to win by not agreeing that the opposite of winning is losing. That's ego's fear. If your body isn't performing in a *winning* fashion on this day, it simply doesn't matter when you aren't identifying exclusively with your ego. Be the observer, noticing and enjoying it all without needing to win a trophy. Be at peace, and match up with the energy of intention. And ironically, although you'll hardly notice it, more of those victories will show up in your life as you pursue them less.

3. Let go of your need to be right. Ego is the source of a lot of conflict and dissension because it pushes you in the direction of making other people wrong. When you're hostile, you've disconnected from the power of intention. The creative Spirit is kind, loving, and receptive; and free of anger, resentment, or bitterness. Letting go of your need to be right in your discussions and relationships is like saying to ego, *I'm not a slave to you. I want to embrace kindness, and I reject your need to be right. In fact, I'm going to offer this person a chance to feel better by saying that she's right, and thank her for pointing me in the direction of truth.*

When you let go of the need to be right, you're able to strengthen your connection to the power of intention. But keep in mind that ego is a determined combatant. I've seen people willing to die rather than let go of being right. I've seen people end otherwise beautiful relationships by sticking to their need to be right. I urge you to let go of this ego-driven need to be right by stopping yourself in the middle of an argument and asking yourself, *Do I want to be right or be happy?* When you choose the happy, loving, spiritual mode, your connection to intention is strengthened. These moments ultimately expand your new connection to the power of intention. The universal Source will begin to collaborate with you in creating the life you were intended to live.

4. Let go of your need to be superior. True nobility isn't about being better than someone else. It's about being better than you used to be. Stay focused on your growth, with a constant awareness that no one on this planet is any better than anyone else. We all emanate from the same creative life force. We all have a mission to realize our intended essence; all that we need to fulfill our destiny is available to us. None of this is possible when you see yourself as superior to others. It's an old saw, but nonetheless true: *We are all equal in the eyes of God.* Let go of your need to feel superior by seeing the unfolding of God in everyone. Don't assess others on the basis of their appearance, achievements, possessions, and other indices of ego. When you project feelings of superiority, that's what you get back, leading to resentments and ultimately hostile feelings. These feelings become the vehicle that takes you farther away from intention. *A Course in Miracles* addresses this need to be special and superior: *Specialness always makes comparisons. It is established by a lack seen in another, and maintained by searching for, and keeping clear in sight, all lacks it can perceive.*

5. Let go of your need to have more. The mantra of the ego is *more.* It's never satisfied. No matter how much you achieve or acquire, your ego will insist that it isn't enough. You'll find yourself in a perpetual state of striving, and eliminate the possibility of ever arriving. Yet in reality, you've already arrived, and how you choose to use this present moment of your life is your choice. Ironically, when you stop needing more, more of what you desire seems to arrive in your life. Since you're detached from the need for it, you find it easier to pass it along to others, because you realize how little you need in order to be satisfied and at peace.

The universal Source is content with itself, constantly expanding and creating new life, never trying to hold on to its creations for its own selfish means. It creates and lets go. As you let go of ego's need to have more, you unify with that Source. You create, attract to yourself, and let it go, never demanding that more come your way. As an appreciator of all that shows up, you learn the powerful lesson St. Francis of Assisi taught: " . . . it is in giving that we receive." By allowing abundance to flow to and through you, you match up with your Source and guarantee that this energy will continue to flow.

6. Let go of identifying yourself on the basis of your achievements. This may be a difficult concept if you think you *are* your achievements. *God writes all the music, God sings all the songs, God builds all the buildings, God is the source of all your achievements.* I can hear your ego loudly protesting. Nevertheless, stay tuned to this idea. All emanates from Source! You and that Source are one! You're not this body and its accomplishments. You are the observer. Notice it all; and be grateful for the abilities you've been given, the motivation to achieve, and the stuff you've accumulated. But give all the credit to the power of intention, which brought you into existence and which you're a materialized part of. The less you need to take credit for your achievements and the more connected you stay to the seven faces of intention, the more you're free to achieve, and the more will show up for you. It's when you attach yourself to those achievements and believe that you alone are doing all of those things that you leave the peace and the gratitude of your Source.

7. Let go of your reputation. Your reputation is not located in you. It resides in the minds of others. Therefore, you have no control over it at all. If you speak to 30 people, you will have 30 reputations. Connecting to intention means listening to your heart and conducting yourself based on what your inner voice tells you is your purpose here. If you're overly concerned with how you're going to be perceived by everyone, then you've disconnected yourself from intention and allowed the opinions of others to guide you. This is your ego at work. It's an illusion that stands between you and the power of intention. There's nothing you can't do, unless you disconnect from the power source and become convinced that your purpose is to prove to others how masterful and superior you are and spend your energy attempting to win a giant reputation among other egos. Do what you do because your inner voice—always connected to and grateful to your Source—so directs you. Stay on purpose, detach from outcome, and take responsibility for what *does* reside in you: your character. Leave your reputation for others to debate; it has nothing to do with you. Or as a book title says: *What You Think of Me Is None of My Business!*

This concludes the three major obstacles to your connecting to intention: *your thoughts, your energy,* and *your self-importance.* Here are five suggestions for overcoming the obstacles and staying permanently connected to the power of intention.

Five Suggestions for Implementing the Ideas in This Chapter

1. *Monitor your inner dialogue.* Notice how much of your inner speech focuses on what's missing, the negative circumstances, the past, and the opinions of others. The more cognizant you become of your inner speech, the sooner you'll be able to shift right in the midst of those habitual inner

proceedings, from a thought of *I resent what's missing*, to *I intend to attract what I want and stop thinking about what I dislike.* That new inner dialogue becomes the link connecting you to intention.

2. *Lighten moments of doubt and depression.* Notice the moments that aren't a part of your higher nature. Reject thoughts that support an inability on your part to match up with intention. *Remain faithful to the light* is good advice. Recently, a friend and teacher learned of a struggle I was personally going through, and wrote to me: "Remember, Wayne, the sun is shining behind the clouds." Be faithful to the light that's always there.

3. *Be aware of low energy.* Recall that everything, which includes your thoughts, has an energy frequency that can be calibrated to determine whether it will strengthen or weaken you. When you find yourself either thinking in low-energy ways, or immersed in low, weakening energy, resolve to bring a higher vibration to the presence of that debilitating situation.

4. *Talk to your ego and let it know that it has no control over you today.* In my children's bedroom here on Maui, I've framed the following observation, which they see each morning. While they joke and laugh about it, they get the essential message and share it out loud when anyone (including me) gets upset during the day.

> *Good morning,*
> *This is God.*
> *I will be handling*
> *All of your*
> *Problems today.*
> *I will not need*
> *Your help, so have*
> *A miraculous day.*

5. *View obstacles as opportunities to circulate the power of your unbending intent.* Unbending means just what it says. *I intend to stay connected to my Source and thereby gain the power of my Source.* This means being at peace, detaching yourself from the circumstances, and seeing yourself as the observer rather than the victim . . . then turning it all over to your Source and knowing that you'll receive the guidance and assistance you require.

※ ※ ※

You've just completed a thorough examination of the three major obstacles to connecting to the power of intention, along with suggestions for eliminating them. In the next chapter, I'll explain how you impact those around you when you raise your energy level to the highest spiritual frequencies and live your days connected to intention. When you're connected to the power of intention, everywhere you go, and everyone you meet, is affected by you and the energy you radiate. As you become the power of intention, you'll see your dreams being fulfilled almost magically, and you'll see yourself creating huge ripples in the energy fields of others by your presence and nothing more.

※ ※ ※ ※ ※

93

Your Impact on Others When Connected to Intention

"It is one of the most beautiful compensations of this life that no man can sincerely try to help another without helping himself. . . . Serve and thou shall be served."

— Ralph Waldo Emerson

As you find yourself being more in harmony with the faces of intention, you're going to discover that you'll be impacting others in new ways. The nature of this impact is profoundly important in your quest to utilize the power of intention. You'll begin seeing in others what you're feeling within yourself. This new way of seeing will enable people in your presence to feel comforted and peaceful, and to indirectly be loving accomplices to your connection to intention.

As you'll read on the next page, the poet Hafiz states that he wants nothing, even if the person is a "drooling mess" and a potential victim. All he perceives is their divine worth, which is what you'll see in others as you connect to the power of intention.

The Jeweler

If a naïve and desperate man
Brings a precious stone
To the only jeweler in town,
Wanting to sell it,
The jeweler's eyes
Will begin to play a game,
Like most eyes in the world when they look at you.

The jeweler's face will stay calm.
He will not want to reveal the stone's true value,
But to hold the man captive to fear and greed
While he calculates
The value of the transaction.

But one moment with me, my dear,
Will show you that there is nothing, nothing Hafiz
    wants from you.
When you sit before a Master like me,
Even if you are a drooling mess,
My eyes sing with Excitement
They see your Divine Worth.

— Hafiz

You Receive What You Desire for Others

As you review the attributes of universal intention and simultane-ously vow to be those attributes, you begin to see the significance of what you desire for all others. If you desire peace for others, you'll receive it. If you want others to feel loved, you'll be the recipient of love. If you see only beauty and worthiness in others, you'll have the same returned to you. You'll only give away what you have in your heart, and attract what you're giving away. This is a matter of great concern to you. Your impact on others—whether it be strangers, family members, co-workers, or neighbors—is evidence of the strength of your connection to the power of intention. Think of your relationships in terms of holy or unholy.

Holy relationships facilitate the power of intention at a high energy level for everyone involved. Unholy relationships keep the energy at the lower, slower levels for all concerned. You'll know your own potential for greatness when you start seeing the perfection in all relationships. When you recognize others' holiness, you'll treat them as divine expressions of the power of intention, wanting nothing from them. The irony is that they become co-creators manifesting all your desires. Want nothing from them, demand nothing from them, have no expectations for them, and they'll return this kindness. Demand from them, insist that they please you, judge them as inferior, and see them as servants, and you'll receive the same. It behooves you to be acutely aware of what you truly want for others, and to know whether you're in a holy or an unholy relationship with every person you're involved with.

The holy relationship. One truth that I've recognized during the years of my own growth is that it's impossible to know my perfection if I'm unable to see and honor that same perfection in others. The ability to see yourself as a temporary expression of intention and to see yourself in all of humanity is a characteristic of the holy relationship. It's the ability to celebrate and honor in all others, the place where we're all one.

In an unholy relationship, you see yourself as separate from others. It's the feeling that others are primarily useful to satisfy ego's urges, and that people are there to help you get what's missing in your life. In any kind of a relationship, this attitude of separation and potential manipulation creates a barrier between

97

you and the power of intention. The signs of unholy relationships are quite clear: People become defensive, fearful, hostile, standoffish, and don't wish to be in your company.

As you change your thought patterns to raise your energy vibrations, and reduce the demands of your ego, you'll begin developing a reverent or holy relationship with others. Then everyone is perceived as complete. When you can celebrate differences in others as interesting or enjoyable, you're loosening your identity with ego. The holy relationship is a way of matching up with the universal Source of Creation and being peacefully joyful. Any relationship—or even an encounter—from the holy perspective, is a coming together with a beloved self-aspect and discovering a stimulating connection with the power of intention.

Recently, in a supermarket, I asked a frenzied clerk behind the seafood counter if he knew where I could find the smoked salmon. I saw myself as connected to him in spite of the frustration showing through his behavior. A man standing next to me heard my request and saw the clerk's harried demeanor. The stranger smiled at me and went to another area of the store, returning with a package of nova lox, which he handed me. He delivered to me what I was seeking! A coincidence? I think not. When I feel myself connected to others and radiate the energy of holy relationship, people react with kindness and go out of their way to assist me with my intentions.

In another example of this, I was transferred from one airline to another because of a mechanical problem that resulted in a cancellation. At my original airline, which is in my hometown, the employees know me and go out of their way to assist me. I've practiced holy relationships with everyone at the counter, at baggage check-in, on the plane, and so on. On this particular day, I was sent to the other end of the airport with seven boxes of books and tapes that had to be checked as baggage. As my assistant, Maya, and I trudged up to the counter of the other airline, pushing a cart with luggage and seven heavy boxes, the passenger agent announced that her airline did not permit more than two pieces of luggage to be checked in, and that I would have to leave three of the boxes behind. I could check in two for me and two for Maya. *Those are the rules.*

Here's where a holy relationship with a stranger has more potential for assisting you with your intentions than an unholy relationship. Rather than countering the agent with an intention that she was a clerk whose job it was to serve my needs, I chose to join her where we both are one. I let her know that I wasn't even mildly upset over this rule, and I imagined how she must feel, having to process a large number of people who weren't scheduled on this flight. I felt connected, and expressed my own feelings of frustration at having this challenge of what to do with these three extra boxes, which my originally scheduled airline had agreed to transport. I invited her to attend a lecture I was giving in town the next month, as my guest. Our entire conversation and the entire interaction was guided by my private intent that this remain a holy relationship.

The energy of this interaction shifted from weak to strong. We bonded, recognized our *self* in the other, and she checked in all of my boxes with a cheerful smile. I've never forgotten what she said to me as she handed me our boarding passes. "When you wheeled up that cart with all those boxes, I was determined that you weren't going to get them on that plane, and after a few moments of being with you, I would've carried them out and put them on the plane myself if I had to. It's a pleasure to know you. Thank you for your business, and I hope you'll consider our airline in the future."

These are two simple examples of what happens when you consciously shift from ego-dominated unholy relationships, to experiencing your connectedness through the power of intention. I urge you to establish a holy relationship with your Source, the world community, your neighbors, acquaintances, family, the animal kingdom, our planet, and yourself. Just as in my examples of the man in the store delivering me the smoked salmon I was looking for, and the airline agent assisting me in realizing my intent, you'll enjoy the power of intention through holy relationships. *It's all about relationship.*

Alone We Can Do Nothing

When you meet anyone, treat the event as a holy encounter. It's through others that we either find or love our *self*. For you see, nothing is accomplished without others. *A Course in Miracles* says this so well:

> *Alone we can do nothing,*
> *But together our minds fuse into something*
> *Whose power is far beyond*
> *The power of its separate parts.*
> *The kingdom cannot be found alone,*
> *And you who are the kingdom*
> *Cannot find yourself alone.*

When you eliminate the concept of separation from your thoughts and your behavior, you begin to feel your connection to everything and everyone. You'll begin having a sense of belonging, which enables you to scoff at any thought of being separate. This feeling of connectedness originates with and helps you process all of your interactions from the point of view of equality. By recognizing others as co-creators, you match up with your Source and move into a state of grace. If you're seeing yourself as either inferior or superior, you've disconnected from the power of intention. Your desires will be frustrated unless you connect with and support other people.

How you interact with your universal support team is significant. How you view others is a projection of how you view yourself. Consistently seeing others as worthless means that you're erecting a roadblock for your potential allies. See others as weak, and you're simultaneously attracting weak energies. Persistently viewing others as dishonest, lazy, sinful, and so on may mean that you need to feel superior. Constantly seeing others critically can be a way of compensating for something you fear. But you don't even need to under-stand this psychological mechanism. All you have to do is recognize how you view others. If there's a pattern of seeing others as failures, you only need to notice the pattern as evidence of what you're attracting into your life.

It's so important to see interactions as holy encounters, because this sets in motion an attractor energy pattern. In a holy relationship, you attract the collaboration of higher energies. In an unholy relationship, the attractor pattern exists, too, attracting low energies and more unholy relationships. By bringing higher spiritual energy to everyone you encounter, you dissolve lower energies. When the energies of kindness, love, receptivity, and abundance are present in your relationships, you have brought the elixir of spiritual Creation or the love of the Creator right into the mix. Now those forces begin to work on everyone in your environment. The right people magically appear. The right materials show up. The phone rings and someone gives you the information you've been wanting for months. Strangers offer suggestions that make sense to you. As I mentioned earlier, these types of coincidences are like mathematical angles that *coincide,* or fit together perfectly. Treat others as co-creators and have divine expectations for them. Don't view anyone as ordinary, unless of course you wish to have more of the ordinary manifest into your world.

From Ordinary to Extraordinary

Leo Tolstoy's famous story *The Death of Ivan Ilyich,* is one of my favorite pieces of literature. Tolstoy describes Ivan Ilyich as a man who's motivated almost exclusively by the expectations of others, and isn't able to live out his own dreams. The opening line of Chapter 2 in this compelling story goes like this: "The story of Ivan Ilyich's life was of the simplest, most ordinary and therefore most terrible." Tolstoy actually defines living an *ordinary* life as terrible. I couldn't agree more!

If your expectations for yourself center on being normal, just getting along, fitting in, and being an ordinary person, you'll resonate to ordinary frequencies, and you'll attract more of normal and ordinary into your life. Furthermore, your impact on others as potential allies in co-creating your intentions will also revolve around ordinary. The *power* of intention occurs when you're synchronized with the all-creating universal force, which is anything but ordinary. This is the power that's responsible for all of creation. It's ever-expansive, and thinks and creates in terms of endless abundance. When you shift to this higher energy and resonate more in harmony with intention, you become a magnet for attracting more of this energy into your world. You also have this kind of impact on everyone and everything you're in contact with.

One of the most effective means for transcending *ordinary* and moving into the realm of *extraordinary* is saying *yes* more frequently and eliminating *no* almost completely. I call it *saying yes to life.* Say yes to yourself, to your family, your children, your co-workers, and your business. Ordinary says, *No, I don't think I can do it. No, that won't work out. No, I've tried that and it's never worked before. No, that intention is impossible for me.* With the idea of *no,* you attract *more of no,* and your impact on others whom you could help and on whom you could rely for help is also *no.* Once again, I urge you to adopt the attitude of the poet Hafiz.

> *I rarely let the word No escape*
> *From my mouth*
> *Because it is so plain to my soul*
> *That God has shouted, Yes! Yes! Yes!*
> *To every luminous movement in Existence*

Shout *yes* to everyone as often as you can. When someone seeks your permission to try something, before saying *no,* ask yourself if you want that person to stay at ordinary levels of living. When my son Sands wished to try out a new surfing area last week, my first inclination was to say, *Too dangerous, you've never been there before, you could get hurt,* and so on. But I reconsidered, and accompanied him on a new adventure. My *yes* impacted his life and mine in a positive manner.

Making *yes* your inner mantra allows you to extend *yes* outside of yourself and attract more of *yes* into your own personal intending. *Yes* is the breath of Creation. Think of a drop of rain merging with a river at the moment it becomes the river. Think of the river merging with the ocean at the moment it becomes the ocean. You can almost hear the sound of *yes* being whispered in those moments. As you merge with the universal force of Creation extending *yes* wherever feasible, you become that force of Creation itself. This will be your impact on others. No more ordinary *nos* in your life. On to the extraordinary.

Ordinary implies being stuck in a rut much like Ivan Ilyich. While in the rut, you'll attract other rut-dwellers, and your mutual impact will be to stay in your ordinary ruts—complaining, finding fault, wishing, and hoping for better days. The universal force of intention never complains; it creates and offers its options for greatness. It judges no one, and isn't stuck wishing and hoping that things will improve. It's too busy creating beauty to be so foolishly engaged. As you move your own energy level up out of a rut mentality, you'll have an uplifting effect on all of the rut-dwellers in your life. Moreover, you'll help many of them have a similar impact, and create new allies in fulfilling your own intentions. Become aware of your identification with normal or ordinary, and begin to vibrate to higher and higher energetic frequencies, which constitute a shift upward into the extraordinary dimensions of pure intent.

How Your Energies Impact Others

When you feel connected and in harmony with intention, you sense a major difference in how other people react to you. Be cognizant of these reactions, because they'll bear directly on your abilities to fulfill your individual intentions. The more closely you automatically resonate to the frequencies of the universal all-creating Source, the more that others will be impacted and their lower energies nullified. They'll gravitate toward you, bringing peace, joy, love, beauty, and abundance into your life. What follows is my opinion on how you'll impact others when you're resonating with intention, and how different your impact is when you're dominated by your ego's separatist attitude.

Here are some of the most significant ways in which you'll impact others:

Your presence instills calmness. When you coincide with intention, your impact on others has a calming influence. People tend to feel more at peace, less threatened, and more at ease. The power of intention is the power of love and receptivity. It asks nothing of anyone, it judges no one, and it encourages others to be free to be themselves. As people feel calmer in your presence, they're inclined to feel safe, by virtue of the energy frequencies that you radiate. Their feelings are encouraged by your energy of love and receptivity, causing them to want to reach out and be with you. As Walt Whitman put it: "We convince by our presence."

If, instead, you bring the lower calibrations of judgment, hostility, anger, hatred, or depression to your interactions, you attract that level of energy if it's lurking in the people you're interacting with. This acts like a counterforce to those same energies if they're present in others. The impact intensifies the lower frequencies at that level and creates a field in which demands are placed as a result of feelings of inferiority or opposition.

Intention doesn't interact *against* anything. It's like gravity, which doesn't move against anything, nor does gravity itself move. Think of impacting others like gravity, with no need to move against or attack anyone. People who feel *empowered* by your presence become kindred spirits. That can only happen if they feel safe rather than attacked, secure rather than judged, calm rather than harassed.

Your presence leaves others feeling energized. I recall leaving a two-hour session with a spiritual master and feeling as if I could conquer the world emotionally and spiritually. The saint was Mother Meera, who'd held my head in her hands and gazed into my eyes with her egoless divinity. I felt so energized that I didn't sleep that entire night. I wanted more of what this joyous being had shown me through her presence alone.

When you bring the frequencies of intention into the presence of others, they'll feel energized just by being in your immediate circle. You don't have to say a word. You don't have to act in any prescribed fashion. Your energy of intention alone will make others in your field feel as if they've mysteriously been empowered. As you begin consciously expressing the seven faces of intention, you'll discover that others begin to comment on the impact you're making on them. They'll want to assist you in fulfilling your own dreams. They'll be energized and volunteer to help you. They'll even begin to offer to finance your dreams with their energized, new ideas. As I've grown in my consciousness of the power of intention, I've been told I've had an impact without my doing anything other than spending an evening having a meal in a restaurant. People tell me they've been energized with greater confidence and determination and inspiration after our time together. I've done nothing. They've felt impacted by the field of high energy we shared.

Your presence allows others to feel better about themselves. Have you ever noticed when you're in the presence of certain people that you feel better about yourself? Their compassionate energy has the noticeably pleasant impact of simply making you feel really good about yourself. You'll impact others with this energy of compassion as you develop your connection to intention. People will sense that you care about them, understand them, and are interested in them as unique individuals. With this kind of connection to intention, you're less likely to focus conversation on yourself and use others to massage your ego.

On the contrary, being in the company of someone who's disdainful or indifferent impacts you quite differently. If this is the low energy you transmit to others, they're quite likely to depart the encounter feeling less than wonderful about themselves, unless they're so strongly connected to intention that they can override the impact of this low energy.

These extremely low-energy thoughts and behaviors are evident if you use every topic that's brought up as an excuse to talk about yourself. Any behavior similar to this displays ego-dominated energy that impacts others unpleasantly. Moreover, it leaves others feeling as if they're insignificant or unimportant, and obviously feeling worse about themselves when it's a repeated pattern in a significant relationship.

Your presence allows others to feel unified. The effect of being in the presence of people expressing high frequencies is to feel unified and connected to all of nature, all of humankind, and to intention. As you raise your frequencies, your impact on others invites them to be on the same team. You are unified and want to assist each other in the fulfillment of a common objective.

The opposite of this feeling of unity is feeling polarized and cut off. Low energy is demanding and always moves against others. Therefore, it will inevitably produce a win/lose condition. The energies of antagonism, judgment, hatred, and the like set up a counterforce in which somebody has to lose. When you have an enemy, you need to establish a defense system, and having to defend yourself becomes the nature of your relationship. One person's need to move against and polarize sets in motion the conditions for war. War is always expensive. This is all avoidable by staying connected to intention and bringing that higher energy to your relationships, allowing those you encounter to feel the oneness with you, with everyone else, with nature, and with God.

Your presence instills a sense of purpose. When you're in the higher spiritual energies, you bring something to others that's almost inexplicable. Your presence and behavior from a space of love, acceptance, nonjudgment, and kindness becomes a catalyst for others feeling *on purpose* in their lives.

By staying at the higher energies of optimism, forgiveness, understanding, reverence for Spirit, creativity, serenity, and bliss, you radiate this energy and convert lower energies to your higher vibrations. These people whom you so nondeliberately impact begin to feel your quiet reverence and serenity. Your own purpose, which revolves around serving others and therefore serving God, becomes fulfilled, and as a bonus, you create allies.

I've had thousands of people tell me that just by attending a lecture or a talk at a church where the primary message is hope, love, and kindness is sufficient motivation for them to make a commitment to pursuing their purpose. When I'm the speaker at such events, I always enter from the rear of the room to take some time to drink in the energy of hope, optimism, and love. I can literally feel their collective energy. It's like a peaceful wave of pleasure, as if there were a warm shower running inside of me. This is energy. It's the stuff of intention, and it's powerfully motivating in helping everyone feel purposeful and hopeful.

Your presence allows others to trust in authentic personal connections. By bringing the traits of intention to others, you allow trust to be present. You'll notice both an inclination and a willingness on the part of others to open up and confide in you. This is related to the quality of trust. In the atmosphere of higher energy, people trust and want to share their personal stories with you. By being so connected to intention, you are more God-like, and who would you trust more than God to share your secrets with?

Recently during an early-morning whale-watching expedition, a woman who had no idea of my identity disclosed to me her history of failed relationships and how unfulfilled she felt. In conversation with me, in an energy field that allows and encourages trust, she let herself take the risk of opening up to a stranger. (This has occurred frequently since I've been living the principles of the seven faces of intention.) As St. Francis of Assisi put it, "It is no use walking anywhere to preach unless our walking is our preaching." You'll ultimately discover that by carrying this energy of intention with you, even strangers will do what they can to serve you and help you accomplish your own intentions.

The opposite results are apparent when you emit the lower-energy frequencies. If your distrustful energy exhibits itself in anxious, judgmental, dictatorial, superior, or demanding ways, others are disinclined to help you get what you want. The truth is that your low-energy emissions often leave others with the desire to interfere with your own intentions. Why? Because your low energies help to create a counterforce, conflict erupts, winners and losers are necessary, and enemies are created—all because of your unwillingness to stay connected to the faces of intention.

Your presence inspires others to greatness. When you're connected to Spirit and quietly reflect this consciousness, you become a source of inspiration to others. In a sense, this is one of the most powerful effects that connecting to intention transmits to others. The word *inspiration* means "in-spirit." The fact that you're primarily in-spirit means that you inspire rather than inform with your presence. You won't inspire others by loudly insisting or demanding that others listen to your point of view.

In all the years that I've been teaching, writing, lecturing, and producing tapes and videos, I've noticed a twofold process at work. I feel on purpose, inspired, and connected to universal Spirit in all of my work, and many thousands or even millions of people become inspired as a result of my own inspiration. The second factor is the vast number of people who have helped me with my work. They've sent me materials, written me inspiring stories that I've used, and literally been my co-creators. When you inspire others by your presence, you're utilizing the originating power of intention for the benefit of all those you touch, including yourself. I wholeheartedly endorse this way of being, and I know without a doubt that you too can be a presence that's inspiring to others.

Your presence aligns others with beauty. When you're connected to intention, you see beauty everywhere and in everything because you're radiating the quality of beauty. Your perceptual world changes dramatically. At the higher energy of intent, you see

beauty in everyone, young or
old, rich or poor, dark or light,
with no distinctions. Everything
is perceived from a perspective
of appreciation rather than judgment. As you bring this feeling
of beauty appreciation to the presence of others, people are inclined
to see themselves as you see them.
They feel attractive and better about
themselves as they circulate that high energy
of beauty. When people feel beautiful, they act in
beautiful ways. Your awareness of beauty impacts others to see the world
around them in the same way. The benefit, once again, is twofold. First,
you'll be helping others become appreciators of life and be happier by
virtue of their immersion into a world of beauty. Second, your own intentions receive the assistance of those people who have acquired newly
enhanced self-esteem. Beauty proliferates in others just by virtue of your
presence when you're connected to intention.

Your presence instills health rather than sickness. Your connection
to your Source keeps you focused on what you intend to manifest into
your life, with no energy given to what you don't want. This internal
focus doesn't permit you to complain about what ails you or to think
about disease, pain, or any physical difficulties. Your energy is always on
creating love, and expanding the perfection from which you originated.
This includes your body and all of your beliefs about your physical self.
You know in your heart that your body is a system of miracles. You have
great reverence for its amazing capacity to heal itself and to function on
its own without your interference. You know that your physical self is
inspired by a divine force that beats its heart, digests its food, and grows its
fingernails, and that this same force is receptive to endlessly abundant
health.

When you bring to the presence of others a healthy appreciation for
the miracle that your body represents, you defuse their efforts to dwell on
disease, ill health, and deterioration. In fact, the higher your energy field
resonates, the more you're able to impact others with your own healing

energy. (See Chapter 13 for a more thorough treatment of healing and intention.) Become aware of your own amazing capacity to affect the healing and health of those around you simply by the silent presence of your high-energy connection to intention. This is a literal energy that emanates from you.

❖❖❖

In the hopes that you will recognize the importance of raising your energy level, I'm going to conclude this chapter with a look at how our entire civilization is impacted when energy levels are synchronized with the Source of our Creation. This will require an open mind and a bit of stretching on your part; however, it's something that I know is true, and I'd be remiss if I left it out. It may appear peculiar or even outlandish to some who fail to see the ways in which all of us on this planet are connected and therefore impact each other from distances not discernible by our senses.

Your Impact on the Consciousness of All of Humanity

Many years ago I was with one of my daughters as she completed a lengthy program in the wilderness to help her deal more effectively with some of her teenage dilemmas. The last thing the counselor at the wilderness camp said to her was, "Remember at all times that what you think and what you do affects other people." This is true even beyond the impact we have on our friends, family, neighbors, and co-workers. I believe that we impact *all* of humanity. Thus, as you read this section, keep in mind that *what you think and do affects all other people.*

In *Power vs. Force,* Dr. David Hawkins writes: "In this interconnected universe, every improvement we make in our private world improves the world at large for everyone. We all float on the collective level of consciousness of mankind, so that any increment we add comes back to us. We all add to our common buoyancy by our efforts to benefit life. It is a scientific fact that what is good for you is good for me." Dr. Hawkins has backed up his remarks and conclusions with 29 years of hard research, which I invite you to examine if you're so inclined. I'll briefly summarize some of these conclusions and how they relate to the impact you have on others when you're connected to intention.

In essence, every single person as well as large groups of people can be calibrated for their energy levels. Generally speaking, low-energy people cannot distinguish truth from falsehood. They can be told how to think, whom to hate, whom to kill; and they can be herded into a group-think mentality based on such trivial details as what side of the river they were born on, what their parents and their grandparents believed, the shape of their eyes, and hundreds of other factors having to do with appearance and total identification with their material world. Hawkins tells us that approximately 87 percent of humanity calibrates at a collective energy level that weakens them. The higher up the ladder of frequency vibration, the fewer people there are in those high levels. The highest levels are represented by the truly great persons who originated spiritual patterns that multitudes have followed throughout the ages. They're associated with divinity, and they set in motion attractor energy fields that influence all of humankind.

Just below the energy level of pure enlightenment are the energy levels associated with the experience designated as transcendence, self-realization, or God consciousness. Here's where those who are called saintly reside. Just below this level is the place of pure joy, and the hallmark of this state is compassion. Those who attain this level have more of a desire to use their consciousness for the benefit of life itself rather than for particular individuals.

Below these supremely high levels, which few ever attain in a permanent way, are the levels of unconditional love, kindness, acceptance of everyone, beauty appreciation, and on a more limited but nonetheless profound level, all of the seven faces of intention described in the opening chapters of this book. Below the levels of energy that strengthen us are the low energy levels of anger, fear, grief, apathy, guilt, hatred, judgment, and shame—all of which weaken and impact us in such a way as to inhibit our connection to the universal energy level of intention.

What I'd like you to do here is take a leap of faith with me, while I present a few of the conclusions that Dr. Hawkins came to in his second book, called *The Eye of the I.* Through his precise kinesiological testing for truth versus falsehood, he's calibrated the approximate number of people whose energy is at or below the level that weakens. I'd like you to consider his findings and conclusions relative to your impact on civilization. Dr. Hawkins suggests that it's crucial for each of us to be aware of the significance of raising our frequency of vibration to the level where we begin to match up with the energy of the universal Source, or in other words, make our connection to the power of intention.

One of the most fascinating aspects of this line of research is the idea of counterbalancing. High-energy people counterbalance the negative effect of low-energy people. But it doesn't happen on a one-to-one basis because of that 87 percent of humanity that's in the lower weakening frequencies. One person connected to intention, as I've described it here in this book, can have an enormous impact on many people in the lower energy patterns. The higher up the scale you move toward actually being the light of enlightenment and knowing God consciousness, the more negatively vibrating energies you can counterbalance. Here are some fascinating figures from Dr. Hawkins's research for you to contemplate as you review the impact you can have on humanity simply by being on the higher rungs of the ladder to intention:

- *One individual who lives and vibrates to the energy of optimism and a willingness to be nonjudgmental of others will counterbalance the negativity of 90,000 individuals who calibrate at the lower weakening levels.*

- *One individual who lives and vibrates to the energy of pure love and reverence for all of life will counterbalance the negativity of 750,000 individuals who calibrate at the lower weakening levels.*

- *One individual who lives and vibrates to the energy of illumination, bliss, and infinite peace will counterbalance the negativity of 10 million people who calibrate at the lower weakening levels (approximately 22 such sages are alive today).*

- *One individual who lives and vibrates to the energy of grace, pure spirit beyond the body, in a world of nonduality or complete oneness, will counterbalance the negativity of 70 million people who calibrate at the lower weakening levels (approximately 10 such sages are alive today).*

Here are two compelling statistics offered by Dr. Hawkins in his 29-year study on the hidden determinants of human behavior:

1. One single avatar living at the highest level of consciousness in this period of history to whom the title *Lord* is appropriate, such as Lord Krishna, Lord Buddha, and Lord Jesus Christ, would counterbalance the collective negativity of *all of mankind* in today's world.

2. The negativity of the entire human population would self-destruct were it not for the counteracting effects of these higher energy fields.

The implications of these figures are immense for discovering ways of improving human consciousness and raising ourselves to the place where we match up with the same energy of intention from which we were intended. By raising your own frequency of vibration only slightly to a place where you regularly practice kindness, love, and receptivity, and where you see beauty and the endless potential of good in others as well as yourself, you counterbalance 90,000 people somewhere on this planet who are living in the low-energy levels of shame, anger, hatred, guilt, despair, depression, and so on.

I can't help thinking of John F. Kennedy's handling of the Cuban missile crisis in the 1960s. He was surrounded by advisors urging the use of nuclear bombs if necessary. Yet his own energy and that of a few trusted colleagues who were steeped in the potential for a peaceful resolution served to counterbalance the vast majority of those who pushed for attack and bellicosity. One person with very high spiritual energy can put the possibility of war into a last-resort category. This is true in your own life. Bring the energy of intention to the presence of conflict even in family matters, and you can nullify and convert the lower antagonistic energy with your presence.

I've done this in a hostile setting where young people influenced by alcohol and drugs were squaring off to fight while a crowd urged them on. On one occasion, I simply walked between two potential combatants humming the song, "Surely the Presence of God Is in This Place," and that energy alone softened the atmosphere, raising the level of energy to peace.

In another instance, I approached a woman who was immersed in having an angry fit with her toddler in a grocery store and screaming hateful epithets at the two-year-old. I quietly moved into the energy field, said nothing, but radiated my desire for a higher energy of love, and it nullified the low energy of hatred. Consider the importance of becoming aware of the impact you have on others, and remind yourself that by raising your own energy level to a place where you're in harmony with intention, you become an instrument, or a channel, of peace. This works everywhere, so be a part of the counterbalance to the human negativity you encounter in your life.

Five Suggestions for Implementing
the Ideas in This Chapter

1. *Become aware of the importance of making all of your relationships divine.* The holy relationship isn't based on any religion. The holy relationship emphasizes the unfolding of Spirit in everyone. Your children are spiritual beings who come *through* you, not *for* you. Your love relationship can focus on wanting for your partner what you want for yourself. If you want freedom, want it for everyone you love. If you want abundance, want it first for others. If you want happiness, want it more for others, and let them know it. The more you have holiness as the centerpiece of your relationships, the more you'll merge with intention.

2. *When a question of morality arises concerning how you should act toward others, simply ask yourself, <u>What would the Messiah do?</u>* This inner inquiry returns you to the tranquility of intention. The Messiah represents the seven faces of intention all manifested in a spiritual being having a human experience. In this way, you're honoring the Christ in you that is also in everyone else. Practice wanting for others what you want for yourself by being Christ-like rather than a Christian, Mohammed-like rather than a Muslim, and Buddha-like rather than a Buddhist.

3. *Keep track of the judgments you direct toward yourself and others.* Make a conscious effort to shift to compassionate thoughts and feelings. Offer a silent blessing to beggars rather than judging them as lazy or a drain on the economy. Your thoughts of compassion raise your level of energy and facilitate your staying connected to intention. Be compassionate toward everyone you meet, all of humanity, the entire kingdom of animal life, and our planet and cosmos as well. In return, the universal Source of all life will bestow compassion upon you, helping you manifest your own individual intention. It's the law of attraction.

Send out compassion, attract it back; send out hostility and judgment, attract it back. Watch your thoughts, and when they're anything other than compassionate, change them!

4. *Whatever others want, want it for them so strongly that you disperse this energy outward and act from this level of spiritual consciousness.* Attempt to feel what would make others most happy and fulfilled. Then send the high energy of intention to that feeling and concentrate on beaming this energy outward, particularly while in their presence. This will help to create a doubly high field for such intentions to manifest.

5. *Be continually alert to the fact that simply by thinking and feeling in harmony with the seven faces of intention, you'll be counterbalancing the collective negativity of a minimum of 90,000 people, and perhaps millions.* Nothing to do. No one to convert. No goals to accomplish. Nothing more than raising your own energy level to the creative, kind, loving, beautiful, ever-expanding, endlessly abundant, and receptive-to-all-without-judgment frequencies. These inner attitudes will raise you to the level where your presence will impact humanity in a positive way. In *Autobiography of a Yogi,* Swami Sri Yukteswar tells Paramahansa Yogananda: "The deeper the self-realization of a man, the more he influences the whole universe by his subtle spiritual vibrations, and the less he himself is affected by the phenomenal flux."

You have a responsibility to the entire human family to stay connected to intention. Otherwise you could be depressing someone in Bulgaria right at this moment!

✵✵✵

With these words, Mahatma Gandhi sums up this chapter on how we can impact the world by staying connected to that which intended us here in the first place: "We must be the change we wish to see in the world." By being it, we connect to the eternal part of us that originates in infinity. This whole idea of infinity and coming to grips with how it affects our ability to know and employ the power of intention is vastly mysterious. It's the subject matter for the final chapter in Part I of this book. We'll explore infinity from a body and a mind that begins and ends in time, yet somehow knows that the *I* that is in here has always been and always will be.

Intention and Infinity

*"Eternity is not the hereafter . . . this is it.
If you don't get it here, you won't get it anywhere."*

— Joseph Campbell

Please indulge me in a little exercise right here, right now. Put this book down, and say out loud: *I'm not from here.* Let the meaning of the words be clear to you. The meaning is that you are *in* this world, but not *of* this world. You've been taught that who you are is a body with your name, made up of molecules, bones, tissue, oxygen, hydrogen, and nitrogen. You know yourself as the person with your particular name, and you identify yourself as the person with the possessions and achievements that you've accumulated. This *self* also possesses some terrifying information. It knows that *if it's lucky,* it's destined to grow old, get sick, and lose everything that it's grown to love. Then it will die. This is a shortened version of what the world has offered you, which probably leaves you mystified and flabbergasted at the absurdity of this thing we call life. Into this bleak picture, which inspires fear and even terror, I'd like to introduce a concept that will eliminate the terror. I want you to know that you needn't subscribe to the idea that you are only this collection of bones and tissues, destined to be annihilated in an aging process.

You've emerged from a universal field of Creation that I've been calling *intention*. In a sense, this universal mind is totally impersonal. It is pure love, fondness, beauty, and creativity, always expanding and endlessly abundant. You emanated from this universal mind. And as I keep telling you, *universal means everywhere and at all times*. In other words, *infinite*. As long as your wishes are aligned with the forward movement of this everlasting principle, there's nothing in nature to restrict you from attaining the fulfillment of those wishes. It's only when you choose to allow ego to oppose the expanding, receptive forward movement of the infinite mind of intention that the realization of your wishes doesn't feel fulfilling. Life itself is eternal, and you spring from this infinite *no thing* called life. Your ability to connect to the eternal and live in the here-and-now will determine your staying connected to intention.

Life Is Eternal

We all live on a stage where many infinities gather. Just take a look outside tonight and contemplate the infinity of space. There are stars so distant from you that they're measured in the distance that light travels in an Earthly year. Beyond those stars that you can see are endless galaxies that stretch out into something we call eternity. Indeed, the space that you occupy is infinite. Its vastness is too huge for us to see. We're in an infinite, never-ending, never-beginning universe.

Now pay close attention to this next sentence. *If life is infinite, then this is not life.* Read that again and consider that life truly is infinite. We can see this in everything that we scrupulously observe. Therefore, we must conclude that life, in terms of our body and all of its achievements and possessions, which without exception begins and ends in dust, isn't life itself. Grasping life's true essence could radically change *your* life for the better. This is an enormous inner shift that eliminates fear of death (how can you fear something that can't exist?) and connects you permanently to the infinite Source of Creation that *intends* everything from the world of infinite Spirit, into a finite world. Learn to be comfortable with the concept of infinity, and see yourself as an infinite being.

While we're in this finite world of beginnings and endings, the power of intention maintains its infinite nature because it's eternal. Anything you experience as other than eternal is simply not life. It's an illusion created by your ego, which strives to maintain a separate address and identity from its infinite Source. This shift toward seeing yourself as an infinite spiritual being having a human experience, rather than the reverse—that is, a human being having an occasional spiritual experience—is loaded with fear for most people. I urge you to look at those fears and face them directly right now; the result will be a permanent connection to the abundance and receptivity of the universal Source that intends all of Creation into temporary form.

Your Fear of the Infinite

We are all in bodies that are going to die, and we know this, yet we can't imagine it for *ourselves,* so we behave as if it weren't so. It's almost as if we're saying to ourselves, *Everybody dies but me.* This is attributable to what Freud observed. Our death is unimaginable, so we simply deny it and live our lives as if we weren't going to die . . . because of the terror that our own death instills. As I sat down to write this chapter, I said to a friend that my goal was to leave the reader with a complete absence of the fear of death. Let me know if it touches you in that way, even on a minor scale.

When I was a seven-year-old, I lived with my older brother, David, in a foster home at 231 Townhall Road, in Mt. Clemens, Michigan. The people who took us in while my mother worked to reunite her family were named Mr. and Mrs. Scarf. I remember this as if it occurred yesterday. David and I were sitting on the back porch of our home, and Mrs. Scarf came outside with two bananas in her hand

and tears flowing down her face. She gave us each a banana, saying, "Mr. Scarf died this morning." It was the first time I'd experienced the concept of death connected to a human being. In my seven-year-old naïveté, I asked her, attempting to soothe her obvious pain, "When will he be back?" Mrs. Scarf responded with one word that I've never forgotten. She simply said, "Never."

I went upstairs to my bunk, peeled my banana, and lay there attempting to comprehend the concept of *never*. What did being dead forever really mean? I could have handled a thousand years, or even a billion light years, but the idea of *never* was so overwhelming, with its no ending, and more no ending, that I was almost sick to my stomach. What did I do to handle this incomprehensible idea of never? Simple, I forgot about it and went on about the business of being seven years old in a foster home. This is what Castaneda meant when he said that we're all in bodies on their way to dying, but we behave as if they're not, and this is our greatest downfall.

Your own death. Essentially, there are two points of view regarding this dilemma of your own death. The first says that we're physical bodies that are born and we go on to live for a while; and then ultimately we deteriorate, our flesh wears out, and then we die and are dead forever. This first perspective, if you embrace it either consciously or otherwise, is terrifying from our alive viewpoint. Unless you embrace the second point of view, it's completely understandable that you fear death. Or you may welcome it if you hate or fear life. The second point of view says very simply that you're eternal, an infinite soul in a temporary expression of flesh. This second point of view says that only your physical body dies, that you were whole and perfect as you were created, and that your physicalness emanated from the universal mind of intention. That universal mind was and is formless—it's the pure energy of love, beauty, kindness, and creativity, and it can't die, since there's no

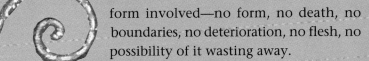

form involved—no form, no death, no boundaries, no deterioration, no flesh, no possibility of it wasting away.

Now which of these two points of view gives you the most comfort? Which is associated with peace and love? Which invokes fear and anxiety? Obviously the idea of your infinite self keeps you on friendly terms with infinity. Knowing you're first and foremost an infinite being consciously connecting with your Source, which is eternal and omnipresent, is surely the more comforting prospect. Because of its infinite nature, it's everywhere, and it then follows that the whole of Spirit must be present at every point in space at the same moment.

Thus, Spirit is present in its entirety everywhere, which includes you. You can never, ever be separate from it. You'll learn to laugh at the absurd idea that you could ever be separate from the universal mind. It's your Source. You are it. God is the mind through which you think and exist. It's always connected to you, even if you don't believe in it. Even an atheist doesn't have to believe in God to experience God. The question then becomes, not whether your body is going to die, but rather, on what side of infinity you wish to live. You have two choices, either you live on the *inactive* or the *active side of infinity*. In either case, you have an appointment with infinity, and there's no way to avoid it.

Your appointment with infinity. Reread the Joseph Campbell quote at the beginning of this chapter. Eternity is now! Right now, right here, you're an infinite being. Once you get past the fear of death as an end, you merge with the infinite and feel the comfort and relief that this realization brings. We identify everything in this material world through a space-time continuum. Yet infinity has no preference for time and space. You aren't the elements that make up your body; you merely make use of the elements. You go beyond space and time and are merged with the infinite universal mind. If you haven't recognized it, it's because of your fear. You can keep your appointment with infinity while you're in your temporary body, with its slavish adherence to time and space. My objective in this chapter is to help you realize and do this. If you make this merger, I assure you of a life without fear of death.

Let's take a look at both of the elements in the space/time prison in which we find our material bodies and all of its treasures. The factor of space means that we're experiencing separation from everyone and everything. This is *my space* as defined by my boundaries; those are *your* spaces. Even your most cherished soul mate lives in a world apart from yours. No matter how close in space you get, the boundaries are separate. In space, we're always separate. Trying to imagine an infinite world without space and separation is extremely difficult, until we make our appointment with infinity.

Time is also a factor of separation. We're separated from all of the events and memories of our past. Everything that has happened is separate from what's happening right now. The future is also separate from the here-and-now where we're living. We can't know the future, and the past is lost to us. Therefore, we're separated from everything that ever was or ever will be by this mysterious illusion we call time.

When your infinite soul leaves the body, it's no longer subject to the constraints of time and space. Separation can no longer interfere with you. So my question to you isn't about whether you believe you have an appointment with infinity. It's about when you're going to keep that inevitable appointment. You can either do it now while you're still alive in your body in the illusion of time and space, or you can do it at death. If you decide to make your appointment with infinity while you still live and breathe, it's like learning to die while you're alive. Once you make this transition to the active side of infinity, your fear of death dissolves and you laugh at the folly of death.

Understand your true essence, look death squarely in the face, and break the shackles of slavery to that fear. *You* do not die. Announce it. Meditate on it. Look at it from this angle: *If you're not an infinite being, what would be the purpose of your life?* Surely not going through the motions of being born, working, accumulating, losing it all, getting sick, and dying. By waking up to your infinite essence and staying connected to the seven faces of intention, you begin to free yourself of the limitations your ego has placed on you. You set in motion the guidance and assistance of the infinite universal mind to work with you. And most of all, you feel the peace that overtakes you when you expel your fear of death and mortality. I'm touched by the stories of great spiritual teachers leaving this Earthly plane feeling blissful and fearless. They banished all doubt, extricated all fear, and met infinity head-on with grace. Here are the final words of a few of the people I've long admired:

The hour I have long wished for is now come.
— Teresa of Avila

Let us be kinder to one another.
— Aldous Huxley

If this is death, it is easier than life.
— Robert Louis Stevenson

This is the last of earth! I am content.
— John Quincy Adams

I shall hear in heaven.
— Ludwig van Beethoven

Light, light, the world needs more light.
— Johann Wolfgang von Goethe

I am going to that country which I have all my life wished to see.
— William Blake

It is very beautiful over there.
— Thomas Edison

Ram, Ram, Ram [God, God, God].
— Mahatma Gandhi

Why not write your own final words now and make your transition to being an infinite being while you still occupy your body? As you consider your appointment with infinity, look at how most of us live our lives. We know we're in a *body* that's going to die, but we behave as if it's not going to happen to us. This viewpoint is from the inactive side of infinity where we don't see our connection to intention and our ability to stay in harmony with our creative Spirit. Let's examine the essential difference between keeping your appointment with infinity now, or at your death. In one case, you'll be on the active side of infinity, and in the other, you'll avoid it by being on the inactive side.

The Active vs. the Inactive Sides of Infinity

On the active side of infinity, you're fully cognizant that you're in a body that's going to die. Furthermore, your inner knowing is that you aren't that body, its mind, or any of its achievements and possessions. On this active side of infinity, you have a good grip on that trolley strap I described earlier, which is connected to intent, and you're an observer of all your sensory experiences. This may not sound like a big deal to you; however, I assure you that once you move your inner awareness to the active side of infinity, you'll begin to notice miraculous happenings in your daily life. On this active side of infinity, you are first and foremost an infinite spiritual being having a temporary human experience, and you do all of your living in all of your relationships from this perspective. On the inactive side of infinity, your experience of life is quite the opposite. Here, you're first and foremost a human being having an occasional spiritual experience. Your life is guided by a fear of death, a separation from others, a competitive style, and a need to dominate and be a winner. The inactive side of infinity separates you from the power of intention.

Here are some of the distinctions that I see between those who live in the active side of infinity and those who deny their eternal nature and opt for the inactive side of infinity:

A sense of destiny. In the active side of infinity, your connection to intention will no longer be thought of as an option, but as a calling that you must heed. The inactive side of infinity leads you to see life as chaotic, purposeless, and meaningless, while your position on the active side of infinity leads you to fulfill a destiny that you feel deep within you.

When I look back at my life, I realize that my sense of destiny was directing me at an early age. I've known since I was a child that I could manifest abundance into my life. While sitting in high school and college classrooms where I was bored to death by teachers who conveyed their lack of passion in their dreary presentations, I dreamed of talking to large audiences. I vowed in those youthful days that I'd live my passion, and somehow knew that I was here for a reason. I couldn't allow anyone or anything to deter me from my path. I've always sensed that I'm really an infinite soul, disguised at various times as a husband, father, author, lecturer, and balding six-foot-plus American male. Because I live on the active side of infinity, I have a sense of destiny that won't allow me to die with my music still in me.

You can make the same kinds of choices. Just let go of the idea that you're a body that's destined to die, and instead seek an awareness of your immortal self. On the active side of infinity, you'll find your greater self, of which a small part has materialized as your body. I guarantee you that simply recognizing yourself as an infinite and therefore indestructible being, your connection to intention and the ability to manifest all that you desire within the confines of your universal Source will become your reality. There's no other way.

Your sense of destiny lets you know that you're playing this game of life on the active side of infinity. Prior to accessing your sense of destiny, your motivation was what you wanted out of life and what you'd like to do. On the active side of infinity, you realize that it's time to do what your destiny intended you to do. Wallowing around hoping things will work out, waiting for your luck to change, and hoping others will come through for you no longer feels right. Your sense of destiny allows you to realize, *I am eternal, and that means that I showed up here from the infinitude of spiritual intention to fulfill a destiny that I must act on.* You begin stating your objectives in the language of intention, knowing they'll materialize. You enlist the power of intention to keep you on track. It can't fail because there's no failure in the infinite.

This 13th-century poem may inspire you to know you have *your* destiny:

> *You were born with potential.*
> *You were born with goodness and trust.*
> *You were born with ideals and dreams.*
> *You were born with greatness.*
> *You were born with wings.*
> *You are not meant for crawling, so don't.*
> *You have wings.*
> *Learn to use them and fly.*
>
> — Rumi

If Rumi composed his poem from the inactive side of infinity, his words might be more like the following.

> *You are an accident of nature.*
> *You are subject to the laws of luck and chance.*
> *You can be pushed around easily.*
> *Your dreams are meaningless.*
> *You were meant to live an ordinary life.*
> *You have no wings.*
> *So forget about flying and stay grounded.*

A sense of the possible. Creation acts upon the everlasting *possibility* that anything that is thought of, can be. Consider some of the numerous great inventions, which we take for granted today: airplanes, electric lights, telephones, television, fax machines, computers. They're all the result of creative ideas by individuals who ignored the ridicule they encountered while they stayed focused on *possible* rather than impossible. In other words, a sense of the possible grows in the fertile terrain of the active side of infinity.

I have here in my writing space a wonderful account of four children who refused to allow the word *impossible* into their hearts:

Eddie was born without hands or feet. At age five, he went to South Africa and saw a mountain he wanted to climb; he climbed it in three hours. And at age 13, he decided to play a trombone. He sees no reason why he shouldn't achieve whatever he sets out to do. He lives on the active side of infinity, consulting that world of infinite possibilities.

Abby was desperately ill and needed a heart transplant. When she saw her mother crying, she told her, "Mommy don't cry, I'm going to get better." At the 11th hour, a heart miraculously became available, and Abby *is* better. Abby's intention came from that world of infinite possibilities. It's the active side of infinity where intentions manifest.

Stephanie was five years old when she came down with meningitis and had to have both of her legs amputated. Today at age 12, she rides her own bicycle and has dreams that go way beyond those of most teenagers who possess all of their limbs. Her personal slogan is: *Push to the limit.*

After two major heart operations while just a toddler, the doctors told little Frankie's parents that they could do no more. Frankie lived only because she was on a life-support machine. When her parents were advised to have the machine turned off because Frankie couldn't survive and would only suffer, they finally agreed. But Frankie survived. She was somehow on the active side of the world of infinite possibilities. The caption beneath her photo says it all: *You didn't think you could get rid of me that easily, did you?*

The power of intention involves staying on the active side of infinite possibilities. George Bernard Shaw, who was still creating into his 90s, has been quoted as saying, "You see things as they are and you say, 'Why?' But I dream things that never were, and I say 'Why not?'" Think of Shaw's words as you practice staying on the active side of infinity and seeing the infinite possibilities that are available to all of us.

A sense of awe. You have to admit that just the concept of infinity is awesome. No beginning. No ending. Everywhere at once. No time. And all of it here and now. The fact that you're a part of this infinite universe and that you emerged into the finite is mind-boggling. It defies description. The active side of infinity inspires a sense of awe. When you're in a state of awe, you're in a persistent state of gratitude. Perhaps the surest way to happiness and fulfillment in life is to thank and praise your Source for *everything* that happens to you. Then, even when a calamity arises, you can be assured that you'll turn it into a blessing.

In the inactive side of infinity, you assume that you're only here temporarily, and therefore you have no obligation to the universe, the planet, or its inhabitants. By denying your infinite nature, you move through life taking everyday miracles for granted. As you become acquainted with your eternal nature, you have a very different point of view. You're in a persistent state of gratitude for all that shows up. This state is the secret to fulfilling your own individual human intentions, and without it, all of your most sincere efforts will amount to naught.

Being in a state of gratitude actually creates magnetism, and of course, a magnet draws things to itself. By giving authentic thanks for all the good you now have, as well as the challenges, through this magnetism you'll start the flow of more good into your life. Every successful person I know is grateful for *everything* he or she has. This process of giving thanks opens the door for more to come. It's how being in active infinity works. Your sense of awe at all of the miracles you see around you allows you to think, see, and live more of these miraculous occurrences. In contrast, a state of ingratitude stops the infinite flow of abundance and health. It's a door closer.

A sense of humility. The active side of infinity fosters a sense of humility. When humility enters your soul, you know that you're not alone in this world, because you sense the heart of the power of intention, which is in each and everyone of us. To quote the Talmud, "Even if you be otherwise perfect, you fail without humility." When you embrace the active side of infinity, you're looking at something so enormous that your little ego is dwarfed in the process. You're looking out at *forever,* and your little life is but a tiny parenthesis in eternity.

One of the reasons for so much contemporary depression and ennui is the inability to see ourselves connected to something greater and more important than our own puny egos. Young people whose primary focus is on their possessions, their appearance, their reputations with their peers—in short, their own egos—have very little sense of humility. When the only thing you have to think about is yourself and how you appear to others, you've distanced yourself from the power of intention. If you want to feel connected to your own purpose, know this for certain: *Your purpose will only be found in service to others, and in being connected to something far greater than your body/mind/ego.*

I always told my young clients in counseling who were desperate for approval from their peers that the more they chase after approval, the more they'll be disapproved of because no one wants to be around those who beg for approval. People who receive the most approval are unconcerned about it. So, if you really want approval, stop thinking about yourself, and focus on reaching out and helping others. The active side of infinity keeps you humble. The inactive side of infinity keeps you focused on me, me, me, and ultimately is a roadblock to your connection to intention.

Wilhelm Stekel made a remarkable comment on the importance of humility (which was quoted by J. D. Salinger in *Catcher in the Rye).* Stekel wrote: "The mark of the immature man is that he wants to die nobly for a cause, while the mark of the mature man is that he wants to live humbly for one."

A sense of generosity. If asked, *Why do you give us light and warmth?* I believe that the sun would answer, *It's my nature to do so.* We must be like the sun, and locate and dispense our giving nature.

When you're on the active side of infinity, giving is your nature.

The more you give of yourself, no matter how little, the more you open the door for life to pour in. This not only compensates you for your gift, it also increases the desire to give, and consequently the ability to receive as well. When you're on the inactive side of infinity, you view life in terms of shortages, and hoarding becomes a way of living. Generosity, as well as the inclination to reach your intentions, is lost when you think in these terms. If you can't see an infinite universe, with infinite supply, and infinite time and an infinite Source, you'll be inclined to hoard and be stingy. The power of intention is paradoxically experienced through what you're willing to give to others. Intention is a field of energy, which is emanating in infinite supply. What can you give if you don't have money to give? I love Swami Sivananda's advice, and I encourage you to consider it here. Everything that he suggests, you own in infinite amounts.

> *The best thing to give*
> *your enemy is forgiveness;*
> *to an opponent, tolerance;*
> *to a friend, your heart;*
> *to your child, a good example;*
> *to your father, deference;*
> *to your mother, conduct that will make her*
> *proud of you;*
> *to your self, respect;*
> *to all men, charity.*

Make giving a way of life. It is, after all, what Source and nature do eternally. I've heard it said about nature that trees bend low with ripened fruit; clouds hang down with gentle rain; noble men bow graciously. This is the way of generous things.

A sense of knowing. Your infinite Source of intention has no doubt. It knows, and consequently it acts upon that knowing. This is what will happen for you when you live on the active side of infinity. All doubt flies out of your heart forever. As an infinite being in a temporary human form, you'll identify yourself primarily on the basis of your spiritual nature.

This sense of knowing that comes from the active side of infinity means that you no longer think in terms of limits. *You* are the Source. The Source is unlimited. It knows no boundaries; it's endlessly expansive, and endlessly abundant. This is what you are, too. Discarding doubt is a decision to reconnect to your original self. This is the mark of people who live self-actualized lives. They think in no-limit, infinite ways. One of the no-limit qualities is the ability to think and act as if what they'd like to have is already present. This is another one of my ten secrets for success and inner peace in the book of the same title. The power of intention is so doubt-deficient that when you're connected to it, your sense of knowing sees what you'd like to have as already present. There are no contrary opinions whatsoever.

Here's my advice for accessing the power of intention: Stay on the active side of the infinite, where all of the energy for creation exists in everlasting supply. Night and day, dream of what you intend to do and what you intend to be, and those dreams will interpret your intentions. Let no doubt into your dreams and intentions. The dreamers are the saviors of the world. Just as the visible world is sustained by the invisible, so too do the manifestations of man find nourishment in the visions of our solitary dreamers. Be one of those dreamers.

A sense of passion. The Greeks have given us one of the most beautiful words of our language: *enthusiasm.* The word *enthusiasm* translates to "a God within." Within you is an infinite passionate soul that wishes to express itself. It's the God within you, urging you to fulfill a deep sense of what you were meant to be. All of our acts are measured by the inspiration from which they originate. When your acts display the faces of intention, they spring from a God residing within you. This is enthusiasm. When you emulate the power of intention, this is where you'll feel the passion you were intended to feel and live.

The beauty of feeling passionate and enthusiastic is the glorious feeling of joy and cheerfulness that comes along with it. Nothing provides me with more joy than sitting here and writing to you from my heart. I enthusiastically allow these teachings to come through me from the Source of all intention, the universal mind of all creativity. Put quite simply, I feel good, I'm in a cheerful mood, and my inspiration provides me with joy. If you want to feel great, look into the mirror, say to your image, *I am eternal; this image will fade, but I am infinite. I am here temporarily for a reason. I will be passionate about all that I do.* Then just notice how you feel as you stare at your reflection. Being cheerful is a wondrous side benefit of enthusiasm. It comes from being in the active side of infinity where there's absolutely nothing to feel bad about.

A sense of belonging. In a world that lasts forever, you certainly must belong! The active side of infinity inspires not only a strong sense of belonging, but a strong feeling of connectedness to everyone and everything in the cosmos. It's impossible for you not to belong, because your presence here is evidence that a divine universal Source intended you here. Yet when you live on the inactive side of infinity, you feel a sense of alienation from others. Your idea that this is all temporary and that you aren't a piece of God's infinite perfection leads you to self-doubt, anxiety, self-rejection, depression, and so many more of the low energies I've written about throughout this book. All it takes is a shift to infinite awareness to leave that feeling of misery. As Sivananda taught his devotees:

> All life is one. The world is one home.
> All are members of one human family.
> All creation is an organic whole. No
> Man is independent of this whole. Man
> Makes himself miserable by separating
> Himself from others. Separation is death.
> Unity is eternal life.

❖ ❖ ❖

This concludes my ideas on the active and inactive side of infinity. I urge you to remind yourself every day, as frequently as possible, of your infinite nature. It may sound like merely an intellectual shift of minor consequence, but I assure you that staying on the active side of infinity and reminding yourself of it regularly will put you in a position to manifest your desires. Of all the quotes on this subject I've read, this observation made by William Blake stands out: "If the doors of perception were cleansed, everything would appear to man as it is: infinite." Remember, we're attempting to clean up the connecting link between ourselves and the field of intention.

Five Suggestions for Implementing the Ideas in This Chapter

1. *Since you already know that you have an appointment with infinity and that you're ultimately required to leave this corporeal world behind, make the decision to do so sooner, rather than later.* In fact today, right now, is a great time to keep that appointment, and get it over with once and for all. Simply announce to yourself: *I'm no longer identified by this body/mind, and I reject this label from this moment on. I'm infinite. I'm one with all of humanity. I'm one with my Source, and this is how I choose to view myself from this day forward.*

2. *Repeat this mantra to yourself each day as you remind yourself that God wouldn't and couldn't create something that doesn't last: I will exist for all eternity. Just as love is eternal, so is this my true nature. I'll never be afraid again, because I am forever.* This kind of inner affirmation aligns you on the active side of infinity and erases doubts about your authentic higher identity.

135

3. *In a meditative stance, consider the two choices of belief on this concept of infinity.* You are in the truest sense, as I've said previously, either a human being having an occasional spiritual experience, or an infinite spiritual being having a temporary human experience. Which of those gives you a feeling of love? And which inspires fear? Now, since love is our true nature and the Source of all, anything that creates fear can't be real. As you see, the feeling of love is associated with yourself as an infinite being. Then you must rely on this feeling to tell you the truth. Your place in the active side of infinity assures you of a feeling of security, love, and permanent connection to intention.

4. *In any moment in which you find yourself thinking low-energy thoughts of fear, despair, worry, sadness, anxiety, guilt, and so on, just for a moment stop and consider whether this makes any sense from the perspective of the active side of infinity.* Knowing that you're here forever, and always connected to your Source, will give you an entirely new outlook. In the context of infinity, living any moment of your life in anything other than appreciation and love is a waste of your life energy. You can quickly dissipate those lower energies and simultaneously connect to the power of intention by cleansing those lenses of perception and seeing everything as it is—*infinite,* as William Blake suggested.

5. *Take a few moments to reflect on the people you were close to and loved who have crossed over.* Being aware of your infinite nature, and staying in infinity's active side, allows you to feel the presence of these souls, who can't die and did not die. In John O'Donohue's book of Celtic wisdom called *Anam Cara,* he offers these words with which I not only concur, but I know to be true from my own personal experience:

I believe that our friends among the dead really mind us and look out for us . . . we might be able to link up in a very creative way with our friends in the invisible world. We do not need to grieve for the dead. Why should we grieve for them? They are now in a place where there is no more shadow, darkness, loneliness, isolation or pain. They are home. They are with God from whom they came.

You can not only communicate with and feel the presence of those who've crossed over, you yourself can die while you're alive and rid yourself now of these shadows and darkness, by living in the active side of infinity.

This concludes Part I of *The Power of Intention.* Part II will be a series of chapters describing how to put this new connection to intention to work in a variety of ways in your life. As with the first part, read on with a mind that is not only open to the possibility of your achieving all that you can imagine, but to knowing that on the active side of infinity all things are possible.

Now, you tell me what that leaves out!

❀❀❀❀❀

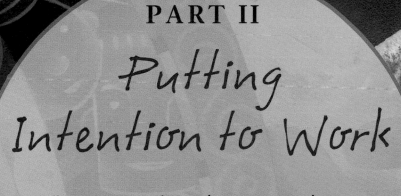

PART II

Putting Intention to Work

"We are already one and we imagine we are not. And what we have to recover is our original unity. Whatever we have to be is what we are."

— Thomas Merton

It Is My Intention to: Respect Myself at All Times

"A man cannot be comfortable without his own approval."

— Mark Twain

ere's a simple truth to begin this chapter: You did not originate from a material particle as you've been led to believe. Your conception at the moment of your parents' blissful commingling was not your beginning. You had no beginning. That particle emanated from the universal energy field of intention, as do all particles. You're a piece of that universal mind of Creation, and you must see God inside of you and view yourself as a divine creation in order to access the power of intention in your life.

Give this idea a healthy dose of your attention—right now in this moment—as you read these words. Contemplate the enormity of what you're reading. You are a piece of God. You are a living, breathing creation that emanated from the universal mind of the all-creating Source. You and God are the same thing. Very simply put, when you love and

trust yourself, you're loving and trusting the wisdom that created you; and when you fail to love and trust yourself, you're denying that infinite wisdom in favor of your own ego. It's important here to remember that at every single moment of your life, you have the choice to either be a host to God or a hostage to your ego.

Host or Hostage?

Your ego is the set of beliefs that I've written about earlier in this book, which define you as what you accomplish and accumulate in a material sense. Your ego is solely responsible for the feelings of self-doubt and self-repudiation that you may carry around. When you attempt to live by the low-level standards of your ego, you're a hostage to that very same ego. Your worth as a person is measured by your acquisitions and accomplishments. If you have less stuff, you're less valuable, and therefore unworthy of respect from others. If others don't respect you, and your value depends on how others see you, then it's unimaginable for you to have self-respect. You become a hostage to this low-level ego energy, which has you constantly striving for self-respect through others.

Your ego's belief that you're separate from everyone, separate from what's missing in your life, and most egregiously, separate from God, further hampers your ability to live up to the intention of respecting yourself. Ego's idea of separation fosters your feelings of being in competition with everyone, and evaluating your worth based on how frequently you emerge as a winner. As a hostage to your ego, self-respect is unavailable because you feel judged for your failures. It's out of this bleak picture, produced by the negative ego, that self-rejection emerges. It captures you and makes a hostage of you, never allowing you to play host to that from which you originated.

Being a host to God means always seeing your authentic connection to your Source. It's knowing that it's impossible for you to ever be disconnected from the Source from which you came. Personally, I thoroughly enjoy being a host to God. As I write here each morning, I feel that I'm receiving words and ideas from the power of intention, which allows me to bring these words to this page. I trust in this Source

to provide me with the words; therefore, I'm trusting in the Source that brought me into this physical world. I'm eternally connected to this Source.

This awareness simply doesn't include a lack of respect for intending this book into form. The conclusion I've come to is that I'm worthy of my intention to write this book and have it published and in your hands today. In other words, I respect the piece of God that I am. I tap in to the power of intention, and my feeling of respect for it enhances my respect for myself.

So, by loving and respecting yourself, you're hosting God *and* inviting the energy of Creation to your consciousness, to your daily life, as you connect to the power of intention.

The energy of intention and your self-respect. If you don't believe that you're worthy of fulfilling your intentions for health, wealth, or loving relationships, then you're creating an obstacle that will inhibit the flow of creative energy into your daily life. Recall that everything in the universe is energy, which moves at various frequencies. The higher the frequency, the closer you are to spiritual energy. In the lower frequencies, you find shortages and problems. Intention itself is a unified energy field that intends everything into existence. This field is home to the laws of nature, and is the inner domain of every human being. This is the *field of all possibilities,* and it's yours by virtue of your existence.

Having a belief system that denies your connection to intention is the only way you're unable to access the power of intention from the infinite field. If you're convinced that you're unworthy of enjoying the field of all possibilities, then you'll radiate this kind of low energy. This will, in fact, become your attracted energy pattern, and you'll send messages to the universe that you're unworthy of receiving the unlimited abundance of the originating Spirit. Soon you'll act on this

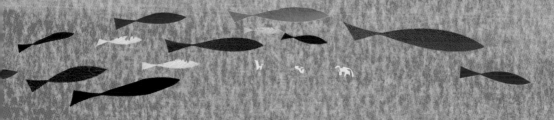

inner conviction of self-disrespect. You'll regard yourself as separate from the possibility of receiving the loving support of the originating field of intention, and you'll stop the flow of that energy into your life. Why? All because you see yourself as unworthy. This disrespect alone is sufficient to impede the arrival of your intentions into your life.

The law of attraction attracts disrespect when you're affirming that you're unworthy of being respected. Send out the message to the provider of all that you're unworthy, and you literally say to the universal Source of all, *Stop the flow of anything I desire, which is coming in my direction, because I don't believe I'm worthy of receiving it.* The universal Source will respond by halting this flow, causing you to reaffirm your inner conviction of unworthiness and attract even more disrespect in a multitude of ways. You'll disrespect your body by overfeeding it and poisoning it with toxic substances. You'll display your lack of self-respect in how you carry yourself, how you dress, how you fail to exercise, how you treat others . . . on and on goes the list.

The antidote to this dreary picture is to make an internal commitment to respect yourself and to feel worthy of all that the universe has to offer. If *anyone* is entitled to success and happiness, *everyone* is, because everyone is always connected to intention. Simply put, disrespecting yourself is not only disrespecting one of God's greatest creations, it's disrespecting God. When you disrespect your Source, you say no to it, and you turn away from the power of intention. This stops the flow of energy that allows you to put your individual unbending intent into practice. All of the positive thinking in the world will do you absolutely no good if those thoughts don't emanate from respect for your connection to intention. The *source* of your thoughts must be celebrated and loved, and this means having the self-respect that's in harmony with the omniscient Source of intelligence. What's the source of your thoughts? Your *beingness*. Your beingness is the place from which your thoughts and actions come. When you disrespect your being, you set into motion a chain reaction culminating in unfulfilled intentions.

Self-respect should be a natural state for you, just as it is for all of the animal kingdom. There's no raccoon out there who believes himself unworthy of what he intends to have. Were that so, the raccoon would simply die by acting on the basis of his inner conviction that he was unworthy of food or shelter, and whatever else raccoons desire. He knows he's respectable, never finds any reason for self-repudiation, and lives out his raccoon-ness in perfect order. The universe provides, and he attracts those provisions into his world.

What You Think of Yourself Is
What You Think of the World

How do you see the world you live in? What do you think people in general are really like? Do you believe that evil is triumphing over good? Is the world filled with egocentric, selfish people? Can the little guy ever get ahead? Are government entities and all their representatives corrupt and untrustworthy? Is life unfair? Is it impossible to get ahead if you don't have connections?

All of these attitudes emerge from your own assessment of your personal interaction with life. If your thoughts reflect a pessimistic view of the world, then that's actually how you feel about yourself. If your thoughts reflect an optimistic view of the world, then *that's* how you feel about your life. Whatever attitude you have about the world in general is a good indicator of the respect you have for your abilities to intend into this world what you desire. Pessimism strongly suggests that you don't subscribe to the idea that you can access the power of intention to help you create your own blissful reality.

I recall hearing the following conversation after the events of 9/11 in New York City. A grandfather was talking to his grandson, telling him, "I have two wolves barking inside of me. The first wolf is filled with anger, hatred, bitterness, and mostly revenge. The second wolf inside of me is filled with love, kindness, compassion, and mostly forgiveness."

"Which wolf do you think will win?" the young boy inquired.

The grandfather responded, "Whichever one I feed."

There are always two ways to look at the conditions of our world. We can see the hate, prejudice, mistreatment, starvation, poverty, and crime and conclude that this is a horrible world. We can feed this barking wolf and see more and more of what we despise. But this will only fill us with the same things that we find so malignant. Or we can look at the world from a position of self-love and self-respect, and see the improvements that have been made in race relations in our lifetime; the fall of so many dictatorships, lower crime rates, the dismantling of the atrocious apartheid systems, the elevated consciousness of the environmental movement, and the desire on the part of so many to rid our world of nuclear weapons and instruments of mass destruction. We can remind ourselves that for every act of evil in the world, there are a million acts of kindness, and we can then feed the second wolf that barks from a position of hope for humanity. If you see yourself as a divine creation, you'll look for this in your worldview, and the gloom-and-doom naysayers will have no impact on you and your self-respect.

When you have a gloomy picture of what the world looks like, you're unreceptive to the potential assistance that's there to help you with your own individual intentions. Why would others want to come to your aid when you view them as contemptible? Why would the universal force be attracted to that which repels it? How could a world that's so corrupt ever be of assistance to someone who has noble intentions? The answers to these questions are obvious. You attract into your life what you feel inside. If you feel that you're not worthy of being respected, you attract disrespect. This weak self-respect is the result of an exceptionally rusty link to the field of intention. This link must be cleansed and purified, and that takes place within your own mind.

I've specifically chosen *self-respect* as the first chapter in Part II on applying intention, because without high esteem for yourself, you shut down the entire process of intention. Without unflagging self-respect, the process of intention is operating at the lowest levels. The universal field of intention is love, kindness, and beauty, which it has for all that it brings into the material world. Those who wish to replicate the works of the universal all-creating mind must be in harmony with the attributes of love, kindness, and beauty. If you disrespect anyone or anything that God creates, you disrespect that creative force. You are one of those creations. If you view yourself disrespectfully, you've forsaken, cast aside, or at the very least, sullied your connection to the power of intention.

It's important that you recognize that your entire worldview is based on how much respect you have for yourself. Believe in infinite possibilities and you cast a vote for your own possibilities. Stand firm on the potential for humans to live in peace and be receptive to all, and you're someone who's at peace and receptive to life's possibilities. Know that the universe is filled with abundance and prosperity and is available to everyone, and you come down on the side of having that abundance show up for you as well. Your level of self-regard must come from your knowing within yourself that you have a sacred connection. Let nothing shake that divine foundation. In this way, your link to intention is cleansed, and you always know that self-respect is your personal choice. It has nothing to do with what others may think of you. Your self-respect comes from the self and the self alone.

The *self* in self-respect. Perhaps the greatest mistake we make, which causes a loss of self-respect, is making the opinions of others more important than our own opinion of ourselves. Self-respect means just what it says—it originates from the self. This *self* originated in a universal field of intention that intended you here—from the infinite formless state to a being of molecules and physical substance. If you fail to respect yourself, you're showing contempt for the process of Creation.

You'll find no shortage of opinions directed at you. If you allow them to undermine your self-respect, you're seeking the respect of others over your own, and you're abdicating yourself. Then you're attempting to reconnect to the field of intention with low-energy attitudes of judgment,

hostility, and anxiety. You'll cycle into low-energy vibrations that will simply force you to attract more and more
of these lower energies into your life. Remember,
it's high energy that nullifies and converts lower
energy. Light eradicates darkness; love dissolves
hate. If you've allowed any of those lower negative
thoughts and opinions directed your way to become the basis of your
self-portrait, you're asking the universal mind do the same. Why? Because
at the high frequencies, the universal Source of intention is pure creativeness, love, kindness, beauty, and abundance. *Self-respect attracts the higher
energy*. Lack of self-respect attracts the lower. It knows no other way.

The negative viewpoints of others represent *their low-energy ego* working on you. Very simply, if you're judging anyone, you aren't loving them
at that moment. The judgments coming your way, likewise, are unloving
but have nothing to do with your self-respect. Their judgments (and yours
as well) distance you from your Source, and therefore away from the *power*
of intention. As my friend and colleague Gerald Jampolsky observed,
"When I am able to resist the temptation to judge others, I can see them
as teachers of forgiveness in my life, reminding me that I can only have
peace of mind when I forgive rather than judge."

This is how you return to the *self* in self-respect. Rather than judging
those who judge you, thereby lowering your self-respect, you send them
a silent blessing of forgiveness and imagine them doing the same toward
you. You're connecting to intention and guaranteeing that you'll always
respect the divinity that you are. You've cleared the path to be able to
enjoy the great power that is yours in the field of intention.

Making Your Intention Your Reality

In this concluding section, you'll find ten ways to practice nurturing
your intention to respect yourself at all times.

**Step 1: Look into a mirror, make eye connection with yourself,
and say *"I love me"* as many times as possible during your day.** *I love
me.* These three magic words help you maintain your self-respect. Now,
be aware that saying these words may be difficult at first because of the

conditions you've been exposed to over a lifetime, and because the words may bring to the surface remnants of disrespect that your ego wants you to hold on to.

Your immediate impulse might be to see this as an expression of your ego's desire to be superior to everyone else. But this is not an ego statement at all—it's an affirmation of self-respect. Transcend that ego mind and affirm your love for yourself and your connection to the Spirit of God. This doesn't make you superior to anyone; it makes you equal to all and celebrates that you're a piece of God. Affirm it for your own self-respect. Affirm it in order to be respectful of that which intended you here. Affirm it because it's the way you'll stay connected to your Source and regain the power of intention. *I love me.* Say it without embarrassment. Say it proudly, and be that image of love and self-respect.

Step 2: Write the following affirmation and repeat it over and over again to yourself: *I am whole and perfect as I was created!* Carry this thought with you wherever you go. Have it laminated, and place it in your pocket, on your dashboard, on your refrigerator, or next to your bed—allow the words to become a source of high energy and self-respect. By simply carrying these words with you and being in the same space with them, their energy will flow directly to you.

Self-respect emerges from the fact that you respect the Source from which you came and you've made a decision to reconnect to that Source, regardless of what anyone else might think. It's very important to keep reminding yourself at the beginning that you're worthy of infinite respect from the one Source you can always count on, the piece of God energy that defines you. This reminder will do wonders for your self-respect, and consequently your ability to use the power of intention in your life. Over and over, remind yourself: *I'm not my body. I'm not my accumulations. I'm not my achievements. I'm not my reputation. I am whole and perfect as I was created!*

Step 3: Extend more respect to others and to all of life. Perhaps the greatest secret of self-esteem is to appreciate other people more. The easiest way to do this is to see the unfolding of God in them. Look past the judgments of others' appearance, failures, and successes, their status in society, their wealth or lack of it . . . and extend appreciation and love to the Source from which they came. Everyone is a child of God—everyone! Try to see this even in those who behave in what appears to be a godless fashion. Know that by extending love and respect, you can turn that energy around so that it's heading back to its Source rather than away from it. In short, send out respect because that is what you have to give away. Send out judgment and low energy and that is what you'll attract back. Remember, when you judge others, you do not define them, you define yourself as someone who needs to judge. The same applies to judgments directed at you.

Step 4: Affirm to yourself and all others that you meet, *I belong!* A sense of belonging is one of the highest attributes on Abraham Maslow's pyramid of self-actualization (which I discuss at the beginning of the next chapter). Feeling that you don't belong or you're in the wrong place can be due to a lack of self-respect. Respect yourself and your divinity by knowing that everyone belongs. This should never come into question. Your presence here in the universe is proof alone that you belong here. No person decides if you belong here. No government determines if some belong and some don't. This is an intelligent system that you're a part of. The wisdom of Creation intended you to be here, in this place, in this family with these siblings and parents,

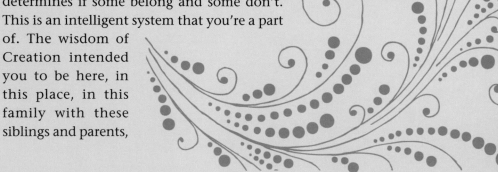

occupying this precious space. Say it to yourself and affirm it whenever necessary: *I belong!* And so does everyone else. No one is here by accident!

Step 5: Remind yourself that you're never alone. My self-respect stays intact as long as I know that it's impossible for me to be alone. I have a *"senior partner"* who's never abandoned me and who's stuck with me even in moments when I had seemingly deserted my Source. I feel that if the universal mind has enough respect to allow me to come here and to work through me—and to protect me in times when I strayed onto dangerous nonspiritual turf—then this partnership deserves my reciprocal respect. I recall my friend Pat McMahon, a talk-show host on KTAR radio in Phoenix, Arizona, telling me about his encounter with Mother Teresa in his studio before interviewing her for his program. He pleaded with her to allow him to do something for her. "Anything at all," he begged. "I'd just like to help you in some way." She looked at him and said, "Tomorrow morning get up at 4:00 A.M. and go out onto the streets of Phoenix. Find someone who lives there and believes that he's alone, and convince him that he's not." Great advice, because everyone who wallows in self-doubt or appears to be lost . . . has lost their self-respect because they've forgotten that they're not alone.

Step 6: Respect your body! You've been provided with a perfect body to house your inner invisible being for a few brief moments in eternity. Regardless of its size, shape, color, or any imagined infirmities, it's a perfect creation for the purpose that you were intended here for. You don't need to work at getting healthy; health is something you already have if you don't disturb it. You may have disturbed your healthy body by overfeeding it, underexercising it, and overstimulating it with toxins or drugs that make it sick, fatigued, jumpy, anxious, depressed, bloated, ornery, or an endless list of maladies. You can begin the fulfillment of this intention to live a life of self-respect by honoring the temple that houses you. You know what to do. You don't need another diet, workout manual, or personal trainer. Go within, listen to your body, and treat it with all of the dignity and love that your self-respect demands.

Step 7: Meditate to stay in conscious contact with your Source, which always respects you. I can't say this enough: Meditation is a way to experience what the five senses can't detect. When you're connected to the field of intention, you're connected to the wisdom that's within you. That divine wisdom has great respect for you, and it cherishes you while you're here. Meditation is a way to ensure that you stay in a state of self-respect. Regardless of all that goes on around you, when you enter into that sacred space of meditation, all doubts about your value as an esteemed creation dissolve. You'll emerge from the solemnity of meditation feeling connected to your Source and enjoying respect for all beings, particularly yourself.

Step 8: Make amends with adversaries. The act of making amends sends out a signal of respect for your adversaries. By radiating this forgiving energy outward, you'll find this same kind of respectful positive energy flowing back toward you. By being big enough to make amends and replace the energy of anger, bitterness, and tension with kindness—even if you still insist that you're right—you'll respect yourself much more than prior to your act of forgiveness. If you're filled with rage toward anyone, there's a huge part of you that resents the presence of this debilitating energy. Take a moment right here and now to simply face that person who stands out in your mind as someone you hurt, or directed hurt to you, and tell him or her that you'd like to make amends. You'll notice how much better you feel. That good feeling of having cleared the air is self-respect. It takes much more courage, strength of character, and inner conviction to make amends than it does to hang on to the low-energy feelings.

Step 9: Always remember the *self* in self-respect. In order to do this, you must recognize that the opinions of others toward you aren't facts, they're opinions. When I speak to an audience of 500 people, there are 500 opinions of me in the room at the end of the evening. I'm none of those opinions. I can't be responsible for how they view me. The only thing I can be responsible for is my own character, and this is true for every one of us. If I respect myself, then I'm relying on the *self* in self-respect. If I doubt myself, or punish myself, I've not only lost my self-respect, I'll continue to attract more and more doubt and lower-energy opinions with which to further punish myself. You can't stay linked to the universal mind, which intends all of us here, if you fail to rely on your self for your self-respect.

Step 10: Be in a state of gratitude. You'll discover that gratitude is the final step in each succeeding chapter. Be an appreciator rather than a depreciator of everything that shows up in your life. When you're saying *Thank you, God, for everything,* and when you're expressing gratitude for your life and all that you see and experience, you're respecting Creation. This respect is within you, and you can only give away what you have inside. Being in a state of gratitude is the exact same thing as being in a state of respect—respect for yourself, which you give away freely, and which will return to you tenfold.

I close this chapter with the words of Jesus of Nazareth, speaking through his apostle Saint Matthew (Matthew 5:48): "Be perfect, therefore, as your heavenly Father is perfect." Reconnect to the perfection from which you originated.

You can't have any more self-respect than that!

It Is My Intention to: Live My Life on Purpose

"Those who have failed to work toward the truth have missed the purpose of living."

— Buddha

"Your sole business in life is to attain God-realization. All else is useless and worthless."

— Sivananda

A sense of purpose is at the very top of the pyramid of self-actualization created by Abraham Maslow more than 50 years ago. Through his research, Dr. Maslow discovered that those who feel purposeful are living the highest qualities that humanity has to offer. During the many years I've been in the fields of human development, motivation, and spiritual awareness, this is the topic that more people inquire about than anything else. I'm repeatedly asked questions such as:

How do I find my purpose? Does such a thing really exist? Why don't I know my purpose in life? Being on purpose is what the most self-actualized people accomplish on their life journeys. But many individuals feel little sense of purpose, and may even *doubt* that they have a purpose in life.

Purpose and Intention

The theme of this book is that intention is a force in the universe, and that everything and everyone is connected to this invisible force. Since this is an intelligent system we're all a part of, and everything that arrives here came from that intelligence, it follows that if it wasn't supposed to be here, then it wouldn't be here. And if it's here, then it's supposed to be, and that's enough for me. The very fact of your existence indicates that you have a purpose. As I mentioned, the key question for most of us is: "What is my purpose?" And I hear that question in as many forms as there are people wondering about it: *What am I supposed to be doing? Should I be an architect, a florist, or a veterinarian? Should I help people or fix automobiles? Am I supposed to have a family or be in the jungle saving the chimpanzees?* We're befuddled by the endless number of options available to us, and wonder whether we're doing the right thing.

In this chapter, I urge you to forget these questions. Move instead to a place of faith and trust in the universal mind of intention, remembering that you emanated from this mind and that you're a piece of it at all times.

Intention and purpose are as beautifully and naturally intertwined as the double helix of your DNA. There are no accidents. You're here for the purpose that you signed up for before you entered the world of particles and form. Many of the things that you refer to as problems result from the fact that you're disconnected from intention and therefore unaware of your true spiritual identity. The process of polishing that connecting link and reconnecting is basic to your intention to live your life on purpose. As you cleanse this link, you'll make two very important discoveries. First, you'll discover that your purpose is not as much about what you do as it is about how you feel. Your second discovery will be that feeling purposeful activates your power of intention to create anything that's consistent with the seven faces of intention.

Feeling purposeful. In response to the question *What should I do with my life?*, I suggest that there's only one thing you *can* do with it, since you came into this life with nothing and you'll leave with nothing: *You can give it away.* You'll feel most on purpose when you're giving your life away by serving others. When you're giving to others, to your planet, and to your Source, you're being purposeful. Whatever it is that you choose to do, if you're motivated to be of service to others while being authentically detached from the outcome, you'll feel on purpose, regardless of how much abundance flows back to you.

So, your intention is to live your life on purpose. But what is the spiritual Source like in this regard? It's perpetually in the process of giving its life force away to create something from nothing. When you do the same, regardless of what you're giving or creating, you're in harmony with intention. You're then on purpose, just as the universal mind is always acting purposefully.

Take this one step further. Does the universal Source of all life have to think about what it's doing with its powers? Is it concerned with bringing in gazelles or centipedes? Does it concern itself with where it lives or what it ultimately creates? No. Your Source is simply in the business of expressing itself through the seven faces of intention. The details are taken care of automatically. Likewise, your feelings of being on purpose in your life flow through expression of the seven faces of intention. Allow yourself to be in the feeling place within you that's unconcerned with such things as vocational choices or doing the things you were destined to do. When you're in the service of others, or extend kindness beyond your own boundaries, you'll feel connected to your Source. You'll feel happy and content, knowing that you're doing the right thing.

I get that feeling of inner completion and contentment that lets me know that I'm on purpose by reading my mail or hearing the comments I so frequently hear when I'm walking through

157

airports or eating at restaurants: *You changed my life, Wayne Dyer. You were there for me when I felt lost.* This is different from receiving a royalty payment or a great review, which I also enjoy. The personal expressions of gratitude are what sustain me in knowing that I'm on purpose.

Outside of my chosen occupation, I feel purposeful in a myriad of ways virtually every single day. When I extend assistance to someone in need, when I take a moment to cheer up a disgruntled employee in a restaurant or a store, when I make a child laugh who sits otherwise ignored in a stroller, or even when I pick up a piece of litter and place it in a trash can, I feel that I'm giving myself away and, as such, feel purposeful.

Essentially what I'm saying is: Stay on purpose by expressing the seven faces of intention, and the details will find you. You'll never have to ask what your purpose is or how to find it.

Your purpose will find you. In a previous chapter, I reviewed the obstacles to connecting to intention and pointed out that our thoughts are one of the major roadblocks. I stressed that we become what we think about all day long. What thoughts do *you* have that inhibit you from feeling as if you're on purpose in your life? For instance, if you think that you're separate from your purpose and that you're drifting without direction through your life, then that's precisely what you'll attract.

Suppose, instead, that you know this is a purposeful universe where your thoughts, emotions, and actions are a part of your free will and are also connected to the power of intention. Suppose that your thoughts of being purposeless and aimless are really a *part* of your purpose. Just as the thought of losing someone you love makes you love them even more, or an illness makes you treasure your health, suppose that it takes the thought of your unimportance to make you realize your value.

When you're awake enough to question your purpose and ask how to connect to it, you're being prodded by the power of intention. The very act of questioning why you're here is an indication that your thoughts are nudging you to reconnect to the field of intention. What's the source of your thoughts about your purpose? Why do you want to feel purposeful? Why is a sense of purpose considered the highest attribute of a fully functioning person? The source of thought is an infinite reservoir of energy and intelligence. In a sense, *thoughts about your purpose are really your purpose trying to reconnect to you.* This infinite reservoir of loving, kind, creative, abundant energy grew out of the originating intelligence, and is stimulating you to express this universal mind in your own unique way.

Reread the two display quotes at the beginning of this chapter. Buddha refers to *the truth,* and Sivananda suggests that *God realization* is our true purpose. This entire book is dedicated to connecting to the power of intention and letting go of ego, which tries to make us believe that we're separate from our divine originating Source and tries to separate us from realizing ultimate truth. This ultimate truth is the source of your thoughts.

That inner beingness knows why you're here, but your ego prods you to chase after money, prestige, popularity, and sensory pleasures and *miss the purpose of living.* You may feel sated and gain a reputation, but inside there's that gnawing feeling typified by the old Peggy Lee song "Is That All There Is?" Focusing on the demands of the ego leaves you feeling unfulfilled. Deep within you, at the level of your being, is what you were intended to become, to accomplish, and to be. In that inner placeless place, you're connected to the power of intention. It will find you. Make a conscious effort to contact it and listen. Practice being what you are at the source of your soul. Go to your soul level, where intention and purpose fit together so perfectly that you achieve the epiphany of simply *knowing this is it.*

Your silent inner knowing. Esteemed psychologist and philosopher William James once wrote: "In the dim background of our mind we know meanwhile what we ought to be doing. . . . But somehow we cannot start. . . . Every moment we expect the spell to break . . . but it does continue, pulse after pulse, and we float with it. . . ."

In my experience as a therapist, and as a speaker talking with thousands of people about their lives, I've come to the same conclusion. Somewhere, buried deep within each of us, is a call to purpose. It's not always rational, not always clearly delineated, and sometimes even seemingly absurd, but the knowing is there. There's a silent something within that *intends* you to express yourself. That something is your soul telling you to listen and connect through love, kindness, and receptivity to the power of intention. That silent inner knowing will never leave you alone. You may try to ignore it and pretend it doesn't exist, but in honest, alone moments of contemplative communion with yourself, you sense the emptiness waiting for you to fill it with your music. It wants you to take the risks involved, and to ignore your ego and the egos of others who tell you that an easier, safer, or more secure path is best for you.

Ironically, it's not necessarily about performing a specific task or being in a certain occupation or living in a specific location. It's about sharing yourself in a creative, loving way using the skills and interests that are inherently part of you. It can involve any activity: dancing, writing, healing, gardening, cooking, parenting, teaching, composing, singing, surfing—whatever. There's no limit to this list. But everything on the list can be done to *pump up your ego* or *to serve others*. Satisfying your ego ultimately means being unfulfilled and questioning your purpose. This is because your Source is egoless, and you're attempting to connect to your Source, where your purpose originates. If the activities on the list are in service to others, you feel the bliss of purposeful living, while paradoxically attracting more of what you'd like to have in your life.

My daughter Skye is an example of what I'm presenting here. Skye has known since she could first speak that she wanted to sing. It was almost as if she showed up here in the world with a destiny to sing for others. Over the years, she's sung at my public appearances, first as a 4-year-old, and then at every age up until now, her 21st year. She has also sung on my public television specials, and the reaction to her singing has always been gratifying.

As a student immersed in a music program at a major university, Skye studied from academic and theoretical perspectives. One day in her junior year, we had a discussion that centered on her purpose and the silent inner knowing she's always had. "Would you be upset," she inquired, "if I left college? I just don't feel like I can do what I know I have to do by sitting in a classroom and studying music theory any longer. I just want to write my own music and sing. It's the only thing I think about, but I don't want to disappoint you and Mom."

How could I, who tells his readers not to die with their music still in them, tell my 21-year-old daughter to stay in college because that's the right way, and it's what I did? I encouraged her to listen to the silent knowing that I've seen evidence of since she was a toddler, and to follow her heart. As Gandhi once said: "To give one's heart is to give all." This is where God exists in Skye . . . and in you.

I did ask Skye to make a supreme effort to live her purpose by serving those who will listen to her music rather than focusing her attention on being famous or making money. "Let the universe handle those details," I reminded her. "You write and sing because you have to express what is in that beautiful heart of yours." I then asked her to think from the end, and act as if all that she wanted to create for herself was already here, waiting for her to connect to it.

Recently she voiced dismay at not having her own CD out in the world, and she was acting with thoughts of *not having a CD out in the world.* Consequently, no CD and lots of frustration. I strongly encouraged her to start thinking from the end by seeing the studio being available, the musicians ready to collaborate with her, the CD as a finished product, and her intention as a reality. I gave her a deadline to have a CD completed that I could make available at my lectures. I told her that she could sing to these audiences, as she has done sporadically in her life as well as on my public-television pledge shows.

Her thinking from the end materialized everything she needed, and the universal Spirit began to work with her unbending intent. She found the studio, the musicians she needed magically appeared, and she was able to have the CD produced.

Skye worked tirelessly day after day singing her own favorites, as well as several that I wanted her to sing at my appearances, including "Amazing Grace," "The Prayer of St. Francis," and her own composition, "Lavender Fields," which she sings from deep pride and passion. And lo and behold, today

161

her CD, *This Skye Has No Limits,* is now out and is being offered to the public whenever she sings at my lectures.

Skye's presence on the stage with me brings so much joy and love to the presentation because she's as closely aligned with those seven faces of intention as any human being I've ever known. So it's no secret why this book is also dedicated to her—one of my angels of spiritual intention.

Inspiration and Purpose

When you're inspired by a great purpose, everything will begin to work for you. Inspiration comes from moving back in-spirit and connecting to the seven faces of intention. When you feel inspired, what appeared to be risky becomes a path you feel compelled to follow. The risks are gone because you're following your bliss, which is the truth within you. This is really love working in harmony with your intention. Essentially, if you don't feel love, you don't feel the truth, and your truth is all wrapped up in your connection to Spirit. This is why inspiration is such an important part of the fulfillment of your intention to live a life on purpose.

When I left the work that no longer inspired me, every single detail that I'd worried about was almost magically taken care of for me. I'd spent several months working for a large corporation where I was offered a salary three times higher than I'd been paid as a teacher, but I wasn't in-spirit. That prodding inner knowing said, *Do what you're here to do,* and teaching/counseling became my manifested daily purpose.

When I left a professorship at a major university for writing and public speaking, it wasn't a risk; it was something I had to do because I knew that I couldn't feel happy with myself if I didn't follow my heart. The universe handled the details, because I was feeling love for what I was doing, and consequently, I was living my truth. By teaching love, that very same love guided me to my purpose, and the financial remuneration flowed to me with that same energy of love. I couldn't see how it would work out, but I followed an inner knowing and never regretted it!

You may think it's too risky to give up a salary, a pension, job security, or familiar surroundings because of a dim night-light in your mind that draws you to see why it's turned on. I suggest that there are no risks at all if you pay attention to that light, which is your knowing. Combine your strong knowing with the faith that Spirit will provide, and you acknowledge the power of intention at work. Your trust in this inner knowing is all you need. I call it *faith*—not faith in an external god to provide you with a purpose, but faith in the call you're hearing from the center of your being. You are a divine, infinite creation making the choice to be on purpose and to be connected to the power of intention. It all revolves around your being harmoniously connected to your Source. Faith eliminates the risk when you choose to trust that inner knowing about your purpose and become a channel for the power of intention.

Making Intention Your Reality

Below are ten ways to practice fulfilling your intention to live your life on purpose from this day forward:

Step 1: Affirm that in an intelligent system, no one shows up by accident, including you. The universal mind of intention is responsible for all of creation. It knows what it's doing. You came from that mind, and you're infinitely connected to it. There's meaning in your existence, and you have the capacity to live from a perspective of purpose. The first step is to know that you're here on purpose. This is not the same as knowing what you're supposed to do. Throughout your life, what you do will change and shift. In fact, the changes can occur from hour to hour in each day of your life. Your purpose is not about what you do, it's about your beingness, that place within you from which your thoughts emerge. This is why you're called a *human being* rather than a *human doing!* Affirm in your own words, both in writing and in your thoughts, that you are here on purpose, and intend to live from this awareness at all times.

Step 2: Seize every opportunity, no matter how small, to give your life away in service. Get your ego out of your intention to live a life of purpose. Whatever it is that you want to do in life, make the primary motivation for your effort something or somebody other than your desire for gratification or reward.

The irony here is that your personal rewards will multiply when you're focused on giving rather than receiving. Fall in love with what you're doing, and let that love come from the deep, inner-dwelling place of Spirit. Then sell the feeling of love, enthusiasm, and joy generated by your efforts. If your purpose is felt by being Supermom, then put your energy and inner drive into those children. If it's felt writing poetry or straightening teeth, then get your ego out of the way and do what you love doing. Do it from the perspective of making a difference for someone or for some cause, and let the universe handle the details of your personal rewards. Live your purpose doing what you do with pure love—then you'll co-create with the power of the universal mind of intention, which is ultimately responsible for all of creation.

Step 3: Align your purpose with the field of intention. This is the most important thing you can do to fulfill your intentions. Being aligned with the universal field means having faith that your Creator knows why you're here, even if you don't. It means surrendering the little mind to the big mind, and remembering that your purpose will be revealed in the same way that *you* were revealed. Purpose, too, is birthed from creativeness, kindness, love, and receptivity to an endlessly abundant world. Keep this connection pure, and you'll be guided in all of your actions.

It's not fatalism to say that *if it's meant to be, then it can't be stopped.* This is having faith in the power of intention, which originated with you and is within you. When you're aligned with your originating Source, then this same Source will aid you in creating the life of your choice. Then, what happens feels exactly as if it was meant to be. And that's because it is! You always have a choice in how to align yourself. If you stay focused on making demands on the universe, you'll feel as if demands are being placed on you in your life. Stay focused on lovingly asking, *How may I use my innate talents and desire to serve?* and the universe will respond with the identical energy by asking you, *How may I serve you?*

Step 4: Ignore what anyone else tells you about your purpose. Regardless of what anyone might say to you, the truth about your feeling purposeful is that only *you* can know it, and if you don't feel it in that inner place where a burning desire resides, it isn't your purpose. Your relatives and friends may attempt to convince you that what *they* feel is *your* destiny. They may see talents that they think will help you make a great living, or they may want you to follow in their footsteps because they think you'll be happy doing what they've done for a lifetime. Your skill at mathematics or decorating or fixing electronic equipment might indicate a high aptitude for a given pursuit—but in the end, if you don't feel it, nothing can make it resonate with you.

Your purpose is between you and your Source, and the closer you get to what that field of intention looks and acts like, the more you'll know that you're being purposefully guided. You might have zero measurable aptitudes and skills in a given area, yet feel inwardly drawn to doing it. Forget the aptitude-test results, forget the absence of skills or know-how, and most important, ignore the opinions of others and *listen to your heart.*

Step 5: Remember that the all-creating field of intention will work on your behalf. Albert Einstein is credited with saying that the most important decision we ever make is whether we believe we live in a friendly universe or a hostile universe. It's imperative that you know that the all-creating field of intention is friendly and will work with you as long as you see it that way. The universe supports life; it flows freely to all and is endlessly abundant. Why choose to look at it in any other way? All of the problems we face are created by our belief that we're separate from God and each other, leading us to be in a state of conflict. This state of conflict creates a counterforce causing millions of humans to be confused about their purpose. Know that the universe is always willing to work with you on your behalf, and that you're always in a friendly, rather than hostile, world.

Step 6: Study and replicate the lives of people who've known their purpose. Whom do you admire the most? I urge you to read biographies of these people and explore how they lived and what motivated them to stay on purpose when obstacles surfaced. I've always been fascinated by Saul of Tarsus (later called St. Paul), whose letters and teachings became the source of a major portion of the New Testament. Taylor Caldwell wrote a definitive fictional account of St. Paul's life called *Great Lion of God,* which inspired me enormously. I was also deeply touched by the purposeful manner in which St. Francis of Assisi lived his life as exemplified in the novel *St. Francis,* by Nikos Kazantzakis. I make it a point to use my free time to read about people who are models for purposeful living, and I encourage you to do the same.

Step 7: Act as if you're living the life you were intended to live, even if you feel confused about this thing called purpose. Invite into your life every day whatever it might be that makes you feel closer to God and brings you a sense of joy. View the events you consider obstacles as perfect opportunities to test your resolve and find your purpose. Treat everything from a broken fingernail to an illness to the loss of a job to a geographical move as an opportunity to get away from your familiar routine and move to purpose. By acting as if you're on purpose and treating the hurdles as friendly reminders to trust in what you feel deeply within you, you'll be fulfilling your own intention to be a purposeful person.

Step 8: Meditate to stay on purpose. Use the technique of Japa, which I mentioned earlier, and focus your inner attention on asking your Source to guide you in fulfilling your destiny. This letter from Matthew McQuaid describes the exciting results of meditating to stay on purpose:

Dear Dr. Dyer,

My wife, Michelle, is pregnant by a miracle—a miracle manifest from Spirit using all of your suggestions. For five years, Michelle and I were challenged by infertility. You name it, we tried it. None of the expensive and sophisticated treatments worked. The doctors had given up. Our own faith was tested over and over with each failed treatment cycle. Our doctor managed to freeze embryos from earlier cycles of treatment. Throughout the years, over 50 embryos had been transferred to Michelle's uterus. The odds of a frozen embryo successfully initiating pregnancy in our case were close to zero. As you know, <u>zero</u> is a word not found in the spiritual vocabulary. One precious frozen embryo, surviving minus 250 degrees for six months, has taken up a new home in Michelle's womb. She is now in her second trimester.

Okay, "So what," you might say. "I get letters like this every day." However, this letter contains proof of God. A tiny drop of protoplasm, as you have so eloquently written on many occasions, a physical mass of cells alive with the future pull of a human being, turned on in a laboratory, then turned off in a freezer. All molecular motion and biochemical processes halted, suspended. Yet, the essence of being was there prior to freezing. Where did the spiritual essence go while frozen? The cells were turned on, then turned off, but the spiritual essence had to prevail despite the physical state of the cells. The frequency of vibration of the frozen cells was low, but the vibrational frequency of its spirit must be beyond measure. The essence of the being had to reside outside of the physical plane or mass of cells. It couldn't go anywhere except to the realm of spirit, where it waited. It waited to thaw and manifest into a being it always has been. I hope you find this story as compelling as I do, as nothing less than a miracle. An example of spirit in body, rather then a body with a spirit.

And now for the million-dollar question. Could this one embryo survive such hostile frozen conditions and still manifest because I practiced the Japa mediation? Just because I opened my mouth and said, "Aaaahhh"? I had a knowing, no question about it. Japa meditation and surrendering to infinite patience are daily practices. During my quiet moments, I can smell this baby. Michelle will thank me for my conviction and faith during the dark times. I praise your work for guiding me. Thank you. Now, nothing is impossible for me. When I compare what I have manifested now in Michelle's womb to anything else I might desire, the process is without effort. After you truly surrender, everything you could ever want just seems to show up, right on schedule. The next amazing manifestation will be to help other infertile couples realize their dreams. Somehow, I will help those who feel there is no hope.

Sincerely,
Matthew McQuaid

Many people have written to me about their success with staying on purpose through the practice of Japa meditation. I'm deeply touched by the power of intention when I read about people who use Japa to help achieve a pregnancy, which they felt was their divine mission. I particularly like Matthew's decision to use this experience to help other infertile couples.

Step 9: Keep your thoughts and feelings in harmony with your actions. The surest way to realize your purpose is to eliminate any conflict or dissonance that exists between what you're thinking and feeling and how you're living your days. If you're in disharmony, you activate ego-dominated attitudes of fear of failure, or disappointing others, which distance you from your purpose. Your actions need to be in harmony with your thoughts. Trust in those thoughts that harmonize, and be willing to act upon them. Refuse to see yourself as inauthentic or cowardly, because those thoughts will keep you from acting on what you know you were meant to be. Take daily steps to bring your thoughts and feeling of your grand heroic mission into harmony with both your daily activities and of course, with that ever-present field of intention. Being in harmony with God's will is the highest state of purpose you can attain.

Step 10: Stay in a state of gratitude. Be thankful for even being able to contemplate your purpose. Be thankful for the wonderful gift of being able to serve humanity, your planet, and your God. Be thankful for the seeming roadblocks to your purpose. Remember, as Gandhi reminded us: "Divine guidance often comes when the horizon is the blackest." Look at the entire kaleidoscope of your life, including all of the people who have crossed your path. See all of the jobs, successes, apparent failures, possessions, losses, wins—everything—from a perspective of gratitude. You're here for a reason; this is the key to feeling purposeful. Be grateful for the opportunity to live your life purposefully in tune with the will of the Source of all. That's a lot to be grateful for.

❈ ❈ ❈

It seems to me that searching for our purpose is like searching for happiness. There's no way to happiness; happiness *is* the way. And so it is with living your life on purpose. It's not something you find; it's how you live your life serving others, and bringing purpose to everything you do. That's precisely how you fulfill the intention that is the title of this chapter. When you're living your life from purpose, you're dwelling in love. When you're not dwelling in love, you're off purpose. This is true for individuals, institutions, business, and our governments as well. When a government gouges its citizens with excessive fees for any service, they're off purpose. When a government pursues violence as a means for resolving disputes, it's off purpose regardless of how it justifies its actions. When businesses overcharge, cheat, or manipulate in the name of profit-making, they're off purpose. When religions permit prejudice and hatred or mistreat their parishioners, they're off purpose. And it's true for you as well.

Your goal in accessing the power of intention is to return to your Source and live from that awareness, replicating the very actions of intention itself. That Source is love. Therefore, the quickest method for understanding and living your purpose is to ask yourself if you're thinking in loving ways. Do your thoughts flow from a Source of love within you? Are you acting on those loving thoughts? If the answers are yes and yes, then you're on purpose. I can say no more!

✺✺✺✺✺

170

CHAPTER

9

It Is My Intention to: Be Authentic and Peaceful with All of My Relatives

"Your friends are God's way of apologizing for your relatives!"

— Dr. Wayne W. Dyer

S omehow we allow the expectations and demands of our family members to be the source of so much unhappiness and stress, when what we want is to be authentically ourselves and at peace with our relatives. The conflict seems too often to be a choice between being authentic, which means no peace with certain relatives, or having peace at the price of being inauthentic. Making the connection to the power of intention in regard to being around your relatives may sound like an oxymoron to you, but it isn't. Being peaceful and authentic can define your relationship with your relatives. First, though, you may have to assess your relationship with the closest relative of all—you. How others treat you, you'll discover, has a lot to do with how you treat yourself and thereby teach others to treat you.

You Get Treated the Way You Teach
Others to Treat You

In an earlier chapter, I urged you to notice your inner dialogue. One of the greatest obstacles to connecting to intention are your thoughts of what others want or expect from you. The more you focus on how upsetting it is that your family doesn't understand or appreciate you, the more you'll attract their misunderstanding or lack of appreciation. Why? Because what you think about expands, even when you think about what you find unnerving, and even when you think about what you don't want in your life.

If you're attracted to this intention, then you most likely already know which family members push your buttons. If you feel as though you're unduly influenced by their expectations, or you're a victim of their way of being, you'll need to begin by shifting from thoughts of what *they're doing* to what *you're thinking.* Say to yourself, *I've taught all these people how to treat me as a result of my willingness to make their opinions of me more important than my own.* You might want to follow this up by emphatically stating, *And it's my intention to teach them how I desire to be treated from now on!* Taking responsibility for how your family members treat you helps you create the kind of relationship with all of your relatives that matches up with the universal mind of intention.

You may be asking yourself how you can possibly be responsible for teaching people how to treat you. The answer is, in large part, your willingness to not only put up with listening to those familial pressures—some of which are long-term traditions running back countless generations—but also with allowing yourself to disconnect from your divine Source and indulge in low-energy emotions as humiliation, blame, despair, regret, anxiety, and even hatred. You and only you taught your kin how to treat you through your willingness to

174

accept critical comments from that well-meaning, but often interfering and bothersome, tribe.

Your family relationships are in your mind. When you close your eyes, your family disappears. Where did they go? Nowhere, but doing this exercise helps you recognize that your relatives exist as thoughts in your mind. And recall that God is the mind with which you're thinking. Are you using your mind to process your relatives in harmony with intention? Or have you abandoned or separated yourself in your mind by viewing your family in ways contrary to the universal Source of intention? These people who are related to you are all ideas in your mind. Whatever power they have, you've given to them. What you feel is wrong or missing in these relationships is an indication that something is amiss within you, because broadly speaking, anything you see in anyone else is a reflection of some aspect of you—otherwise you wouldn't be bothered by it, because you wouldn't notice it in the first place.

In order to change the nature of family relationships, you'll have to change your mind about them and do a somersault into the inconceivable. And what is the inconceivable? It's the idea that *you are the source of the anguish* in your relationships, rather than the individual whom you've pegged as the most outrageous, the most despicable, or the most infuriating. Over the years, all of these individuals have been treating you exactly as you've allowed them to with your reactions and behaviors. All of them exist as ideas in your mind that have separated you from your source of intention. This can miraculously change when you choose to be at peace with everyone in your life—most particularly, your relatives.

If the focus of your inner dialogue about your family members is on what they're doing that's wrong, then that's precisely how your relationship with them will be experienced. If your inner speech centers on what's annoying about them, that's what you'll notice. As much as you're inclined to blame them for your annoyance, it's yours, and it's coming from your thoughts. If you make a decision to put your inner attention, your life energy, on something quite different, your relationship will change. In your thoughts, where your family relationships exist, you'll no longer be annoyed, angry, hurt, or depressed. If in your mind you're thinking, *My intention is to be authentic and peaceful with this relative,* then that's what you'll experience—even if that relative continues to be exactly the way he or she has always been.

Changing your mind is changing your relationships. Being authentic and peaceful with your relatives is only a thought away. You can learn to change your thoughts by intending to create authentic and peaceful feelings within yourself. No one is capable of making you upset without your consent, and you've given your consent too frequently in the past. When you begin practicing the intention to be authentic and peaceful, you withdraw your consent to be in the lower energy. You connect to peace itself, and decide to bring peace to your relatives, thereby immediately gaining the power to change the energy of family gatherings.

Think of the relatives whom you've blamed for your feelings of anxiety, annoyance, or depression. You've focused on what you disliked about them or how they treated you, and your relationship has always had an uncomfortable edge to it. Now imagine yourself doing this from a new point of view: Rather than reacting to their low energy of hostility or bragging with a hostile or bragging reaction of your own—lowering the energy field for everyone involved—you instead bring your intention of peace to the interaction. Remember, it's the higher energy of love that can dissolve all the lower energies. When you react to low energy with more of the same, you're not being peacefully authentic or connected to the power of intention. In the low energy, you say or think sentences like, *I disrespect you for being so disrespectful. I'm angry at you for being so angry at the world. I dislike you because you're such a braggart.*

By putting your attention on what you intend to manifest rather than on the same low energy that you encounter, you make a decision to connect to intention and bring the attributes of your universal Source to the presence of that low energy. Try to imagine Jesus of Nazareth saying to his followers, "I despise those people who despise me, and I want nothing to do with them." Or, "It makes me so angry when people judge me. How can I have peace when there are so many hostile people around me?" This is absurd, because Jesus represents the highest loving energy in the universe. That's precisely what he brought to the presence of doubting, hostile people, and his presence alone would raise the energy of those around him. Now I know you're not the Christ, but you do have some great spiritual lessons to learn from our greatest teachers. If you have the intention to bring peace to a situation and you're living at the level of intention, you'll leave that situation feeling peaceful. I learned this lesson years ago with my in-laws.

Prior to my waking up to the power of intention, family visits were events that caused me consternation because of the attitudes and behavior of some of my wife's relatives. I'd prepare for a Sunday-afternoon family visit by getting anxious and upset over what I anticipated to be a fretful, lousy experience. And I seldom disappointed myself! I'd focus my thoughts on what I didn't like, and I defined my relationship with my in-laws in this manner. Gradually, as I began to understand the power of intention and left my ego behind, I substituted kindness, receptivity, love, and even beauty for my former annoyed and angry assessments.

Before family get-togethers, I'd remind myself that I am what I choose to be in any and all circumstances, and I chose to be authentically peaceful and have a good time. In response to something that used to annoy me, I'd now say to my mother-in-law in a loving way, "I never thought of it that way; tell me more." In response to what I previously considered to be an ignorant comment, I'd respond, "That's an interesting point of view; when did you first learn about this?" In other words, I was bringing my own intention to be in a state of peace to this encounter, and was refusing to judge them.

The most amazing thing began to happen: I started looking forward to having these family members at our home. I began to see them as much more enlightened than I'd previously thought. I actually enjoyed our times together, and every time something came up that I'd found annoying in the past, I'd overlook it and respond with love and kindness instead. At an earlier stage of my life, expressions of racial or religious prejudice were a stimulus for my anger and resentment. Now I'd quietly respond with a kind and gentle reminder of my own opinions, and simply let the matter drop.

Over the years, I found that not only did the racial and religious slurs diminish to zero, but I noticed that my in-laws were expressing tolerance—and even love—toward minorities, as well as those who practiced religions different from their own.

Although my primary intention was to stay in a state of peace, I discovered that by not joining in the low energies of my in-laws, not only was the entire family more peaceful, but many enjoyable and even enlightening conversations developed. I had as much to learn from my in-laws as I had to teach. Even when I disagreed vehemently with a judgment directed at me, if I remembered my intention to have a peaceful relationship with them, I was able to do just that. No longer did I think about what I disliked, what was missing, or what always had been. I stayed focused on making these gatherings fun, loving, and most important to me, peaceful.

※ ※ ※

Let's take a look at the steps you need to take in order to make the stated intention of this chapter and all succeeding ones a reality.

Step 1: Identify your intention verbally and in writing, and develop a deep yearning for it. When you create a great longing for the experience of a peaceful family, everything will begin to happen to fulfill this yearning spontaneously and naturally. Rather than praying to a saint or God for a miracle, pray for the miracle of the inner awakening, which will never leave you. The awakening of this inner light, once experienced, will become your constant companion, regardless of who you are with or where you are. The dynamic force is within you. This force is felt as great joy running through your body. Ultimately, your thinking will become sublime, and your inner and outer world will become one. Yearn for this awakening to the inner light, and long for your intention to manifest.

   Step 2: Intend for all of your relatives what you intend for yourself. When anyone criticizes, judges, acts angry, expresses hatred, or finds fault with you, they're not at peace with themselves. Want this peace for them even more than you desire it for yourself. By having this kind of intention for them, you take the focus off of you. This doesn't require words or actions on your part. Simply picture the people in your family with whom you're not at peace, and feel the peace you crave for them. Your inner speech will change, and you'll begin to experience the peaceful authenticity of both your beings.

   Step 3: Be the peace you're seeking from others. If peace is missing in your relationships with your family, it means that you have a place within you that's occupied by non-peace. It may be filled with anxiety, fear, anger, depression, guilt, or any low-energy emotions. Rather than attempting to rid yourself of these feelings all at once, treat them the same as you do your relatives. Say a friendly *Hello* to the non-peace, and let it be. You're sending a peaceful feeling to the non-peace feeling. The lower energies you're experiencing will be strengthened by your peaceful *Hi* or *Hello,* and eventually vanish as the divine grows within you. The way to this peace is through any form of quiet and meditation that works for you. Even if it's only a two-minute respite during which time you're silent, concentrate on the name of the divine, or repeat that sound of "Aaahh" as an inner mantra.

Step 4: Match up with the seven faces of intention. If you've forgotten what the universal mind of intention looks like, it's creative, kind, loving, beautiful, always expanding, endlessly abundant, and receptive to all of life. Play the match game that I introduced earlier in this book, and very quietly and with unbending intent bring the face of the universal Source of all to the presence of everyone whom you feel brings you down or interferes with your peace. This kind of spiritual energy will be transformative—not only for you, but also for your relatives. Your intention to be in peaceful relationships is now taking form—first in your mind, then in your heart—and ultimately, it will materialize.

Step 5: Review all the obstacles that have been erected on your path to familial peace. Listen to any inner dialogue that focuses on your resentment of others' expectations for you. Remind yourself that when you think about what you resent, you act upon what you think about, while simultaneously attracting more of it to you. Examine your energy level for your tendency to react to lower energies with more of the same, and give your ego a reminder that you'll no longer opt to be offended, or need to be right in these relationships.

Step 6: Act *as if*. Begin the process of acting *as if what you intend to manifest is already true.* See everyone in your family in the love and light that is their true identity. When someone asked Baba Muktananda, a great saint in India, "Baba, what do you see when you look at me?" Baba said, "I see the light in you." The person replied, "How can that be, Baba? I am an angry person. I am terrible. You must see all that." Baba said, "No, I see light." (This story is told by Swami Chidvilasananda Gurumayi in *Kindle My Heart.*)

So, see the light in those *others,* and treat them *as if* that is all you see.

Step 7: Detach from the outcome. Don't let your authentic and peaceful attitude depend on your relatives' behavior. As long as you remain connected to intention and radiate outward the high energy,

180

you've achieved your peace. It's not your place or your purpose to make everyone else in your family think, feel, and believe as you do. The likelihood is great that you'll see dramatic changes in your relatives as you teach them with your own persona how you intend to be treated. But if they don't change, and if they continue their nonpeaceful ways, let go of your need to see them transformed. It all works in divine order, and the saying *Letting go and letting God* is a helpful reminder for you. By letting go, you guarantee your own peace, and you dramatically increase the odds of helping others to do the same.

Step 8: Affirm: *I attract only peace into my life.* I remind myself of this affirmation many times on a given day, particularly with my children and other more distant relatives. I also practice this in grocery stores, when greeting flight attendants, when visiting the post office, and while driving my automobile. I say this silently to myself as an absolute truth with unbending intent on my part, and it works for me all the time. People respond to me with smiles, acknowledgments, friendly gestures, and kind greetings all day long. I also remind myself of the cogent observation from *A Course in Miracles* when I feel other than peaceful in any given moment with my family: *I can choose peace, rather than this.*

Step 9: Hold no grudges, and practice forgiveness. The key to having peace in all your family relationships is forgiveness. Your relatives are simply doing what they've been taught to do over a lifetime, and the lifetimes of many of their ancestors. Shower them with understanding and forgiveness from your heart.

This passage from *A Course in Miracles* offers so much in the fulfillment of this intention:

> *Do you want peace? Forgiveness offers it.*
> *Do you want happiness, a quiet mind,*
> *a certainty of purpose,*
> *and a sense of worth and beauty*
> *that transcends the world?*
> *Do you want a quietness that cannot be disturbed,*

a gentleness that can never be hurt,
a deep abiding comfort,
and a rest so perfect it can never be upset?
All this forgiveness offers you.

Step 10: Be in a state of gratitude. Rather than being in a state of non-peace concerning any family members, say a prayer of gratitude for their presence in your life and all that they have come to teach you.

❀ ❀ ❀

These are the ten steps that you can practice each day. As you work toward the absolute knowing that this intention will manifest for you, remind yourself on a daily basis that you can never remedy a bad relationship by condemning it.

❀ ❀ ❀ ❀ ❀

It Is My Intention to: Feel Successful and Attract Abundance into My Life

"God is able to provide you with every blessing in abundance."

— St. Paul

*"When you realize there is nothing lacking,
the whole world belongs to you."*

— Lao Tzu

O ne of my secrets for feeling successful and attracting bountiful abundance into my life has been an internal axiom that I use virtually every day of my life. It goes like this: *Change the way you look at things, and the things you look at change.* This has always worked for me.

The truth of this little maxim is actually found in the field of quantum physics, which, according to some, is a subject that's not only stranger than you think it is, it's stranger than you can *think*. It turns out that at the tiniest subatomic level, the actual act of observing a particle changes the particle. The way we observe these infinitely small building blocks of life is a determining factor in what they ultimately become. If we extend this metaphor to larger and larger particles and begin to see ourselves as particles in a larger body called humanity or even larger— life itself—then it's not such a huge stretch to imagine that the *way* we observe the world we live in affects that world. It's been said repeatedly in a number of different ways: *As is the microcosm, so is the macrocosm.* As you read this chapter, remember this little journey into quantum physics as a metaphor for your life.

This being the case, your intention to feel successful and experience prosperity and abundance depends on what view you have of yourself, the universe, and most important, the field of intention from which success and abundance will come. My little maxim about changing the way you look at things is an extremely powerful tool that will allow you to bring the intention of this chapter into your life. First examine how *you* look at things, and then how the spirit of intention does the same.

How Do You Look at Life?

The way you look at life is essentially a barometer of your expectations, based on what you've been taught you're worthy of and capable of achieving. These expectations are largely imposed by external influences such as family, community, and institutions, but they're also influenced by that ever-present inner companion: your ego. These sources of your expectations are largely based on the beliefs of limitation, scarcity, and pessimism about what's possible for you. If these beliefs are the basis for how you look at life, then this perception of

186

the world is what you expect for yourself. Attracting abundance, prosperity, and success from these limiting viewpoints is an impossibility.

In my heart, I know that attracting abundance and feeling successful is possible, because, as I touched on earlier, *I* had an early life of enormous scarcity. I lived in foster homes, away from my mother and my absentee, alcoholic, often-imprisoned father. I know that these truths can work for you, because if they've worked for any one of us, they can work for *all* of us, since we all share the same abundant divine force and emanated from the same field of intention.

Take an inventory of how you look at the world, asking yourself how much of your life energy is focused on explaining away potentially optimistic viewpoints by preferring to see the inequities and inconsistencies in the abundance-for-all philosophy. Can you change the way you look at things? Can you see potential for prosperity where you've always seen scarcity? Can you change *what is* by simply changing the way you see it? I say a resounding *yes* to these questions. And the way to work at changing the way you see things is to take a hard look at something you may not have previously considered.

How Does the Universal All-Creating Field of Intention Look at Life?

The field of intention, which is responsible for all creation, is constantly giving—in fact, it knows no bounds to its giving. It just keeps on converting pure formless spirit into a myriad of material forms. Furthermore, this field of intention *gives* in unlimited supplies. There is no such concept as shortage or scarcity when it comes to the originating Source. So we're looking at two major conceptualizations when we think of the universal mind's natural abundance. The first is that it's perpetually giving, and the second is that it offers an infinite supply.

The power of intention is perpetually giving and infinite, so it seems obvious that you'll need to adopt these same two attributes if you're to fulfill your own personal intention to live successfully and attract abundance into your life. What should your message back to the universe be if you want to *be* abundance and success rather than strive for it? Your Source is abundant and you are your Source; therefore, you must communicate this back. Since your Source is always serving and giving, and you are your Source, then you must be always in a state of serving and giving. *This Source can only work with you when you are in harmony with it!*

A message to the field of intention that says *Please send me more money* is interpreted as your seeing yourself in a state of scarcity, but this Source has no concept of scarcity. It doesn't even know what not having enough money means. Thus, its response back to you will be: *Here's a state of needing more money because that's how you think, and I'm the mind with which you think, so here's more of what you don't want and don't have.* Your ego-dominated response will be: *My desires are being denied!* But the real truth is, the universal Source knows only abundance and giving, and will respond with money flowing to you if your intention is: *I have enough money, and I allow what I already have enough of to flow to me.*

Now this may appear to be mumbo jumbo and nothing more than twisting words around, but I assure you that it's exactly how the universal mind of intention operates. The more you get back into gear with that which intended you here, the more you'll see that unlimited abundance showing up. Get rid of the concept of shortages, because God hasn't got a clue about such things. The creative Source reacts to your belief in shortages with a fulfillment of your belief.

Now, think back to my opening observation in this chapter: *Change the way you look at things, and the things you look at change.* I can guarantee you that the universal mind only flows in harmony with its own nature, which is providing endless abundance. Stay in harmony with this nature, and all of your desires *have* to manifest for you—the universe knows no other way to be. If you tell the universal mind what you want, it will respond by leaving you in a state of wanting, never arriving and always needing more. If, however, you feel that what you intend to manifest has already manifested, you're unified with your intention. Never allowing a moment of doubt or listening to naysayers, you'll be in the presence of that all-creating field of intention.

You can't come from shortage, you can't come from scarcity, and you can't come from wanting. You must come from the same attributes as that which allows everything. This is a key word, *allowing.* Let's take a look at how *allowing* is so often ignored in attempts to manifest feeling successful and attracting abundance.

The Art of Allowing

The universal mind of Creation is in a constant state of supplying. It never shuts down, it takes no vacations, there are no days off, and it's perpetually giving forth. Everything and everyone, without exception, emanates from this universal mind we're calling intention. So if everything comes from this infinite field of invisible energy, why is it that some are able to partake of it, while others seem so separated from it? If it's always giving forth in an endless stream of abundance, somehow there must be resistance to allowing it to come into your life if you're experiencing shortages or scarcity in any way.

Allowing this all-giving Source into your life means becoming aware of the resistance that you may be placing in the way of the abundance that's always being supplied. If the universe is based on energy and attraction, this means that everything is vibrating to

189

particular frequencies. When the frequency with which you're vibrating is in contradiction with the frequency of the universal supply, you create a resistance, thereby inhibiting that flow of abundance into your life space. Your individual vibrations are the key to understanding the art of allowing. The nonharmonious vibrations are largely in the form of your thoughts and feelings. Thoughts that emphasize what you don't believe you deserve set up a contradiction in energy. That contradiction puts a stop to a hooking up of identical energies, and you've created a field of disallowing. Remember, it's always about being in harmony with your Source. Your thoughts can either emerge from a beingness that's in rapport with intention or in contradiction with it.

Keep in mind that you're a part of the universal mind, so if you see yourself in a harmonious way with the seven faces of intention, the universal mind can only work harmoniously with you. For example, suppose that you want a better job with a higher salary. Imagine yourself as already having it, knowing in your thoughts that you're entitled to it, with no doubts about the job showing up because you can see it within. The universal mind now has no choice in the matter, since you're a part of that all-creating mind and there's no vibrational contradiction. So what can go wrong here? The art of allowing gets hampered by your habit of disallowing.

There's a long history of countless thoughts that have formed a field of resistance to allowing the free flow of abundance. This habit of disallowing grew from the belief system that you've cultivated over the years and that you rely on. Furthermore, you've allowed the resistance of others to enter this picture, and you surround yourself with the need for their approval in these matters. You solicit their resistant opinions, read newspaper accounts of all those who've failed to manifest the jobs of their choice, examine government reports about the poor job prospects and the declining economy, watch the television reports belaboring the sorry state of affairs in the world, and your resistance becomes even more convincingly entrenched. You've aligned yourself with the proponents of disallowing.

What you need to do is look at this belief system and all of the factors that continue to support it and say, *It's too big of a job to change the entire thing. Instead, I'm going to start changing the thoughts that activate disallowing right here, right now.* It doesn't matter what you thought before, or for how long, or how many pressures you're under to maintain your resistance. Instead, stop activating disallowing thoughts today, one thought at a time. You can do so by stating, *I feel successful, I intend to feel the abundance that is here, now.* Repeat these words, or create your arrangement of words, which continually inundate your thoughts during your waking hours, with a new belief of being successful and abundant. When you've activated these thoughts enough times, they'll become your habitual way of thinking, and you will have taken the steps to eliminating your resistance to allowing.

Those thoughts will then become what you say in silent, prayerlike messages to yourself: *I am success; I am abundance.* When you're success itself, when you're abundance itself, you're in harmony with the all-creating Source, and it will do the only thing it knows how to do. It will be endlessly giving and forthcoming with that which has no resistance to it—namely, you. You're no longer vibrating to scarcity; your every individual vibrational utterance is in concert with what you summon from your Source. You and your Source are one in your thoughts. You've chosen to identify thoughts of resistance and have simultaneously decided to stay out of your own way.

As you practice allowing and living the faith of least resistance, success is no longer something you choose; it's something that you are. Abundance no longer eludes you. You are it, and it is you. It flows unimpeded beyond your resistance. Herein lies another clue to the free flow of abundance: *You must avoid becoming attached to and hoarding what shows up in your life.*

Abundance, Detachment, and Your Feelings

While it's crucial for you to have a firm vibrational match-up with the all-creating abundance of intention, it's just as crucial for you to know that you can't hang on to and own any of the abundance that will be coming your way. This is because the you that would like to hang on to and become attached to your success and your wealth is not really you, it's that troublesome ego of yours. You're not what you have and what you do; you're an infinite, divine being disguised as a successful person who has accumulated a certain amount of stuff. *The stuff is not you.* This is why you must avoid being attached to it in any way.

Detachment comes from knowing that your true essence is a piece of the infinitely divine field of intention. It's then that you become aware of the importance of your feelings. Feeling good becomes much more valuable than polishing your jewelry. Feeling abundant surpasses the money in your bank account and transcends what others may think of you. Genuinely feeling abundant and successful is possible when you detach yourself from the things you desire and allow them to flow to you, and just as important, *through* you. Anything that inhibits the flow of energy stops the creating process of intention right where the obstacle is erected.

Attachment is one such roadblock. When you hang on to that which arrives, rather than allowing it to move through you, you stop the flow. You hoard it or decide to own it, and the flow is disrupted. You must keep it circulating, always knowing that nothing can stop it from coming into your life except any resistance you place in its way. Your feelings and emotions are sensational barometers for detecting resistance and evaluating your ability to experience success and abundance.

Paying attention to your feelings. Your emotions are the inner experiences that tell you how much of the divine energy you're summoning for the manifestation of your desires. Feelings can be measuring tools that gauge how you're doing in the manifestation process. An exceptionally positive emotional response indicates that you're summoning the divine energy of intention and allowing that energy to flow to you in a nonresistant manner. Feelings of passion, pure bliss, reverence, unmitigated optimism, unquestioned trust, and even illumination indicate that your desire to manifest success and abundance, for example, have an extremely strong pulling power from the universal Source to you. You must learn to pay close attention to the presence of these feelings. These emotions aren't just facets of your life that are empty of energy—they're agents that are in charge of how you clean and purify the connecting link to intention. These emotions tell you precisely how much of the life force you're summoning, and how much *pulling power* you have going for you at that moment.

Abundance is the natural state of the nature of intention. Your desire for abundance must flow free of resistance. Any discrepancy between your individual intention or desire, and your belief concerning the possibility of summoning it into your life, creates resistance. If you want it but believe it's impossible or that you're unworthy, or that you don't have the skills or perseverance, then you've created resistance and you're disallowing. Your feelings indicate how well you're attracting the energy necessary for the fulfillment of your desire. Strong feelings of despair, anxiety, blame, hate, fear, shame, and anger are sending you the message that you want success and abundance but you don't believe it's possible for you. These negative feelings are your clues to get busy and balance your desires with those of the universal mind of intention, which is the only source of that which you desire. Negative emotions tell you that your pulling power from intention is weak or even nonexistent. Positive emotions tell you that you're connecting to and accessing the power of intention.

Concerning abundance, one of the most effective ways to increase that pulling power from intention to you is to take the focus off of dollars and place it on creating abundant friendship, security, happiness, health, and high energy. It's here that you'll begin to feel those higher emotions, which let you know that you're back in the match game with the all-creating Source. As you focus on having abundant happiness, health, security, and friendship, the means for acquiring all of this will be flowing toward you. Money is only one of those means, and the faster your vibrational energy around abundance radiates, the more money will show up in significant amounts. These positive feelings as indicators of your pulling power for success and abundance will put you into an active mode for co-creating your intentions.

I'm not suggesting that you just wait for everything to fall into place. I'm suggesting that by declaring, *I intend to feel successful and attract prosperity*, your emotional energy will shift and you'll act as if what you desire were already true. Your actions will be in harmony with the faces of intention, and you'll be provided with what you *are,* rather than attempting to be provided with what's missing.

At this point in my life, I refuse to participate in any desire unless I have total, nonresistant knowing that it can and will manifest into my life from the all-creating Source of intention. My desires for personal indicators of abundance have all manifested by practicing what I write here, and in the ten-step program that follows. I've been able to *allow* by removing resistance and connecting to my originating, all-creating Source. I trust in it completely. Over the years, I've learned that when I've desired something seemingly impossible, I felt poorly as a result. I then figured that I should desire less, but all that did was make me even further removed from the unlimited power of intention. I was still in vibratory *disharmony* with the abundance of the universe.

I began to understand that my being in harmony with abundance didn't cause others to be poor or hungry. On the contrary, the abundance I created gave me the chance to help eradicate poverty and hunger. But the significant awareness was realizing that I had less of a chance to help others when I was in the lower frequencies. I learned that I had to get myself into vibratory harmony with my Source. One of my reasons for writing this chapter in this fashion is to convince you that you don't have to ask for less, or feel guilty about wanting abundance—it's there for you and everyone in an unlimited supply.

❖❖❖

I live and breathe what I'm writing here about success and abundance. I know beyond any doubt (resistance) that you can attract abundance and feel successful by absorbing the messages of this chapter, which, like the abundance you seek, have flowed from that universal Source through me and onto these pages. There's no discrepancy between my desire to write it all out here and my willingness to allow it to flow unimpeded to you. How do I know this? My emotion in this moment is ineffable bliss, serenity, and reverence. I trust this emotional state, which indicates to me that I've been utilizing a very strong pulling power to create these messages from the all-creating Spirit of intention. I'm in vibratory harmony and abundance, and feelings of success are my intentions herewith manifested. Try it on anything you'd like to see flowing abundantly into your life.

Making Your Intention Your Reality

Below is a ten-step program for implementing the intention of this chapter—that is, to feel successful and attract abundance into your life:

Step 1: See the world as an abundant, providing, friendly place. Again, when you change the way you look at things, the things you look at change. When you see the world as abundant and friendly, your intentions are genuine possibilities. They will, in fact, become a certainty, because your world will be experienced from the higher frequencies. In this first step, you're receptive to a world that provides rather than restricts. You'll see a world that wants you to be successful and abundant, rather than one that conspires against you.

Step 2: Affirm: *I attract success and abundance into my life because that is who I am.* This puts you into vibratory harmony with your Source. You goal is to eliminate any distance between what you desire and that from which you pull it into your life. Abundance and success aren't out there waiting to show up for you. You are already it, and the Source can only provide you with what it is, and, consequently, what you are already.

Step 3: Stay in an attitude of allowing. *Resistance* is disharmony between your desire for abundance and your beliefs about your ability or unworthiness. *Allowing* means a perfect alignment. An attitude of allowing means that you ignore efforts by others to dissuade you. It also means that you don't rely on your previous ego-oriented beliefs about abundance being a part of or not a part of your life. In an attitude of *allowing,* all resistance in the form of thoughts of negativity or doubt are replaced with simply knowing that you and your Source are one and the same. Picture the abundance you desire freely flowing directly to you. Refuse to do anything or have any thought that compromises your alignment with Source.

Step 4: Use your present moments to activate thoughts that are in harmony with the seven faces of intention. The key phrase here is *present moments*. Notice right now, in this moment, if you're thinking that it's hopeless at this stage of your life to change the thoughts that comprise your belief system. Do you defeat yourself with thoughts of having had such a long life practicing affirmations of scarcity and creating resistance to your success and abundance that you don't have enough time left to counterbalance the thoughts that comprise your past belief system?

Make the choice to let go of that lifetime of beliefs, and begin activating thoughts right now that allow you to feel good. Say *I want to feel good* whenever anyone tries to convince you that your desires are futile. Say *I want to feel good* when you're tempted to return to low-energy thoughts of disharmony with intention. Eventually your present moments will activate thoughts that make you feel good, and this is an indicator that you're reconnecting to intention. Wanting to feel good is synonymous with wanting to feel *God*. Remember, "God is good, and all that God created was good."

Step 5: Initiate actions that support your feelings of abundance and success. Here, the key word is *actions*. I've been calling this *acting as if* or *thinking from the end* and acting that way. Put your body into a gear that pushes you toward abundance and feeling successful. Act on those passionate emotions as if the abundance and success you seek is already here. Speak to strangers with passion in your voice. Answer the telephone in an inspired way. Do a job interview from the place of confidence and joy. Read the books that mysteriously show up, and pay close attention to conversations that seem to indicate you're being called to something new.

Step 6: Remember that your prosperity and success will benefit others, and that no one lacks abundance because you've opted for it. Once again, the supply is unlimited. The more you partake of the universal generosity, the more you'll have to share with others. In writing this book, wonderful abundance has flowed into my life in many ways. But even more significantly, book editors and graphic designers, the truck drivers who deliver the book, the auto workers who build the trucks, the farmers who feed the auto workers, the bookstore clerks . . . all receive abundance because I've followed my bliss and have written this book.

Step 7: Monitor your emotions as a guidance system for your connection to the universal mind of intention. Strong emotions such as passion and bliss are indications that you're connected to Spirit, or *inspired,* if you will. When you're inspired, you activate dormant forces, and the abundance you seek in any form comes streaming into your life. When you're experiencing low-energy emotions of rage, anger, hatred, anxiety, despair, and the like, that's a clue that while your desires may be strong, they're completely out of sync with the field of intention. Remind yourself in these moments that you want to feel good, and see if you can activate a thought that *supports* your feeling good.

Step 8: Become as generous to the world with your abundance as the field of intention is to you. Don't stop the flow of abundant energy by hoarding or owning what you receive. Keep it moving. Use your prosperity in the service of others, and for causes greater than your ego. The more you practice detachment, the more you'll stay in vibratory harmony with the all-giving Source of everything.

Step 9: Devote the necessary time to meditate on the Spirit within as the source of your success and abundance. There's no substitute for the practice of meditation. This is particularly relevant with abundance.

You must have an understanding that your *consciousness of the presence* is your supply. By repeating the sound that is in the name of God as a mantra, you're using a technique for manifesting as ancient as recorded history. I am particularly drawn to the form of meditation I've mentioned previously, called Japa. I know it works.

Step 10: Develop an attitude of gratitude for all that manifests into your life. Be thankful and filled with awe and appreciation, even if what you desire hasn't arrived yet. Even the darkest days of your life are to be looked on with gratitude. Everything coming from Source is on purpose. Be thankful while empowering your reconnection to that from which you and everything else originated.

The energy that creates worlds and universes is within you. It works through attraction and energy. Everything vibrates; everything has a vibratory frequency. As St. Paul said, "God is able to provide you with every blessing in abundance." Tune in to God's frequency, and you will know it beyond any and all doubt!

It Is My Intention to: Live a Stress-Free, Tranquil Life

"Anxiety is the mark of spiritual insecurity."

— Thomas Merton

"So long as we believe in our heart of hearts that our capacity is limited and we grow anxious and unhappy, we are lacking in faith. One who truly trusts in God has no right to be anxious about anything."

— Paramahansa Yogananda

Fulfilling this intention to live a stress-free and tranquil life is a way of manifesting your grandest destiny. It seems to me that what our Source had in mind when we were intended here is for us to have happy and joyous experiences of life on Earth. When you're in a state of joy and happiness, you've returned to the pure, creative, blissful, nonjudgmental joy that intention truly is. Your natural state—the state from which you were created—is that feeling of well-being. This chapter is concerned with having you return to, and access, this natural state.

You were created from a Source that is peaceful and joyful. When you're in that state of exuberant joy, you're at peace with everything. This is what intended you here and what you're determined to match up with in your thoughts, feelings, and actions. In a state of joy, you feel fulfilled and inspired in all facets of your life. In short, gaining freedom from anxiety and stress is a pathway to rejoicing with the field of intention. The moments of your life, which you spend being happy and joyful and allowing yourself to be fully alive and on purpose, are the times when you're aligned with the all-creating universal mind of intention.

There's nothing natural about living a life filled with stress and anxiety, having feelings of despair and depression, and needing pills to tranquilize yourself. Agitated thoughts that produce high blood pressure, a nervous stomach, persistent feelings of discomfort, an inability to relax or sleep, and frequent displays of displeasure and outrage are violating your natural state. Believe it or not, you have the power to create the naturally stress-free and tranquil life you desire. You can utilize this power to attract frustration or joy, anxiety or peace. When you're in harmony with the seven faces of intention, you can access and pull from the Source of all in order to fulfill your intention of being stress free and tranquil.

So if it's natural to have feelings of well-being, why is it that we seem to experience so much "unwellness" and tension? The answer to this question provides you with the key that leads to the peaceful life you desire.

Stress Is a Desire of the Ego

That pesky ego is at work when you're experiencing stress or anxiety. Perhaps your ego-self feels more effective dealing and coping with stress because you feel you're actually doing something in the world. Perhaps it's habit, custom, or believing that this is the right way to be. Only you can analyze the *why*. But the fact is that stress is familiar, and tranquility is unfamiliar, so ego desires stress.

But there's no actual stress or anxiety in the world; it's your thoughts that create these false beliefs. You can't package stress, touch it, or see it. There are only people engaged in stressful thinking. When we think stressfully, we create reactions in the body, valuable messages or signals requesting our attention. These messages might reveal themselves as nausea, elevated blood pressure, stomach tension, indigestion, ulcers, headaches, increased heart rate, difficulty breathing, and a zillion other feelings—from minor discomfort to serious, life-threatening illness.

We speak of stress as if it were present in the world as something that attacks us. We say things like *I'm having an anxiety attack* as if anxiety is a combatant. But the stress in your body is rarely the result of external forces or entities attacking you; it's the result of the weakened connecting link to intention caused by your belief that ego is who you are. You are peace and joy, but you've allowed your ego to dominate your life. Here's a short list of stress-inducing thoughts that originate in your ego self:

- *It's more important to be right than to be happy.*

- *Winning is the only thing. When you lose, you should be stressed.*

- *Your reputation is more important than your relationship with your Source.*

- *Success is measured in dollars and accumulations rather than in feeling happy and content.*

- *Being superior to others is more important than being kind to others.*

The following lighthearted way to stop taking yourself so seriously is from a book by Rosamund and Benjamin Zander (he's the conductor of the Boston Philharmonic) titled *The Art of Possibility*. It illustrates in a delightful way how we allow ego to create many of the problems we encounter that we label stress and anxiety.

> Two prime ministers are sitting in a room discussing affairs of state. Suddenly a man bursts in, apoplectic with fury, shouting and stamping and banging his fist on the desk. The resident prime minister admonishes him: "Peter," he says, "kindly remember Rule Number 6," whereupon Peter is instantly restored to complete calm, apologizes, and withdraws. The politicians return to their conversation, only to be interrupted yet again twenty minutes later by an hysterical woman gesticulating wildly, her hair flying. Again the intruder is greeted with the words: "Marie, please remember Rule Number 6." Complete calm descends once more, and she too withdraws with a bow and an apology. When the scene is repeated for a third time, the visiting prime minister addresses his colleague: "My dear friend, I've seen many things in my life, but never anything as remarkable as this. Would you be willing to share with me the secret of Rule Number 6?" "Very simple," replies the resident prime minister. "Rule Number 6 is 'Don't take yourself so goddamn seriously.'"
> "Ah," says his visitor, "that is a fine rule." After a moment of pondering, he inquires, "And what, may I ask, are the other rules?"
> "There aren't any."

As you encounter stress, pressure, or anxiety in your life, remember "Rule Number 6" at the moment you realize you're thinking stressful thoughts. By noticing and discontinuing the inner dialogue that's causing stress, you may be able to prevent its physical symptoms. What are the inner thoughts that produce stress? *I'm more important than those around me. My expectations aren't being met. I shouldn't have to wait, I'm too important. I'm the customer here, and I demand attention. No one else has these pressures.* All of the above, along with a potentially endless inventory of "Rule Number 6" thoughts are from the ego's bag of tricks.

You aren't your work, your accomplishments, your possessions, your home, your family . . .

your anything. You're an aspect of the power of intention, dressed in a physical human body intended to experience and enjoy life on Earth. This is the intention that you want to bring to the presence of stress.

Bringing intention to the presence of stress. In any given day, you have hundreds of opportunities to implement "Rule Number 6" by bringing the power of intention into the moment and eliminating the potential for stress. Here are a few examples of how I've employed this strategy. In each of these examples, I activated an inner thought that was in vibrational harmony with the universal field of intention, and I fulfilled my personal intention to be tranquil. These examples occurred in a three-hour period of a normal day. I offer them to you to remind you that stress and anxiety are choices that we make to process events, rather than entities that are out there waiting to invade our lives.

— I'm dropping off a prescription at the drugstore and the person ahead of me is talking to the pharmacist, asking a series of seemingly inane questions—all of which, my stress-producing ego tells me, are intended to deliberately delay and annoy me. My inner dialogue might go like this: *I'm being victimized! There's always someone just ahead of me in line who fumbles with money, can't find what's needed to prove participation in some kind of an insurance plan, and has to ask silly questions designed to keep me from dropping off a prescription.*

I use those thoughts as a signal to change my inner dialogue to: *Wayne, stop taking yourself so goddamn seriously!* I immediately make the shift from pissed to blissed. I take the focus off of myself, and at the same time, I remove resistance to my intention to live a stress-free and tranquil life. I now see this person as an angel who's ahead of me in line to assist me in reconnecting to intention. I stop judging, and actually see beauty in the slow, deliberate gestures. I'm kind in my mind toward this *angel*. I've moved from hostility to love in my thoughts, and my emotions have shifted from discomfort to ease. Stress is absolutely impossible in the moment.

— My 17-year-old daughter tells me about her disagreement with a school official who's taken action against some of her friends, an act she considers totally unfair. It's Saturday morning and nothing can be done until Monday. The choice? Spend two days in misery replaying the details of her story, and have a weekend of inner stress, or remind her how to activate thoughts that will make her feel good. I ask her to describe her feelings. She responds that she's "angry, upset, and hurt." I ask her to think about "Rule Number 6" and see if there's any other thought she could activate.

She laughs at me, telling me how crazy I am. "But," she admits, "it really doesn't make any sense to be upset for the entire weekend, and I'm going to stop thinking thoughts that make me feel bad."

"On Monday we'll do what we can to rectify the situation," I tell her. "But for now—and now is all you have—put 'Rule Number 6' into play and rejoin the field of intention where stress, anxiety, and pressure don't exist."

To fulfill the intention of this chapter, *to live a stress-free and tranquil life,* you must become conscious of the need to activate thought responses that match your intention. These new responses will become habitual, and replace your old habit of responding in stress-producing ways. When you examine segments of stress-producing incidents, you always have a choice: *Do I stay with thoughts that produce stress within me, or do I work to activate thoughts that make stress impossible?* Here's another easy tool that will help you replace the habit of choosing anxiety and stress.

Five magic words: I want to feel good! In an earlier chapter, I described how your emotions are a guidance system informing you of whether or not you're creating resistance to your intentions. Feeling bad lets you know that you're not connected to the power of intention. Your intention here is to be tranquil and stress free. When you feel good, you're connected to your intentions, regardless of what goes on around you or what others expect you to feel. If there's a war going on, you still have the option to feel good. If the economy goes further into the toilet, you have the option to feel good. In the event of any catastrophe, you can still feel good. Feeling good isn't an indication that you're callous, indifferent, or cruel—it's a choice you make. Say it out loud: *I want to feel good!* Then convert it to: *I intend to feel good.* Feel the stress, and then send it the love and respect of the seven faces of intention. The seven faces smile and say hello to what you label as feeling bad. It's that feeling that wants to feel good. You must be to your feelings as your Source is to you, in order to counteract the desires of your ego.

Many events will transpire in which your conditioned response is to feel bad. Be aware of these outer incidents, and say the five magic words: *I want to feel good.* In that precise moment, ask yourself if feeling bad is going to make the situation any better. You'll discover that the only thing that feeling bad accomplishes in response to outer situations is to plummet you into anxiety, despair, depression, and of course, stress. Instead, ask yourself in that moment what thought you can have that will make you feel good. When you discover that it's responding with kindness and love to the bad feeling (which is quite different from wallowing in it), you'll begin experiencing a shift in your emotional state. Now you're in vibrational harmony with your Source, since the power of intention knows only peace, kindness, and love.

This newly activated thought, which allows you to feel good, may only last a few moments, and you might go back to your previous way of processing unpleasant events. Also treat that old way of processing with respect, love, and understanding, but remember that it's your ego-self trying to protect you from its perception of danger. Any stress signal is a way of alerting you to say the five magic words *I want to feel good.* Stress wants your attention! By saying the five magic words and extending love to your bad feelings, you'll have begun the process of fulfilling your stated intention of being tranquil and stress free. Now you can practice activating these thoughts in the toughest of moments, and before long, you'll be living the message offered to all of us in the book of Job: "You will decide on a matter and it will be established for you, and light will shine on your ways" [Job 22:28]. The word *light* in this biblical reference means that you'll have the assistance of the divine mind of intention once you decide on a matter that is consistent with that light.

I assure you that your decision to feel good is a way of connecting to Spirit. It isn't an indifferent response to events. By feeling good, you become an instrument of peace, and it's through this channel that you eradicate problems. By feeling bad, you stay in the energy field that creates resistance to positive change; and experience a stressful, anxious state as a by-product. The things you call problems will perpetually present themselves to you. They'll never go away. Resolve one . . . and another will surface!

You'll never get it done. In Chapter 6, I reminded you of your infinite nature. Since you're an infinite spiritual being disguised as a temporary human being, it's essential to understand that in infinity there's no beginning and no ending. Therefore, your desires, goals, hopes, and dreams will never be finished—ever! As soon as you manifest one of your dreams, another will most assuredly pop up. The nature of the universal force of intention from which you emigrated into a temporary material being is always creating and giving forth. Furthermore, it's in a continuous state of expansion. Your desires to manifest into your life are a part of this infinite nature. Even if you desire to have no desires, that's a desire!

I urge you to simply accept the fact that you'll never get it all done, and begin to live more fully in the only moment that you have—now! The secret to removing the harmful effects of feeling stressed and under pressure is to be in the now. Announce out loud to yourself and all who are willing to listen to you: *I'm an incomplete being. I'll always be incomplete because I can never get it done. Therefore, I choose to feel good while I'm in the moment, attracting into my life the manifestations of my desires. I am complete in my incompleteness!* I can assure you that a follow-up on this statement will eradicate all anxiety and stress, which is precisely the intention of this chapter. All resistance melts away when you can feel complete in your incompleteness.

The Path of Least Resistance

You live in a universe that has limitless potential for joy built into the creation process. Your Source, which we call the universal mind of intention, adores you beyond anything you can possibly imagine. When you adore yourself in the same proportion, you're matched up with the field of intention, and you've opted for the path of no resistance. As long as you have even a pinch of an ego, you'll retain some resistance, so I urge you to take the path in which resistance is minimized.

The shape and quantity of your thoughts determine the amount of resistance. Thoughts that generate bad feelings are resistant thoughts. Any thought that puts a barrier between what you would like to have and your ability to attract it into your life is resistance. Your intention is to live a tranquil life, free of stress and anxiety. You know that stress doesn't exist in the world, and that there are only people thinking stressful thoughts. Stressful thoughts all by themselves are a form of resistance. You don't want stressful, resistant thoughts to be your habitual way of reacting to your world. By practicing thoughts of minimal resistance, you'll train yourself to make this your natural way of reacting, and eventually you'll become the tranquil person you desire to be, a stress-free person free of the "dis-ease" that stress brings to the body. Stressful thoughts *all by themselves* are the resistance that you construct that impedes your connection to the power of intention.

We're in a world that advertises and promotes reasons to be anxious. You've been taught that feeling good in a world where so much suffering exists is an immoral stance to take. You've been convinced that choosing to feel good in bad economic times, in times of war, in times of uncertainty or death, or in the face of any catastrophe anywhere in the world is crass and inappropriate. Since these conditions will always be in the world someplace, you believe you can't have joy and still be a good person. But it may not have occurred to you that in a universe based on energy and attraction, thoughts that evoke feeling bad originate in the same energy Source that attracts more of the same into your life. These are resistant thoughts.

Here are some examples of sentences on the **path of resistance**, which are then changed to sentences on the *path of least resistance*.

I feel uneasy about the state of the economy;
I've already lost so much money.
I live in an abundant universe; I choose to think about what I have
and I will be fine. The universe will provide.

I have so many things to do that I can never get caught up.
I'm at peace in this moment. I'll only think about the one thing I'm
doing. I will have peaceful thoughts.

I can never get ahead in this job.
I choose to appreciate what I'm doing right now, and I'll attract an
even greater opportunity.

My health is a huge concern. I worry about getting
old and becoming dependent and sick.
I'm healthy, and I think healthy. I live in a universe
that attracts healing, and I refuse to anticipate
sickness.

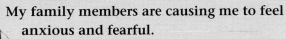

My family members are causing me to feel anxious and fearful.
I choose thoughts that make me feel good, and this will help me uplift those family members in need.

I don't deserve to feel good when so many people are suffering.
I didn't come into a world where everyone is going to have the same identical experiences. I'll feel good, and by being uplifted, I'll help eradicate some of the suffering.

I can't be happy when the person I really care about loves another and has abandoned me.
Feeling bad won't change this scenario. I trust that love will return to my life if I'm in harmony with the loving Source. I choose to feel good right now and focus on what I have, rather than what's missing.

All stressful thoughts represent a form of resistance you wish to eradicate. Change those thoughts by monitoring your feelings and opting for joy rather than anxiety, and you'll access the power of intention.

Making Your Intention Your Reality

Below is my ten-step program for creating a stress-free, tranquil life:

Step 1: Remember that your natural state is joy. You are a product of joy and love; it's natural for you to experience these feelings. You've come to believe that feeling bad, anxious, or even depressed is natural, particularly when people and events around you are in low-energy modes. Remind yourself as frequently as necessary: *I come from peace and joy. I must stay in harmony with that from which I came in order to fulfill my*

211

dreams and desires. I choose to stay in my natural state. Anytime I'm anxious, stressed out, depressed, or fearful, I've abandoned my natural state.

Step 2: Your thoughts, not the world, cause your stress. Your thoughts activate stressful reactions in your body. Stressful thoughts create resistance to the joy, happiness, and abundance that you desire to create in your life. These thoughts include: *I can't, I'm too overworked, I worry, I'm afraid, I'm unworthy, It will never happen, I'm not smart enough, I'm too old (young),* and so on. These thoughts are like a program to resist being tranquil and stress free, and they keep you from manifesting your desires.

Step 3: You can change your thoughts of stress in any given moment, and eliminate the anxiety for the next few moments, or even hours and days. By making a conscious decision to distract yourself from worry, you've inaugurated the process of stress reduction, while simultaneously reconnecting to the field of all-creating intention. It's from this place of peace and tranquility that you become a co-creator with God. You can't be connected to your Source and be stressed at the same time—this is mutually exclusive. Your Source doesn't create from a position of anxiety, nor does it need to swallow antidepressants. You've left behind your capacity to manifest your desires when you don't choose in the moment to eliminate a stressful thought.

Step 4: Monitor your stressful thoughts by checking on your emotional state right in the moment. Ask yourself the key question: *Do I feel good right now?* If the answer is no, then repeat those five magic words: *I want to feel good,* then shift to: *I intend to feel good.* Monitor your emotions, and detect how much stress- and anxiety-producing thinking you're engaging in. This monitoring process keeps you apprised of whether you're on the path of least resistance or going in the other direction.

Step 5: Make a conscious choice to select a thought that will activate good feelings. I urge you to choose your thought based exclusively on how it makes you feel, rather than on how popular it is or how well advertised. Ask yourself: *Does this new thought make me feel good? No? Well, how about this thought? Not really? Here's another.* Ultimately you'll come up with one that you agree makes you feel good, if only temporarily. Your choice might be the thought of a beautiful sunset, the expression on the face of someone you love, or a thrilling experience. It's only important that it resonate within you emotionally and physically as a good feeling.

In the moment of experiencing an anxious or stressful thought, change to the thought you chose, which makes you feel good. Plug it in. Think it and feel it in your body if you can. This new thought that makes you feel good will be of appreciation rather than depreciation. It will be of love, beauty, receptivity to happiness, or in other words, it will align perfectly with those seven faces of intention I've been harping about since the opening pages of this book.

Step 6: Spend some time observing babies, and vow to emulate their joy. You didn't come forth into this world to suffer, to be anxious, fearful, stressful, or depressed. You came from the God-consciousness of joy. Just watch little babies. They've done nothing to be so happy about. They don't work; they poop in their pants; and they have no goals other than to expand, grow, and explore this amazing world. They love everyone, they're completely entertained by a plastic bottle or goofy faces, and they're in a constant state of love—yet they have no teeth, no hair, and they're pudgy and flatulent. How could they possibly be so joyful and easily pleased? Because they're still in harmony with the Source that intended them here; they have no resistance to being joyful. Be like that baby you once were in terms of being joyful. You don't need a reason to be happy . . . your desire to be so is sufficient.

Step 7: Keep "Rule Number 6" in mind. This means to suspend the demands of your ego, which keep you separated from intention. When you have a choice to be right or to be kind, pick kind, and push the ego's demand out of the way. Kindness is what you emanated from, and by practicing it, rather than being right, you eliminate the possibility of stress in your moment of kindness. When you find yourself being impatient with anyone, simply say to yourself: "Rule Number 6," and you'll immediately laugh at the piddly little ego that wants you to be first, faster, number one, and to be treated better than the other guy.

Step 8: Accept the guidance of your Source of intention. You will only come to know the Father by being as He is. You'll only be able to access the guidance of this field of intention by being as *it* is. Stress, anxiety, and depression will be lifted from you with the assistance of that same force that created you. If it can create worlds out of nothing, and you out of nothing, surely the removal of some stress isn't such a big task. I believe that God's desire for you is that you not only know joy, but that you become it.

Step 9: Practice being in silence and meditation. Nothing relieves stress, depression, anxiety, and all forms of low-energy emotions like silence and meditation. Here, you make conscious contact with your Source and cleanse your connecting link to intention. Take time every day for moments of quiet contemplation, and make meditation a part of your stress-reducing ritual.

Step 10: Stay in a state of gratitude and awe. Go on a rampage of appreciation for all that you have, all that you are, and all that you observe. Gratitude is the tenth step in every ten-step program for manifesting your intentions, because it's the surest way to stop the incessant inner dialogue that leads you away from the joy and perfection of the Source. You can't feel stressed and appreciative at the same time.

❖ ❖ ❖

I conclude this chapter on your intention to lead a tranquil life with a poem by the famous Bengali poet of Calcutta, Rabindranath Tagore, one of my favorite spiritual teachers:

> *I slept and dreamt that life was joy*
> *I awoke and saw that life was service*
> *I acted and behold service was joy*

It can all be joy in your inner world. Sleep and dream of joy, and remember above all else: *You feel good not because the world is right, but your world is right because you feel good.*

❀ ❀ ❀ ❀ ❀

It Is My Intention to: Attract Ideal People and Divine Relationships

"The moment one definitely commits oneself, then Providence moves too. All sorts of things occur to help one that would never otherwise have occurred . . . unforeseen incidents, meetings, and material assistance, which no man could have dreamed would have come his way."

— Johann Wolfgang von Goethe

I f you saw the 1989 movie *Field of Dreams*, you probably came away remembering the concept that if you pursue a dream, you will succeed (or, "If you build it, they will come"). I thought of this as I began writing this chapter because I'm suggesting that if you commit yourself to matching up with the field of intention, everyone you desire or need to fulfill your personal intention will appear. How can that be? In the quote above, Goethe, one of the most brilliantly gifted scholars and achievers in the history of humanity, gives you the answer. The moment you definitely commit yourself to being a part of the power of intention, "then Providence moves too," and unforseen assistance comes your way.

The right people will arrive to assist you in every aspect of your life: The people who will support you in your career are there; the people who will help you create your perfect home show up; the people who will arrange the finances for whatever you desire are available; the driver you need to get you to the airport is waiting for you; the designer you've admired wants to work with you; the dentist you need in an emergency when you're on vacation just happens to be there; and your spiritual soul mate finds you.

The list is endless, because we're all in relationship to each other, we all emanate from the same Source, and we all share the same divine energy of intention. There's no place that this universal mind is not; therefore, you share it with everyone you attract into your life.

You'll have to let go of any resistance to your ability to attract the right people, or you won't recognize them when they show up in your everyday life. Resistance may be difficult to recognize at first, because it's such a familiar form of your thoughts, your emotions, and your energy levels. If you believe that you're powerless to attract the right people, then you've attracted powerlessness to your experience. If you're attached to the idea of being stuck with the wrong people or no people at all, then your energy isn't aligned with the power of intention, and resistance reigns. The field of intention has no choice but to send you more of what you're desiring. Once again, make a somersault into the inconceivable, where you have faith and trust in the universal mind of intention, and allow the right people to arrive in your life space right on schedule.

Removing Resistance by Allowing

Your intention is absolutely clear here. You want to attract the people who are

218

intended to be part of your life, and you want to have a happy, fulfilling, spiritual relationship. The universal all-creating field is already cooperating with your intention. These very people are obviously already here, otherwise you'd want something that hasn't been created. Not only are the right people here, but you also share the same divine Source of all life with them, since everyone emanates from that Source. In some invisible way, you're already connected spiritually to those *perfect-for-you* people. So why can't you see them, touch them, or hold them, and why aren't they there when you need them?

What you need in the way of the *right people* showing up will appear for you only when you're ready and willing to receive them. They've always been there. They're there right now. They'll always be there. The questions you need to ask yourself are: *Am I ready? Am I willing?* and *How much am I willing to have it?* If your responses to these questions are a readiness and willingness to experience your desires, then you'll begin seeing people not only as a body with a soul, but as a spiritual being clothed in a unique body. You'll see the infinite souls that we all are: *infinite,* meaning always and everywhere; and *everywhere,* meaning with you right now if that's your spiritual desire.

Giving forth what you want to attract. Once you've formed a picture in your mind of the person or people that you intend to show up in your immediate life space, and you know how you want them to treat you and what they'll be like, you must be what it is that you're seeking. This is a universe of attraction and energy. You can't have a desire to attract a mate who's confident, generous, nonjudgmental, and gentle, and expect that desire to be manifested if you're thinking and acting in nonconfident, selfish, judgmental, or arrogant ways—which is why most people don't attract the right people at the right time.

Almost 30 years ago, I wanted to attract a publisher into my life for my book, *Your Erroneous Zones.* This publisher would have to be understanding, since I was an unknown writer at the time, and would have to be a risk taker, willing to let go of any doubts about me.

My literary agent arranged a meeting with an executive editor, whom I'll refer to as George, at a large New York publishing house. As I sat down to talk with him, it was obvious to me that he was personally distraught. I asked him what was troubling him, and we proceeded to spend the next three to four hours talking about a devastating personal matter that had just transpired the night before. George's wife had told him that she was going to seek a divorce, and he felt as though he'd been blindsided by this news. I let go of my own desires to talk about getting my book published and became what it was that I was seeking: an understanding, confident, risk-taking person. By being that very thing and detaching from my ego-dominated desires, I was able to help George out that afternoon, which I've never forgotten.

I left George's office that day without even discussing my book proposal. When I told my literary agent this story, he was convinced that I'd blown my one opportunity with a major publishing house by not making a strong pitch for my book. The following day, George called my agent, telling him, "I really don't even know what Dyer's book proposal entails, but I want that man as one of our authors."

At the time, I didn't realize what was happening. Now, with a quarter century of living in this world of spiritual inquiry, I see it quite clearly. The right people will show up precisely when you need them and when you're able to match up. You must be that which you desire. When you *are* what you desire, you attract it by radiating it outward. You have this ability to match up with the power of intention and fulfill your intention to attract ideal people and divine relationships.

Attracting Spiritual Partnerships

There's no point whatsoever in an unloving man or woman bemoaning their inability to find a partner. They're doomed to endless frustration because they don't recognize the perfect match when it appears. That loving person could be right there, right now, and their resistance doesn't allow them to see it. The unloving person continues to blame bad luck or a series of external factors for their not having a loving relationship. Love can only be attracted by and returned by love. The best advice I can give for attracting and maintaining spiritual partnerships, as I've been empha-sizing in this chapter, is to *be what it is that you're seeking.* Most relationships that fail to sustain themselves are based on one or both of the partners feeling as if their freedom has been compromised in some way. Spiritual partner-ships, on the other hand, are never about making another person feel inferior or ignored in any way. The term *spiritual partnership* simply means that the energy that holds the two of you together is in close har-mony with the Source energy of intention.

This means that an *allowing* philosophy flows through the partnership, and you need never fear that your freedom to ful-fill your own inner knowing about your purpose is ques-tioned. It's as if each person has whispered silently to the other, *You are Source energy in a physical body, and the better you feel, the more of this loving, kind, beautiful, receptive, abundant, expanding, and creative energy is flow-ing through you. I respect this Source energy, and I share it with you as well. When either of us feels downhearted, there's less of this energy of intention flowing. We must always remember that nothing is disallowed by the universal mind. Whatever is not allowing us to be happy is being disallowed by us. I'm committed to staying in this energy field of intention and watching myself whenever I slip. It's that very Source that brought us together, and I'll work to stay in harmony with it.* This kind of inner commitment is what Goethe was speaking about in that opening quotation. It allows providence to move and helps things to occur, "which no man could have dreamed would come his way."

You're already connected to those you want in your life—so act like it. Mystically speaking, there's no difference between you and another person. A weird concept, perhaps, but nevertheless valid. This explains why you can't hurt another person without hurting yourself, nor can you help another person without helping yourself. You share the same Source energy with everyone, and consequently, you must begin to think and act in a way that reflects your awareness of this principle. When you feel the need to have the right person show up, begin to change your inner dialogue to reflect this awareness. Rather than saying, *I wish this person would show up because I need to get out of this rut,* activate a thought that reflects your connection, such as: *I know the right person will be arriving in divine order at precisely the perfect time.*

Now you'll act on this inner thought. You'll be *thinking from the end,* and anticipating this arrival. Your anticipation will make you alert. You've revised your energy level to the same receptivity as the power of intention that intends everything and everyone here. When you reach these higher energy levels, you access higher information. Your intuition clicks in, and you can feel the presence of the person or people you want in your life. Now you act on that intuition with a deep sense of knowing that you're on track. You're acting in accordance with this new awareness. You become a co-creator. New insight becomes activated within you as well. You're looking at the face of the Creator, and you see yourself co-creating. You know whom to call, where to look, when to trust, and what to do. You're being guided to connect to that which you're bringing forth.

If a friendship or partnership requires the submission of your higher original nature and dignity, it's simply wrong. When you truly know what it is to love, as you're loved by your Source, you won't experience the kind of pain you did in the past when your love was unnoticed or rejected. It will, instead, be similar to how a friend described her experience of choosing to leave a relationship: "My heart was broken, but it felt like it was stuck in the open position. I felt love flowing toward this person who couldn't love me the way I wanted to be loved, even as I left that relationship to seek the love I felt inside of me. It was strange to feel the pain of my broken heart, and at the same time feel its openness. I kept thinking, *My heart's broken, but it's broken open.* I shifted to an entirely new level of loving and being loved. The relationship I'd dreamed of having manifested 18 months later!"

You are love. You emanated from pure love. You're connected to this Source of love at all times. Think this way, feel this way, and you'll soon act this way. And all that you think, feel, and do will be reciprocated in exactly the same fashion. Believe it or not, this principle of the right person showing up has been in place forever. It's only your ego that's kept you from seeing it clearly.

It's all unfolding in divine order. By now you should be affirming that everyone you need for this journey of yours will show up, and that they'll be perfect in every way for whatever needs you have at this time. Furthermore, they'll arrive at precisely the right moment. In this intelligent system that you're a part of, everything arrives from the field of intention where the infinite, invisible life force flows through everyone and everything. This includes you, and everyone else as well. Trust in this invisible life force and the all-creating mind that intends everything into existence.

I suggest that you do a quick review, and note all of the people who've shown up as characters in this play called your life. It has all been perfect. Your ex-spouse showed up at just the right time—when you needed to create those children you love so much. The father who walked out on you so that you could learn self-reliance left right on time. The lover who abandoned you was a part of this perfection. The lover who stayed with you was also taking his or her cues from Source. The good times, the struggles, the tears, the abuse—all of it involved people coming into your life and then leaving. And all of your tears will not and cannot wash out one word of it.

This is your past, and whatever your energy level at the time, whatever your needs, whatever your station in life, you attracted the right people and events to you. You may feel that they didn't show up when you needed them, that in fact, you were alone and no one showed up at all, but I urge you to see it from the perspective of all of life being in divine order. If no one showed up, it was because you needed to handle something on your own and therefore attracted no one to fulfill your energy level at that time. Viewing the past as a play in which all characters and all entrances and exits were scripted by your Source and was what you attracted at the time, frees you from the very low energies of guilt, regret, and even revenge.

As a result, you'll go from being an actor who's influenced by others playing the roles of producer and director, to being the writer, producer, director, and star of your glorious life. You'll also be the casting director who possesses the ability to audition anyone you choose. Base your choices on taking the path of no resistance and staying harmonized with the ultimate producer of this entire drama: the universal all-creating mind of intention.

A few words about patience. There's a wonderfully paradoxical line in *A Course in Miracles:* "Infinite patience produces immediate results." To be infinitely patient means to have an absolute knowing within you that you're in vibrational harmony with the all-creating force that intended you here. You are, in fact, a co-creator of your life. You know that the right people will show up on divinely ordained schedule. Attempting to rush the schedule based on your own timetable is akin to getting down on your knees and tugging at an emerging tulip shoot, insisting that you need the flower now. Creation reveals its secrets by and by, not according to your agenda. The immediate result that you'll receive from your infinite patience is a deep sense of peace. You'll feel the love of the creation process, you'll stop making incessant demands, and you'll start being on the lookout for exactly the right person.

I write this with the idea of infinite patience producing immediate results. I know that I'm not alone as I sit here writing. I know that the right people will magically appear to provide me with whatever incentive or material I might need. I have total faith in this process, and I stay harmoniously in tune with my Source. The phone will ring, and someone has a tape they think I'll like. Two weeks ago, it wouldn't have clicked with me, but on this day, I listen to that tape while exercising, and it provides me with exactly what I need. I pass someone on a walk, and they stop to talk. They tell me about a book they're sure I'd love. I jot down the title, look it up, and sure enough, I have what I need.

This goes on every day in some way or another as I surrender my ego-mind to the universal mind of intention, and allow precisely the right people to help me with my individual intention. The immediate result of infinite patience is the inner peace that comes from knowing that I have a "senior partner" who will either send me someone, or leave me alone to work it out myself. This is called practical faith, and I urge you to trust in it, be infinitely patient with it, and have an attitude of radical appreciation and awe each time the right person mysteriously appears in your immediate life space.

Making Your Intention Your Reality

Below is my ten-step program for implementing the intention of this chapter:

Step 1: Move away from hoping, wishing, praying, and begging for the right person or people to show up in your life. Know that this is a universe that works on energy and attraction. Remind yourself that you have the power to attract the right people to assist you with any desire as long as you're able to shift from ego-driven energy to match up with the all-providing Source of intention. This first step is crucial, because if you can't banish all doubt about your ability to attract helpful, creative, loving people, then the remaining nine steps will be of little use to you. Intending ideal people and divine partners begins with knowing in your heart that it's not only a possibility, but a certainty.

Step 2: Conceptualize your invisible connection to the people you'd like to attract to your life. Let go of your exclusive identification with the appearance of your body and its possessions. Identify with the invisible energy within you that sustains your life by directing the functions of your body. Now recognize that same energy Source flowing through the people you perceive to be missing from your life, and then realign yourself in thought with that person or persons. Know within you that this power of intention connects the two of you. Your thoughts of creating this merger also emanate from that same field of universal intention.

Step 3: Form a picture in your mind of meeting the person(s) you'd like to have assist you or be in partnership with you. Manifesting is a function of spiritual intention matching up in vibrational harmony with your desires. Be as specific as you'd like, but don't share this visualizing technique with anyone because you'll be asked to explain yourself, defend yourself, and have to deal with the low energy of doubt that will inevitably occur. This is a private exercise between you and God. Never, *never* allow your picture to be blurred or corroded by negativity or doubt. Regardless of any obstacles that may surface, hang on to this picture, and stay in loving, kind, creative, peaceful harmony with your always-expanding and endlessly receptive Source of intention.

Step 4: Act upon the inner picture. Begin to act as if everyone you meet is a part of your intention to attract ideal people into your life. Share with others your needs and desires without going into detail about your spiritual methodology. Make calls to experts who might be of assistance, and state your desires. They'll want to help you. Don't expect anyone else to do the work of attracting the right people for whatever you seek—be it a job, admission to a college, a financial boost, or a person to repair your automobile. Be proactive, and stay alert for signs of synchronicity, never ignoring them. If a truck drives by with a phone number advertising what you need, jot the number down and call. See all so-called bizarre coincidences surrounding your desires as messages from Source, and act upon them immediately. I assure you that they'll occur repeatedly.

Step 5: Take the path of least resistance. I use the word *resistance* here, as I have several times in Part II of this book. Thoughts such as the following are actually a form of resistance to having your intentions manifest: *This stuff isn't practical. I can't just materialize my ideal person by my thoughts. Why should I be treated any better than all of those others who are still waiting for Mr. Right? I tried this before, and a real idiot came into my life.* These are thoughts of resistance that you're placing right in the way of Source sending you someone. Resistance is lowered energy. Source is high, creative, expansive energy. When your thoughts are low-energy vibrations, you simply can't attract the high-energy people you need or desire. Even if they came rushing up to you announcing: *Here I am, how can I serve you, I'm willing and able,* and carrying a sign saying *I'M YOURS,* you wouldn't recognize or believe them while you're so busy trying to attract more of what you *can't have and don't deserve.*

Step 6: Practice being the kind of person you wish to attract. As I've touched on before, if you want to be loved unconditionally, *practice* loving unconditionally. If you want assistance from others, *extend* assistance whenever and wherever you have the opportunity. If you'd like to be the recipient of generosity, then *be* as generous as you can, as frequently as you can. This is one of the simplest and most effective ways of attracting the power of intention. Match up with the *forthcomingness* of the universal mind from which everyone and everything originates while extending it outward, and you'll attract back to yourself all that you intend to manifest.

Step 7: Detach from the outcome, and practice infinite patience. This is the crucial step of faith. Don't make the mistake of evaluating your intentions as successes or failures on the basis of your little ego and its time schedule. Put out your intention, and practice everything that's written in this chapter and in this book . . . and then let go. Create a knowing within, and let the universal mind of intention handle the details.

Step 8: Practice meditation, particularly the Japa meditation, to attract ideal people and divine relationships. Practice the repetition of the sound that is in the name of God as a mantra, literally seeing in your mind's eye the energy you're radiating, bringing the people you desire into your life. You will be astounded at the results. I've provided examples throughout this book of how the practice of Japa meditation has helped people manifest their dreams, almost like magic.

Step 9: Look upon everyone who has ever played any role in your life as having been sent to you for your benefit. In a universe peopled by a creative, divine, organizing intelligence, which I'm calling *the power of intention,* there are simply no accidents. The wake of your life is like the wake of a boat. It's nothing more than the trail that's left behind. The wake doesn't drive the boat. The wake is not driving your life. Everything and everyone in your personal history had to be there when they were. And what's the evidence for this? *They were there!* That's all you need to know. Don't use what transpired in the wake, or the wrong people who showed up in your wake, as a reason why you can't attract the right people today. It's your past . . . nothing more than a trail you've left behind.

Step 10: As always, remain in a state of eternal gratitude. Even be grateful for those whose presence may have caused you pain and suffering. Be thankful to your Source for sending them, and to yourself for attracting them to you. They all had something to teach you. Now be grateful for everyone God sends to your path, and know as a co-creator that it's up to you to either resonate with the high, loving energy of intention and keep those like-energized people in your life, or to give them a silent blessing and a pleasant *no thank you.* And the emphasis is on the *thank you,* for that is true gratitude in action.

❖ ❖ ❖

In Lynne McTaggart's fabulous book *The Field: The Quest for the Secret Force of the Universe,* she offers us this scientific perspective on what I've written in this chapter: "Our natural state of being is a relationship, a tango, a constant state of one influencing the other. Just as the subatomic particles that compose us cannot be separated from the space and particles surrounding them, so living beings cannot be isolated from each other. . . . By the act of observation and *intention,* we have the ability to extend a kind of super-radiance to the world." [Emphasis mine]

Through relationships with others and by using the power of intention, we can radiate outward all of the energy necessary to attract what we desire. I urge you to move into this awareness now and know in your heart, just as the farmer in *Field of Dreams* knew, that *if you build this inner dream, surely, it will come!*

❀❀❀❀❀

It Is My Intention to: Optimize My Capacity to Heal and Be Healed

"No one can ask another to be healed. But he can let himself be healed, and thus offer the other what he has received. Who can bestow upon another what he does not have? And who can share what he denies himself?"

— *A Course in Miracles*

Every single person on the planet has within them the potential to be a healer. In order to make conscious contact with your inherent healing powers, you must first make the decision to be healed yourself. As *A Course in Miracles* reminds us: "Those who are healed become the instruments of healing," and "The only way to heal is to be healed." Thus, there's a twofold advantage in this intention to be healed. Once you've accepted your power to heal yourself and optimize your health, you become someone who's capable of healing others as well.

One of the many fascinating observations that David Hawkins made in his book *Power vs. Force* is the relationship between a person's calibrated level of energy and their capacity to heal. People who calibrated above 600 on his map of consciousness scale (which is an exceptionally high-energy score indicating illumination and supreme enlightenment) radiated healing energy. Disease, as we know it, can't exist in the presence of such high spiritual energy. This explains the miraculous healing powers of Jesus of Nazareth, St. Francis of Assisi, and Ramana Maharshi. Their exceptionally high energy is sufficient to counterbalance disease.

As you read this, keep in mind that you too emanated from the highest spiritual loving energy field of intention, and you have within you this capacity. In order to fulfill the intention of this chapter, you must, as Gandhi states in the quotation above, "be the change that you wish to see in others." You must focus on healing yourself so you'll have this healing ability to offer others. If you reach a level of blissful illumination where you're reconnected to Source and are harmonized vibrationally, you'll begin to radiate the energy that converts disease to health.

In St. Francis's powerful prayer, he asks of his Source, "Where there is injury, let me sow pardon," meaning, *allow me to be a person who gives others healing energy.* This principle has been repeated throughout the pages of this book: Bring higher/spiritual energy to the presence of lower/diseased energy, and it not only nullifies the lower energy, but converts it to healthy spiritual energy. In the field of energy medicine where these principles are being applied, tumors are bombarded with exceptionally high-laser energy that dissolves and converts them to healthy tissue.

Energy medicine is the discipline of the future, and relies on the ancient spiritual practice of *being the change,* or healing others by first healing ourselves.

Becoming the Healing

Reconnect to the disease-free loving perfection from which you came is a succinct statement of what the self-healing process requires. The universal mind of intention knows precisely what you need in order to optimize your health. What *you* must do is notice your thoughts and behaviors, which are creating *resistance,* and interfering with healing, which is the flow of intentional energy. Recognizing your resistance is something that's entirely up to you. You must dedicate yourself to this awareness so that you can make a shift to pure healing intention.

While I was on the treadmill at the gym yesterday, I talked to a gentleman for five minutes, and in that brief span of time, he regaled me with a laundry list of ailments, surgeries, heart procedures, diseases, and projected joint replacements—all in five minutes! This was his calling card. Those thoughts and recapitulations of bodily afflictions are resistance to the healing energy that's available.

As I talked to the complaining man on the treadmill, I attempted to get him to shift even momentarily away from his resistance to receiving healing energy. But he was absolutely determined to wallow in his disabilities, wearing them as a badge of honor, arguing vehemently for his limitations. He seemed to cherish and cling to his self-loathing for his deteriorating body. I attempted to surround him with light and sent him a silent blessing, congratulating him for doing a treadmill exercise as I moved on to my own workout. But I was struck by how much of this man's inner focus was on dis-order, dis-harmony, and dis-ease as he related to his own body.

Reading about the role of thoughts in reports of spontaneous recovery from irreversible and incurable disease is fascinating. Dr. Hawkins, writing in *Power vs. Force,* offers us this wisdom: "In every studied case of recovery from hopeless and untreatable disease, there has been a major shift in consciousness, so that the attractor patterns that resulted in the pathologic process no longer dominated." Every case! Imagine that. And look at that term *attractor patterns:* We attract into our lives through our level of consciousness, and we can change what we attract. This is a very powerful idea and the basis for accessing the power of intention not only in healing, but in every area where we have desires, aspirations, and individual intentions. Hawkins goes on to say that "in spontaneous recovery, there is frequently a marked increase in the capacity to love and the awareness of the importance of love as a healing factor."

Your intention in this chapter is facilitated by looking at the larger objective of returning to your Source, and vibrating more in harmony with the energy of the power of intention. That Source is never focused on what's wrong, what's missing, or what's sickly. True healing takes you back to the Source. Anything short of this connection is a temporary fix. When you clean up the connecting link to your Source, *attractor patterns* of energy are drawn to you. If you don't believe that this is possible, then you've created resistance to your intention to heal and be healed. If you believe that it *is* possible, but not for you, then you have more resistance. If you believe you're being punished by the absence of health, that's also resistance. These inner thoughts about your ability to be healed play a dominant role in your physical experience.

Becoming a healer by healing oneself involves another one of those imaginary somersaults into the inconceivable, wherein you land upright and balanced in your thoughts, face-to-face with your Source. You realize, perhaps for the first time, that you and your Source are one when you let go of the ego-mind, which has convinced you that you're separate from the power of intention.

Healing others by healing yourself. In Lynne McTaggart's book *The Field,* which I've mentioned previously, the author has taken the time and trouble to report the hard scientific research conducted around the world in the past 20 years regarding this field I'm calling intention. In a chapter that is relevant here, called "The Healing Field," McTaggart describes a number of research studies. Here are just five of the intriguing conclusions that researchers have come to concerning intention and healing. I present these to you to stimulate an awareness of your potential for healing the physical body you've opted for in this lifetime, as well as the corollary capacity to offer healing to others. (I haven't reiterated the obvious need for a healthy diet and a sensible exercise routine, which I'm assuming you're aware of and practicing. Bookstores now have entire sections on healthy alternatives for this purpose.)

**Five Conclusions about Healing from the
World of Hard Research**

1. **Healing through intention is available to ordinary people, and
   healers may be more experienced or naturally talented in tapping in to the field.** There's physical evidence that those who are
   capable of healing through intention have a greater coherence
   and a greater ability to marshal quantum energy and transfer it
   to those in need of healing. I interpret this scientific evidence to
   mean that deciding to focus life energy on being in coherence with
   the power of intention gives you the capacity to heal yourself and
   others. This means essentially abandoning the fear that permeates
   your consciousness. And it also means recognizing the fear-based
   energy promoted by much of the health-care industry. The field
   of intention has no fear in it. Any disease process is evidence that
   something is amiss. Any fear associated with the disease process
   is further evidence that something is amiss in the working of
   the mind. Health and peace are the natural state when that
   which prevents them is removed. Research shows that healing through intention, which is actually healing through
   connecting to the field of intention, is possible for everyone.

2. **Most authentic healers claim to
   have put out their intention and
   then stepped back and surrendered
   to some other kind of healing
   force, as though they were opening a door and allowing something greater in.** The most effective healers ask for assistance from the universal
   Source, knowing that their job is to be uplifting
   and allow the Source of healing to flow. Healers know that the body is the hero, and the
   life force itself is what does the healing. By
   removing ego and allowing that force to flow
   freely, healing is facilitated. Medically trained
   professionals often do the opposite of allowing

and uplifting. They frequently convey the message that the medicine does the healing, and communicate disbelief in anything other than their prescribed procedures. Patients often feel anything but uplifted and hopeful, and diagnosis and prognosis are usually fear based and excessively pessimistic to avoid legal proceedings. *Tell them the worst and hope for the best* is often the medical operating philosophy.

The ability to heal yourself seems to be available to those who have an intuitive knowing about the power of the Spirit. The healing inner speech has to do with relaxing, removing thoughts of resistance, and allowing the spirit of light and love to flow. A powerful healer from the island of Fiji once told me about the efficacy of the native healers. He said, "When a knowing confronts a belief in a disease process, the knowing will always triumph." *A knowing is faith in the power of intention.* A knowing also involves an awareness of always being connected to this Source. And finally, a knowing means getting one's ego out of the way and surrendering to the omnipotent, omnipresent, and omniscient Source, the power of intention, which is the source of all, including all healing.

3. **It didn't seem to matter what method was used, so long as the healer held an intention for a patient to heal.** Healers relied upon profoundly different techniques, including a Christian image, a kabbalist energy pattern, a Native American spirit, a totem, a statue of a saint, and incantations and chants to a healing spirit. As long as the healer held firm to an intention and had a knowing beyond any and all doubts that he could touch the patient with the spirit of intention, the healing was effective as measured by scientific validation.

It's crucial for you to hold an absolute intention for yourself to heal, regardless of what goes on around you, or what others might offer you in the way of discouragement or "getting real." Your intention is strong because it isn't ego's intention, but a match-up with the universal Source. It's God-realization at work in your approach to healing and being healed.

As an *infinite being,* you know that your own death, and the death of everyone else, is programmed in the energy field from which you emanated. Just as all of your physical characteristics were determined by that future pull, so, too, is your death. So let go of fear of your death, and decide to hold the same intention that intended you here from the world of formlessness. You came from a natural state of well-being, and you intend to be there in your mind, regardless of what transpires in and around your body. Hold that intention for yourself until you leave this body, and hold that same invisible intention for others. This is the one quality that all healers shared. I encourage you to emphasize it, too, right here, right now, and don't let anyone or any prognosis deter you from it.

4. **Research suggests that intention on its own heals, but that healing is a collective memory of a healing spirit, which can be gathered as a medicinal force.** Healing itself may in fact be a force that's available to all of humankind. It's the universal mind of intention. Further, research suggests that individuals and groups of individuals can gather this collective memory and apply it to themselves and to those who suffer with epidemic diseases as well. Since we're all connected to intention, we all share the same life force, and we all emanated from the same universal mind of God, it's not so far-fetched to assume that by tapping in to this energy field, we can gather healing energy and spread it to all who enter our

enlightened spheres. This would explain the enormous collective healing power of saints, and make the case for each of us holding the intention to eradicate such things as AIDS, smallpox, worldwide influenzas, and even the cancer epidemic we live with today.

When illness is viewed in isolation, it's disconnected from the collective health of the universal field. Several studies report that the AIDS virus seems to feed on fear, the kind of fear that's experienced when a person is shunned or isolated from the community. Studies on heart patients reveal that those who felt isolated from their family, their community, and especially their spirituality, were more susceptible to disease. Studies on longevity show that those who live longer have a strong spiritual belief and a sense of belonging to a community. The capacity to heal collectively is one of the powerful benefits that's available when you raise your energy level and connect to the faces of intention.

5. **The most important treatment any healer can offer is hope for the health and well-being of those who suffer disease or trauma.** Healers do a self-analysis of what's present in their consciousness before they focus on someone in need of healing. The key word here is *hope*. The presence of hope conveyed boils down to faith. I would also call it *knowing*, a knowing that connection to one's Source is a connection to the source of all healing. When we live this way, we always see hope. We know that miracles are always a possibility. Staying in that mind-set, fear and doubt are banished from the landscape. If you give up hope, you change the energy level of your life to vibrate at fear and doubt levels. Yet we know that the all-creating Source of intention knows no fear or doubt.

My favorite quote from Michelangelo is on the value of hope: "The greater danger for most of us is not that our aim is too high and we miss it, but that it is too low and we reach it." Just imagine—the intention of healers and the hopes they have for themselves and others may be even more important than the medicine being offered. The simple thought of dislike toward another impedes the potential for healing. Lack of faith in the power of Spirit to heal plays a deleterious role in the healing process. Any low-energy thoughts you have undermine your ability to heal yourself. All five of these research-backed conclusions lead us to an awareness of the importance of shifting our focus and connecting to the all-healing field of intention and harmonizing with it.

From Thoughts of Sickness to Intentions of Wellness

You're probably familiar with the phrase "And God intended, 'Let there be light!' and there was light," from the Old Testament. If you look in an English-Hebrew dictionary, you'll find that the English translation of the Hebrew can be read as: "And god *intended . . .*" The decision to *create* is the decision to *intend*. To create healing, you can't have thoughts of illness and anticipate your body falling victim to disease. Become aware of the thoughts you have that support the idea of sickness as something to be expected. Begin noticing the frequency of those thoughts. The more they occupy your mental landscape, the more resistance you're creating to realizing your intention.

You know what those thoughts of resistance sound like: *I can't do anything about this arthritis. It's the flu season. I feel okay now, but by the weekend, it will be in my chest and I'll have a fever. We live in a carcinogenic world. Everything is either fattening or filled with chemicals. I feel so tired all the time.* On and on they go. They're like huge barricades blocking the realization of your intention. Notice the thoughts that represent a decision on your part to buy into the illness mentality of the huge profit-making drug companies and a health-care industry that thrives on your fears.

But you're the divine, remember? You're a piece of the universal mind of intention, and you don't have to think in these ways. You can opt to think that you have the ability to raise your energy level, even if all of the advertising around you points to a different conclusion. You can go within and hold an intention that says: *I want to feel good, I intend to feel good, I intend to return to my Source, and I refuse to allow any other thoughts of dis-order or dis-ease in.* This is the beginning. You'll feel empowered by this unique experience. Then in any given moment of not feeling well, choose thoughts of healing and feeling good. In that instant, feeling good takes over, if only for a few seconds.

When you refuse to live in low energy, and you work moment by moment to introduce thoughts that support your intention, you've effectively decided that wellness is your choice and that being a healer is a part of that decision. At this time, wheels of creation are set in motion, and what you've imagined and created in your mind begins to take form in your everyday life.

Give it a shot the next time you're low-energy thinking of any kind. Just note how quickly you can change how you feel by refusing to think thoughts that are out of harmony with your Source of intention. It works for me, and I encourage you to do so as well. I simply will not think any longer that I must be a victim of illness or disability, and I will not spend the precious moments of my life discussing illness. I am a healer. I heal myself by co-creating health with God, and I give this gift to others as well. This is my intention.

Illness Is Not a Punishment

Illness became a component of the human condition when we separated ourselves from the perfect health from which we were intended. Rather than attempting to intellectualize reasons why people get sick and come up with a rationale for understanding illness, I encourage you to think of yourself as having the potential to become a master healer. Try visualizing all of human illness from the perspective of something that the human race has collectively brought upon itself by identifying with the ego rather than staying with the divinity from which we emanated. Out of this collective ego identification, we brought about all that goes with the ego problems—fear, hate, despair, anxiety, depression—all of it. The ego feeds on these emotions because it's insistent on its own identity as a separate entity apart from this God-force that intended us here. In one way or another, virtually every single member of the human race bought into this idea of separation and ego identification. Consequently, illness, disease, sickness, and the need for healing simply come with the territory of being human.

However, you needn't feel stuck there. The power of intention is about returning to the Source of perfection. It's about knowing that the power to heal is all wrapped up in making that divine connection, and that the Source of all life does not punish, offering karmic paybacks through suffering and hardship. You don't have a need for healing because you were bad or ignorant, or as retribution for past-life offenses. You've taken on whatever you're experiencing for whatever lessons you need to learn on this journey, which is being orchestrated by the all-providing intelligence that we're calling intention.

In an eternal universe, you must view yourself and all others in infinite terms. Infinite terms mean that you have an infinite number of opportunities to show up in a material body to co-create anything. As you view the sickness of the mind and body that permeates your own life as well as the rest of humanity, try viewing it as part of the infinite nature of our world. If starvation, pestilence, or disease are a part of the perfection of the universe, then so is your intention to end these things a part of that same perfection. Now decide to stay with that intention—first in your own life, then in the lives of others. Your intention will match up with the intention of the universe, which knows nothing of egos and separation, and all thoughts of illness as punishment and karmic paybacks will cease to exist.

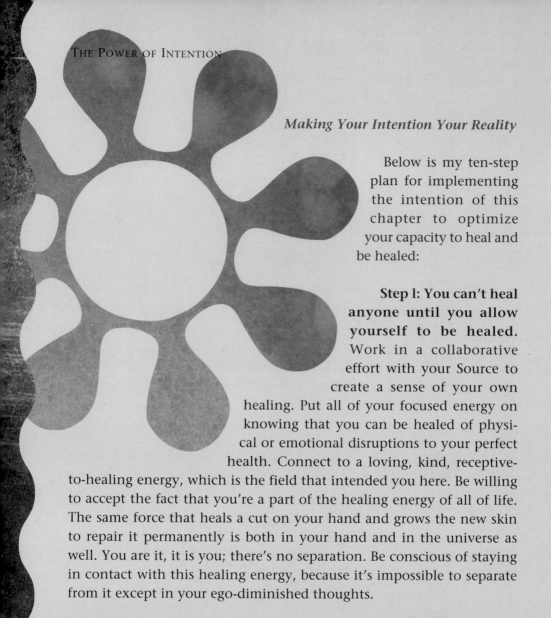

Making Your Intention Your Reality

Below is my ten-step plan for implementing the intention of this chapter to optimize your capacity to heal and be healed:

Step 1: You can't heal anyone until you allow yourself to be healed. Work in a collaborative effort with your Source to create a sense of your own healing. Put all of your focused energy on knowing that you can be healed of physical or emotional disruptions to your perfect health. Connect to a loving, kind, receptive-to-healing energy, which is the field that intended you here. Be willing to accept the fact that you're a part of the healing energy of all of life. The same force that heals a cut on your hand and grows the new skin to repair it permanently is both in your hand and in the universe as well. You are it, it is you; there's no separation. Be conscious of staying in contact with this healing energy, because it's impossible to separate from it except in your ego-diminished thoughts.

Step 2: The healing energy that you're connected to at all times is what you have to give away to others. Offer this energy freely, and keep your ego entirely out of the healing process. Remember how St. Francis responded when asked why he didn't heal himself of his diseases, which would cause his death at the age of 45: "I want everyone to know that it is God who does this healing." St. Francis was healed of ego domination, and he deliberately held on to his infirmities to teach others that it was God's energy working through him that provided the energy for all of his miraculous healings.

Step 3: By raising your energy to a vibrational match with the field of intention, you're strengthening your immune system and increasing the production of well-being enzymes in the brain. A change in personality from being spiteful, pessimistic, angry, sullen, and disagreeable to one of passion, optimism, kindness, joy, and understanding is often the key when witnessing miraculous acts of spontaneous recovery from fatalistic prognostications.

Step 4: Practice surrender! *Let go and let God* is a great theme in the recovery movement. It's also a wonderful reminder in the world of healing. By surrendering, you're able to have reverence for, and commune with, the Source of all healing. Remember that the field of intention doesn't know anything about healing *per se,* because it's spiritual perfection already, and it creates from that perspective. It's ego consciousness that creates the dis-order, dis-harmony, and dis-eases of our world, and it is in returning to that spiritual perfection that harmony of body, mind, and spirit are realized. When this balance or symmetry is restored, we call it healing, but the Source knows nothing of healing because it creates only perfect health. It's to this perfect health that you must surrender.

Step 5: Don't ask to be healed, ask to be restored to that perfection from which you emanated. Here's where you want to hold an intention for yourself and for others in an unbending, nonnegotiable way. Let nothing interfere with the intention you have to heal and be healed. Discard all negativity that you encounter. Refuse to let in any energy that will weaken your body or your resolve. Convey this to others as well. Remember, you're not asking your Source to heal you, because this assumes health is missing from your life. It assumes scarcity, but the Source can only recognize and respond to what it is already, and you too are a component of that Source. Come to the Source as whole and complete, banish all thoughts of illness, and know that by connecting back to this Source—filling yourself with it and offering it to others—you become healing itself.

Step 6: Know that you are adored. Look for reasons to praise and feel good. In the moment in which you're experiencing thoughts that make you feel sick or bad, do your best to change them to thoughts that support your feeling good, and if that seems impossible, then do your very best to say nothing at all. Refuse to talk about disease, and work to activate thoughts that predict recovery, feeling good, and perfect health. Picture yourself as healthy and free of disability. Be on the lookout for the opportunity to literally say to yourself, *I feel good. I intend to attract more of this good feeling, and I intend to give it away to any and all in need of it.*

Step 7: Seek out and cherish the silence. Many people who have suffered with long-term illnesses have been able to return to their Source through the channel of nature and contemplative silence. Spend time in quiet meditation visualizing yourself coupled with the perfectly healthy field of intention. Commune with this Source of all that is good, all that is well, and practice accessing this high spiritual energy, bathing your entire being in this light.

Meditation is always healing for me. When I'm fatigued, a few moments in silence accessing higher, loving, kind vibrations energizes me. When I feel out of sorts, a few moments in quietude making conscious contact with God provides me with all that I need to not only feel good, but to help others do the same. I always remember Herman Melville's timely words: "Silence is the only Voice of our God."

Here's an excerpt from a letter written to me by Darby Hebert, who now lives in Jackson Hole, Wyoming. For more than two decades, she struggled with feeling used as well as watching her own physical condition deteriorate. She opted for nature, silence, and meditation. I repeat her words (with her permission) below:

For a year I lived out of boxes in an empty house. Then, to remove myself from this negative energy field and the scorn of people who were sitting in judgment, I moved 2,000 miles away to Jackson Hole. The magnificence, grandeur, and peace of this sacred, enchanted place began to work its magic immediately. I have lived in silence for almost *two years. Meditation and appreciation have become my way of life. Leaving low energy, and moving into high energy, with your help, has worked miracles. I have moved from hemorrhaging eyes, internal lesions, aseptic meningitis, and severe muscle pain to a health that includes all-day mountain hiking and cross-country skiing. I am slowly getting off of the dangerous drugs used to control the diseases, and I <u>know</u> I can do it. You have shown me the way to being well, and I will forever be grateful. God bless you a thousandfold, Wayne, for following your bliss and helping others to find theirs. I hope there will come a time when I can express my gratitude in person. Until then, I'll see you in the Gap.*

Step 8: To *be* health, you must totally identify with the wholeness that you are. You can stop seeing yourself as a physical body and immerse yourself in the idea of absolute well-being. This can become your new identification card. Here, you breathe only wellness, you think only perfect health, and you detach from appearances of illness in the world. Soon you recognize only perfection in others. You stand firm in your truth, reflecting only thoughts of well-being, and speaking only words of the infinite possibility for healing any and all disease processes. This is your rightful identity of wholeness, and you live it as if you and the Source that creates all are one and the same. This is your ultimate truth, and you can allow this dynamic aura of wholeness to saturate and animate your every thought until it is all that you have to give away. This is how you heal, from that inner knowing and trust of your wholeness.

Step 9: Allow health to stream into your life. Become conscious of resistance, which interferes with the natural flow of healthy energy to you. This resistance is in the form of your thoughts. Any thought that's out of sync with the seven faces of intention is a resistant thought. Any thought that says that *it's impossible to heal* is a resistant thought. Any thought of doubt or fear is a resistant thought. When you observe these thoughts, note them carefully, and then deliberately activate thoughts that are in energetic, vibrational balance with the all-providing Source of intention.

Step 10: Stay immersed in a state of gratitude. Be grateful for every breath you take . . . for all of your internal organs that work together in harmony . . . for the wholeness that is your body . . . for the blood streaming through your veins . . . for your brain that allows you to process these words and the eyes that allow you to read them. Look in the mirror at least once every day and give thanks for that heart that continues to beat and the invisible force on which those heartbeats depend. Stay in gratitude. This is the surest way to keep the connecting link to perfect health clean and pure.

❊ ❊ ❊

One of the messages of Jesus of Nazareth is apropos of all that I've presented in this chapter on having a healing intention:

If you bring forth what is inside you,
what you bring forth will save you.
If you don't bring forth what is inside you,
what you don't bring forth will destroy you.

What is inside you is the power of intention. No microscope will reveal it. You can find the command center with x-ray technology, but the *commander* in the command center remains impervious to our sophisticated probing instruments. *You are that commander*. You must allow yourself to be in vibrational harmony with the greatest commander of all and bring it forth to serve you, rather than allowing yourself to be in a state of disrepair.

It Is My Intention to: Appreciate and Express the Genius That I Am

"Everyone is born a genius, but the process of living de-geniuses them."

— Buckminster Fuller

Consider that all human beings have within themselves the same essence of consciousness, and that the process of creativity and genius are attributes of human consciousness. Therefore, genius is a potential that lives within you and every other human being. You have many moments of genius in your lifetime. These are the times when you have a uniquely brilliant idea and implement it even if only you are aware of how fantastic it is. Perhaps you created something absolutely astonishing and you even amazed yourself. Then there are the moments when you make exactly the right shot in a round of golf or a tennis match and you realize with immense pleasure what you've just accomplished. You are a genius.

You may never have thought of yourself as a person who has genius residing within. You may have thought that *genius* is a word reserved for the Mozarts, Michelangelos, Einsteins, Madame Curies, Virginia Woolfs, Stephen Hawkings, and others whose lives and accomplishments have been publicized. But keep in mind that they share the same essence of consciousness that you do. They emanated from the same power of intention as you did. They have all shared the same life force animating them as you do. Your genius is in your very existence, awaiting the right circumstances to express itself.

There is no such thing as *luck* or *accidents* in this purposeful universe. Not only is everything connected to everything else, but no one is excluded from the universal Source called intention. And genius, since it's a characteristic of the universal Source, must be universal, which means that it's in no way restricted. It's available to every single human being. It certainly can and does show up differently in every single one of us. The qualities of creativity and genius are within you, awaiting your decision to match up with the power of intention.

Changing Your Energy Level to Access the Genius Within You

In his illuminating book, *Power vs. Force*, David Hawkins wrote: "Genius is by definition a style of consciousness characterized by the ability to access high energy attractor patterns. It is not a personality characteristic. It is not something that a person *has*, nor even something that someone *is*. Those in whom we recognize genius commonly disclaim it. A universal characteristic of genius is humility. The genius has always attributed his insights to some higher influence." Genius is a characteristic of the creative force (the first of the seven faces of intention) that allows all of material creation to come into form. It is an expression of the divine.

No one who's considered a genius—be it Sir Laurence Olivier onstage as Hamlet; Michael Jordan gracefully gliding toward a dunk on the basketball court; Clarence Darrow speaking to a jury; Joan of Arc inspiring a nation; or Mrs. Fuehrer, my eighth-grade teacher making a story come alive in the classroom—can explain where the energy to perform at those levels came from. Sir Laurence Olivier is said to have been distraught after giving one of the greatest stage performances of *Hamlet* ever seen in London. When asked why he was so upset after the thundering ovation from the audience, he replied (I paraphrase), "I know it was my best performance, but I don't know how I did it, where it came from, and if I can ever do it again." Ego and genius are mutually exclusive. Genius is a function of surrendering to the Source or reconnecting to it so dramatically that one's ego is substantially minimized. This is what Dr. Hawkins means by *accessing higher energy patterns.*

Higher energy is the energy of light, which is a way of describing spiritual energy. The seven faces of intention are the ingredients of this spiritual energy. When you shift your thoughts, emotions, and life activities into these realms and deactivate the lower energies of the ego, the God force within you begins to take over. It's so automatic that it travels faster than your thoughts. This is why your thoughts about how you did something are so bewildering. The higher energy level actually transcends thought, moving into vibrational harmony with the Source energy of intention. As you release ego-dominated thoughts (which convince you that you're doing these amazing things and are responsible for these unbelievable accomplishments), you tap in to the power of intention. This is where the genius that you truly are resides.

Many people never get acquainted with this inner world of their personal genius, and think that genius is only measured in intellectual or artistic endeavors. Genius remains in the shadows of their thoughts, unnoticed during their occasional forays inward, and may even be padlocked and chained! If you've been taught to avoid thinking too highly of yourself, and that genius is reserved for a handful of select individuals, you probably resist this idea. You won't recognize your genius aspect if you've been conditioned to believe that you should accept your lot in life, think small, try to fit in with *normal* groups of people, and not aim too high in order to avoid disappointment.

I'd like you to consider what may seem like a radical idea: *Genius can show up in as many ways as there are human beings.* Anything in any field that anyone has ever accomplished is shared by you. You're connected to every being that has ever lived or ever will live, and you share the exact same energy of intention that flowed through Archimedes, Leonardo da Vinci, the Virgin Mother, and Jonas Salk. You can access this energy. At the deepest level, all things and all people are composed of vibrations organized into fields that permeate the entire structure of the universe. You share these vibrations, and you are in this field.

The starting point is knowing and understanding that this level of creativity and functioning called *genius* resides within you. Then begin to deconstruct doubts about your role here. Make a commitment to raise your energy levels to vibrate harmoniously with the field of intention despite attempts by your ego and others' egos to dissuade you.

Dr. Valerie Hunt in *Infinite Mind: Science of Human Vibrations of Consciousness,* reminds us: "Lower vibrations exist with material reality, higher ones with mystical reality, and a full vibrational spectrum with expanded reality." To fulfill this intention of appreciating and expressing the genius that you are, you're going to have to strive for that *full vibrational spectrum.* This is the idea of expansion, which is crucial to knowing your true potential. It's what you signed up for when you left the formless world of spiritual intention. You co-created a body and a life to express that inner genius, which you may have locked away in an almost inaccessible chamber.

252

Expanding Your Reality

The universal force that created you is always expanding, and your objective is to achieve harmony with that Source and thereby regain the power of intention. So what is it that keeps you from expanding to the mystical reality and full vibrational spectrum that Dr. Hunt refers to? I like this answer from William James, who is often referred to as the father of modern psychology: "Genius means little more than the faculty of perceiving in an unhabitual way." To expand your reality to match the expansiveness of the all-creating field of intention, you have to peel away your old habits of thought. These habits have pigeonholed you to a point where you allow labels to be attached to you. These labels define you in many ways.

Most of the labels are from other people who need to describe what you are not, because they feel safer predicting what can't be than what can be: *She's never been very artistic. He's a tad clumsy, so he won't be an athlete. Mathematics was never her strong suit. He's a bit shy, so he won't be good dealing with the public.* You've heard these pronouncements for so long that you believe them. They've become a habitual way of thinking about your abilities and potentialities. As William James suggested, *genius means making a shift in your thinking* so that you let go of those habits and open yourself to possibilities of greatness.

I've heard the stereotype about writers and speakers since I was a young man. If you're a writer, you're introverted, and writers don't make dynamic speakers. I chose to shift from that programmed and stereotypical way of thinking and decided that I could excel at anything I affirmed and intended for myself. I chose to believe that when I came into this world of boundaries and form, there were no restrictions on me. I was intended here from an expansive energy field that knows nothing of limits or labels. I decided that I'd be both an introverted writer *and* a dynamic extroverted speaker. Similarly, I've broken through many socially imposed habitual ways of labeling people. I can be a genius in any area if, according to the father of modern psychology, I learn to *perceive in unhabitual ways.* I can sing tender songs, write sentimental poetry, create exquisite paintings, and at the same time in the same body, excel as

253

an athlete in any sport, build a fine piece of furniture, repair my automobile, wrestle with my children, and surf in the ocean.

Pay attention to yourself in ways that allow the expansion of the infinite possibilities that you're potentially capable of. You may decide, as I have, that repairing an automobile and surfing in the ocean aren't what you enjoy doing. So leave those activities to others, and use your genius to engage in pursuits that please and attract you. Expand your reality to the point where you pursue what you love doing and excel at it. Involve yourself in the high-energy levels of trust, optimism, appreciation, reverence, joy, and love. That means love for what you're doing, love for yourself, and love for your genius, which allows you to immerse yourself in any activity and enjoy the process of experiencing it fully.

Trusting your insights. The process of appreciating your genius involves trusting those inner flashes of creative insight that are worthy of expression. The song you're composing in your head. The weird storyline that you keep dreaming about that would make a fabulous movie. The crazy idea about combining peas and carrots in a seed and growing *parrot* vegetables. The new car design you've always contemplated. The fashion idea that would become the next fad. The toy that every child will yearn to have. The musical extravaganza you've seen in your mind. These ideas and thousands like them are the creative genius within you at work. These ideas in your imagination are *distributions of God* taking place. They're not from your ego, which squashes them with fear and doubt. Your insights are divinely inspired. Your creative mind is how your higher self vibrates harmoniously with the field of intention, which is always creating.

Banishing doubt regarding those brilliant flashes of insight will allow you to express these ideas and begin the process of acting on them. Having the thoughts and squelching them because you think they aren't good enough or they don't merit any action is denying the connection that you have to the power of intention. You have a connecting link to intention, but you're allowing it to be weakened by living at ordinary levels of ego consciousness. Remember that you're a piece of God, and the inner spark of genius in your imagination—that intuitive inner voice—is really God reminding you of your uniqueness. You're having these inner insights because this is precisely how you stay connected to the all-creating genius that intended you here. As I've said earlier, trusting in yourself is trusting in the wisdom that created you.

Never, ever regard any creative thought that you're having as anything other than a worthy potential expression of your inner genius. The only caveat here is that these thoughts must be in vibrational harmony with the seven faces of intention. Inner thoughts of hatred, anger, fear, despair, and destruction simply don't foster creative insights. The low-energy, ego-dominated thoughts must be replaced and converted to the power of intention. Your creative impulses are real, they're vital, they're worthy, and they crave expression. The fact that you can conceive of them is proof of this. Your thoughts are real. They're pure energy, and they're telling you to pay attention and get that connecting link to the power of intention polished through living at different levels than you've accepted as normal or ordinary. At these levels, everyone is a genius.

Appreciating the genius in others. Every person you interact with should feel the inner glow that comes from being appreciated, particularly for the ways in which they express their creativity. A core theme, which strengthens the flow of the power of intention, is wanting for others as much as you intend for yourself. Appreciating the genius in others attracts high levels of competent energy to you. By seeing and celebrating the creative genius, you open a channel within yourself for receiving the creative energy from the field of intention.

My 15-year-old son, Sands, has a unique way of riding a surfboard unlike everyone around him in the ocean. I encourage him to do what comes naturally and express it with pride. He also created a unique language of communication, similar to my brother David, which others in the family and close personal acquaintances emulate. Creating a language that others use is the work of a genius! I tell Sands this, and my brother, too, whose unique language I've spoken for over half a century. My daughter Skye has a distinctive one-of-a-kind singing voice that I love. I tell her so, and point out that it's an expression of her genius.

All of my children, and yours as well (including the child within you) have unparalleled characteristics in many of the ways they express themselves. From the way that they dress, to the little tattoo, to their signature, to their mannerisms, to their unmatched personality quirks, you can appreciate their genius. Notice and appreciate *your* genius, too. When you're just like everybody else, you've nothing to offer other than your conformity.

Take the road of *seeing the face of God in everyone* you encounter. Look for something to appreciate in others, and be willing to communicate it to them and anyone who's willing to listen. When you see this quality in others, you'll soon begin to realize that this potential is available to all of humanity. This obviously includes you. Recognizing genius in yourself is an integral part of the dynamic. As Dr. Hawkins tells us in *Power vs. Force:* "Until one acknowledges the genius within oneself, one will have great difficulty recognizing it in others."

Genius and simplicity. Begin to realize the intention of this chapter by uncomplicating your life as much as possible. Genius thrives in a contemplative environment, where every minute isn't filled with obligations or hoards of people offering advice and insisting on your constant participation in ordinary, mundane endeavors. The genius in you isn't seeking confirmation from others, but quiet space for its ideas to blossom. Genius isn't as much about achieving a high IQ on a standardized test, as it is the exceptionally high level of plain old savvy in any given field of human endeavor. Genius-at-work may be the person who finds tinkering with an electronic gadget for hours on end exhilarating, and also can be entranced by puttering in the garden or observing the communication patterns between bats on a starry night. An uncomplicated life with fewer intrusions tolerated, in a simple setting, allows your creative genius to surface and express itself. The simplicity establishes a link to the power of intention, and your genius will flourish.

Making Your Intention Your Reality

Below is my ten-step program for putting this intention to appreciate and express the *genius* within you to work.

Step 1: Declare yourself to be a genius! This shouldn't be a public pronouncement, but a statement of intention between you and your Creator. Remind yourself that you're one of the masterpieces that emanated from the universal field of intention. You don't have to prove that you're a genius, nor do you need to compare any of your accomplishments to those of others. You have a unique gift to offer this world, and you are unique in the entire history of creation.

Step 2: Make a decision to listen more carefully to your inner insights, no matter how small or insignificant you may have previously judged them to be. These thoughts, which you may have viewed as silly or unworthy of attention, are your private connection to the field of intention. Thoughts that seem to persist, particularly if they relate to new activities and adventures, aren't in your mind accidentally. Those tenacious thoughts that don't go away should be viewed by you as intention talking to you, saying, *You signed up to express your unique brilliance, so why do you keep ignoring the genius in favor of settling for less?*

Step 3: Take constructive action toward implementing your inner intuitive inclinations. Any step in the direction of expressing your creative impulses is a step in the direction of actualizing the genius that resides within you—for example, writing and submitting a book outline, regardless of how you may have doubted yourself up until now; recording a CD of yourself reading poetry or singing the songs you've written; purchasing an easel and art paraphernalia and spending an afternoon painting; or visiting an expert in the field that interests you.

During a recent photo shoot, a photographer told me that years earlier he'd arranged a meeting with a world-renowned photographer, and that visit sent him on the road to doing the work that he loved. To me, this man was a genius. Photography had always intrigued him. The early prodding in his life that he acted on allowed him to *appreciate the genius* within him, then one meeting with one man taught him to trust in that *intrigue* and to use it as a means for communicating his genius to the entire world.

Step 4: Know that any and all thoughts that you have regarding your own skills, interests, and inclinations are valid. To reinforce the validity of your thoughts, *keep them private.* Tell yourself that they're between you and God. If you keep them in the spiritual domain, you don't have to introduce them to your ego or expose them to the egos of those around you. This means that you'll never have to compromise them by explaining and defending them to others.

Step 5: Remind yourself that aligning with spiritual energy is how you will find and convey the genius within you. In *Power vs. Force,* David Hawkins concluded: "From our studies it appears that the alignment of one's goals and values with high energy attractors is more closely associated with genius than anything else." This is completely in line with understanding and implementing the power of intention. Shift your energy to harmonize vibrationally with the energy of Source. Be an appreciator of life, and refuse to have thoughts of hatred, anxiety, anger, and judgment. Trust yourself as a piece of God and your genius will flourish.

Step 6: Practice radical humility. Take no credit for your talents, intellectual abilities, aptitudes, or proficiencies. Be in a state of awe and bewilderment. Even as I sit here with my pen in my hand, observing how words appear before me, I'm in a state of bewilderment. Where do these words come from? How does my hand know how to translate my invisible thoughts into decipherable words, sentences, and paragraphs? Where do the thoughts come from that precede the words? Is this really Wayne Dyer writing, or am I watching Wayne Dyer put these words on the paper? Is God writing this book through me? Was I intended to be this messenger before I showed up here as a baby on the 10th of May, 1940? Will these words live beyond my lifetime? I'm bewildered by it all. I'm humble in my inability to know where any of my accomplishments come from. Practice radical humility, and give credit everywhere except to your ego.

Step 7: Remove resistance to actualizing your genius. Resistance always shows up in the form of your thoughts. Watch for thoughts that convey your inability to think of yourself in genius terms . . . thoughts of doubt about your abilities . . . or thoughts that reinforce what you've been taught about a lack of talent or lack of aptitude. All of these kinds of thoughts are a misalignment and don't allow you to be in vibrational harmony with the universal all-creating field of intention. Your Source knows that you're a genius. Any thought you have that challenges this notion is resistance, which will inhibit you from realizing your intention.

Step 8: Look for the genius in others. Pay attention to the greatness you observe in as many people as possible, and if you don't see it at first, then spend some mental energy looking for it. The more you're inclined to think in genius terms, the more natural it becomes for you to apply the same standards to yourself. Tell others about their genius. Be as complimentary and authentic as you can. In doing so, you'll radiate loving, kind, abundant, creative energy. In a universe that operates on energy and attraction, you'll find these same qualities returning to you.

Step 9: Simplify your life. Take the complications, rules, *shoulds*, *musts*, *have tos*, and so on out of your life. By uncomplicating your life and removing the trivial pursuits that occupy so much of it, you open a channel for the genius within you to emerge. One of the most effective techniques for simplifying life is to take time each day to spend 20 or so minutes in silence and meditation. The more conscious contact you make with your Source, the more you come to appreciate your own highest self. And it's from this highest self that your own genius will be manifested.

Step 10: Remain humble while staying in a state of gratitude. This genius that you are has nothing at all to do with your ego-mind. Be ever so grateful to the Source of intention for providing you with the life force to express the genius that resides within you. Those who attribute their inspiration and success to their ego soon lose this capacity, or they allow the approval and attention of others to destroy them. Remain humble and grateful, and more of your genius will surface as you remain in a constant state of expansion. Gratitude is a sacred space where you *allow* and *know* that a force greater than your ego is always at work and always available.

❋ ❋ ❋

The man who inspires me every day, Ralph Waldo Emerson, whose photograph looks back at me as I write, put it this way: "To believe your own thoughts, to believe that what is true for you in your private heart is true for all men—that is genius."

Take this awareness and apply it in your life. Another genius tells us just how to do this. Thomas Edison said, "Genius is one percent inspiration, and ninety-nine percent perspiration." Are you sweating yet?

❋ ❋ ❋ ❋ ❋

PART III

The Connection

"Man is in the process of changing, to forms that are not of this world; grows he in time to the formless, a plane on the cycle above. Know ye, ye must become formless before ye are one with the light."

— adapted from
The Emerald Tablets of Thoth

A Portrait of a Person Connected to the Field of Intention

"Self-actualizing people must be what they can be."

— Abraham Maslow

A person who lives in a state of unity with the Source of all life doesn't look any different from ordinary folks. These people don't wear a halo or dress in special garments that announce their godlike qualities. But when you notice that they go through life as the *lucky ones* who seem to get all the breaks, and when you begin to talk to them, you realize how distinctive they are compared to people living at ordinary levels of awareness. Spend a few moments in conversation with these people who are connected to the power of intention and you see how unique they are.

These people, whom I call *connectors* to signify their harmonious connection with the field of intention, are individuals who have made themselves available for success. It's impossible to get them to be pessimistic about achieving what they desire in their lives. Rather than using language that indicates that their desires may not materialize, they speak from an inner conviction that communicates their profound and simple knowing that the universal Source supplies everything.

They don't say, *With my luck things won't work out.* Instead, you're much more likely to hear something like, *I intend to create this and I know it will work out.* No matter how you might attempt to dissuade them by pointing out all the reasons why their optimism ought to be curtailed, they seem blissfully blind to reality-check repercussions. It's almost as if they're in a different world, a world in which they can't hear the reasons why things won't work out.

If you engage them in conversation about this idea, they simply say something like, *I refuse to think about what can't happen, because I'll attract exactly what I think about, so I only think about what I know will happen.* It doesn't matter to them what's happened before. They don't relate to the concepts of *failure* or *it's impossible.* They simply, without fanfare, are unaffected by reasons for being pessimistic. They've made themselves available for success, and they know and trust in an invisible force that's all-providing. They're so well connected to the all-providing Source that it's as if they have a natural aura preventing anything from getting through that might weaken their connection to the   creative energy of the power of intention.

Connectors don't place their thoughts on what they don't want, because, as they'll tell you: *The Source of all can only respond with what it is, and what it is, is infinite supply. It can't relate to scarcity, or things not working out, because it's none of these things. If I say to the Source of all things, "It probably won't work out," I'll receive back from it precisely what I sent to it, so I know better than to think anything other than what my Source is.*

To the average person who has fears about the future, this all sounds like mumbo jumbo. They'll tell their connector friend to do a reality check and look realistically at the world they live in. But connectors aren't distracted from their inner knowing. They'll tell you, if you choose to listen, that this is a universe of energy and attraction, and that the reason so many people live lives of fear and scarcity is because they rely on their ego to fulfill their desires. *It's simple, they'll tell you. Just reconnect to your Source, and be like your Source, and your intentions will match up perfectly with the all-providing Source.*

To connectors, it all seems so simple. Keep your thoughts on what you intend to create. Stay consistently matched up with the field of intention, and then watch for the clues that what you're summoning from the all-creative Source is arriving in your life. To a connector, there are simply no accidents. They perceive seemingly insignificant events as being orchestrated in perfect harmony. They believe in synchronicity and aren't surprised when the perfect person for a situation appears, or when someone they've been thinking about calls out of the blue, or when a book arrives unexpectedly in the mail giving them the information they needed, or when the money to finance a project they've been intending mysteriously shows up.

Connectors won't attempt to win you over to their point of view with debates. They know better than to place a lot of energy on arguing or being frustrated, because that attracts argumentation and frustration into their lives. They know what they know, and they aren't seduced into constructing a counterforce of resistance to people who live otherwise. They accept the idea that there are no accidents in a universe that has an invisible force of energy as its Source that continuously creates and provides an infinite supply to all who wish to partake of it. They'll tell you plain and simple if you inquire: *All you have to do to tap in to the power of intention is to be in a perfect match with the Source of everything, and I'm choosing to be as closely aligned to that Source as I can.*

To connectors, everything that shows up in their life is there because the power of intention intended it there. So they're always in a state of gratitude. They feel thankful for everything, even things that might seem to be obstacles. They have the ability and desire to see a temporary illness as a blessing, and they know in their heart that somewhere an opportunity exists in the setback, and that is what they look for in everything that shows up in their life. Through their thanks, they honor all possibilities, rather than asking their Source for something, because that seems to give power to what's missing. They commune with the Source in a state of reverent gratitude for all that's present in their lives, *knowing* that this empowers their intention to manifest precisely what they need.

Connectors describe themselves as living in a state of appreciation and bewilderment. You're unlikely to hear them complain about anything. They aren't faultfinders. If it rains, they enjoy it, knowing that they won't get where they want to go if they only travel on sunny days. This is how they react to all of nature, with appreciative harmony. The snow, the wind, the sun, and the sounds of nature are all reminders to connectors that they're a part of the natural world. The air—regardless of its temperature or wind velocity—is the revered air that is the breath of life.

Connectors appreciate the world and everything in it. The same connection that they experience with nature they feel toward all beings, including those who lived before and those who have yet to arrive. They have a consciousness of the oneness, and therefore they make no distinctions such as *them* or *those other people*. To a connector, it is all *we*. If you could observe their inner world, you'd discover that they're hurt by pain inflicted on others. They don't have the concept of enemies, since they know that all of us emanate from the same divine Source. They enjoy the differences in the appearance and customs of others rather than disliking, criticizing, or feeling threatened by them. Their connection to others is of a spiritual nature, but they don't separate themselves spiritually from anyone regardless of where they might live or how different their appearances or customs may be from their own. In their heart, connectors feel an affinity to all of life, as well as to the Source of all of life.

It's because of this connecting link that connectors are so adept at attracting into their lives the cooperation and assistance of others in fulfilling their own intentions. The very fact of feeling connected means that in the connectors' minds, there's no one on this planet who they're not joined up with in a spiritual sense. Consequently, living in the field of intention, the entire system of life in the universe is available to access anything their attention is on, because they're already connected to this life-giving energy system and all of its creations. They appreciate this spiritual connection, and expend no energy on depreciating or criticizing it. They never feel separated from the assistance that this entire life-giving system offers.

Therefore, connectors aren't surprised when synchronicity or coincidence brings them the fruits of their intentions. They know in their hearts that those seemingly miraculous happenings were brought into their immediate life space because they were already connected to them. Ask connectors about it and they'll tell you, *Of course, it's the law of attraction at work. Stay tuned vibrationally to the Source of all life that intended you, and everyone else here and all of the powers of that field of intention will cooperate with you to bring into your life what you desire.* They know that this is how the universe works. Others may insist that connectors are just plain lucky, but the people who enjoy the power of intention know otherwise. They know that they can negotiate the presence of anything they place their attention on as long as they stay consistent with the seven faces of intention.

Connectors don't brag about their good fortune, but are in a perpetual state of gratitude and radical humility. They understand how the universe works, and they stay blissfully in tune with it, rather than challenging or finding fault with it. Ask them about this and they'll tell you that we're part of a dynamic energy system. *Energy that moves faster,* they explain, *dissolves and nullifies slower-moving energy.* These people choose to be in harmony with the invisible spiritual energy. They've trained their thoughts to move at the levels of the higher vibrations, and consequently they're able to deflect lower/slower vibrations.

Connectors have an uplifting effect when they come into contact with people who are living in lower energy levels. Their peacefulness causes others to feel calm and assured, and they radiate an energy of serenity and peace. They're not interested in winning arguments or accumulating allies. Rather than trying to persuade you to think like they do, they're convincing through the energy they exude. People feel loved by connectors, because they're merged with the Source of all life, which is love.

Connectors tell you without hesitation that they choose to feel good regardless of what's going on around them or how others might judge them. They know that feeling bad is a choice, and that it isn't useful for correcting unpleasant situations in the world. So they use their emotions as a guidance system to determine how attuned they are to the power of intention. If they feel bad in any way, they use this as an indicator that it's time to change their energy level so that it matches up with the peaceful, loving energy of the Source. They'll repeat to themselves: *I want to feel good,* and they'll bring their thoughts into harmony with this desire.

If the world is at war, they still opt to feel good. If the economy takes a nosedive, they still want to feel good. If crime rates go up or hurricanes rage somewhere on the planet, they still choose to feel good. If you ask them why they don't feel bad when so many bad things are happening in the world, they'll smile and remind you that *the world of spirit from which all is intended works in peace, love, harmony, kindness, and abundance, and that is where I choose to reside within myself. My feeling bad will only ensure that I attract more of feeling bad into my life.*

Connectors simply don't allow their well-being to be contingent on anything external to themselves—not the weather, not the wars some-place on the globe, not the political landscape, not the economy, and certainly not anyone else's decision to be low energy. They work with the field of intention, emulating what they know is the creative Source of all.

Connectors are always in touch with their infinite nature. Death is not something that they fear, and they'll tell you, if you ask, that they were never truly born nor will they ever die. They see death as taking off a garment or moving from one room into another—merely a transition. They point to the invisible energy that intends everything into existence and see this as their true self. Because connectors always feel aligned to everyone and everything in the universe, they don't experience the feeling of being separate from anyone else or from what they'd like to attract into their lives. Their connection is invisible and nonmaterial, but it's never doubted. Consequently, they rely on this inner, invisible spiritual energy that permeates all things. They live in harmony with Spirit, never seeing themselves as separate. This awareness is key to their seeing the power of intention at work on a daily basis.

You simply can't convince connectors that what they're intending won't materialize, because they trust in their connection to Source energy so strongly. They'll invite you to choose which possibility you're going to identify with, and then encourage you to live as if it had already occurred. If you can't do it, and are stuck in worry, doubt, and fear, they'll wish you well, but they'll continue what they call *thinking from the end*. They can see what it is they intend to manifest into their lives as if it already had materialized, and for them, because it's so real in their thoughts, it's their reality. They'll tell you forthrightly: *My thoughts, when harmonized with the field of intention, are God's thoughts, and this is how I choose to think.* You'll see if you follow them closely enough that they're exceptional at realizing the fruits of their intentions.

Connector people are exceptionally generous. It's as if what they want for themselves is dwarfed only by wanting it even more for other people. They take great pleasure in giving. Others may wonder how they ever accumulate anything for themselves, yet their lives are filled with abundance, and they seem to lack nothing that they desire. *The secret to the power of intention, they'll tell you, is in thinking and acting the same as the all-providing Source from which all originates. It's always providing, and I choose to be a provider, too. The more I give of myself and all that flows to me, the more I see flowing back to me.*

Connectors are highly inspired people. They live more in spirit than in form. Consequently, they're inspired and inspiring, as opposed to informed and filled with information. These are people who have a strong sense of their own destiny. They know why they're here, and they know that they're more than an encapsulated collection of bones, blood, and organs in a skin- and hair-covered body. They're all about living this purpose and choosing to avoid being distracted by the demands of the ego. They have great reverence for the world of Spirit, and by communing with this Source, they stay inspired.

Their level of energy is exceptionally high. It's an energy that defines them as connectors. It's the energy of the Source, a fast vibrational frequency that brings love to the presence of hatred and converts that hatred to love. They bring a peaceful countenance to the presence of chaos and disharmony, and convert the lower energies to the higher energy of peace. When you're around those who dwell in the field of intention, you'll feel energized, cleansed, healthier, and inspired. They have a noticeable absence of judgment toward others, and they aren't immobilized by the thoughts or actions of others. They often get labeled as aloof and distant because they don't gravitate toward small talk and gossip. They'll tell you that it is the Spirit that gives life, and that everyone on this planet has this Spirit within them as an all-powerful force for good. They believe it, they live it, and they inspire others.

They'll even go so far as to tell you that imbalances in the earth such as earthquakes, volcanic eruptions, and extreme weather patterns are the result of a collective imbalance in human consciousness. They'll remind you that our bodies are made up of the same materials as the earth, that the fluid that comprises 98 percent of our blood was once ocean water, and that the minerals in our bones were components of the finite supply of minerals in the earth. They view themselves as one with the planet, and feel a responsibility to stay in balanced harmony with the field of intention to help to stabilize and harmonize the forces of the universe that can get out of balance when we live from excessive ego. They'll tell you that all thoughts, feelings, and emotions are vibrations, and that the frequency of these vibrations can create disturbances—not only in ourselves, but in everything that's made of the same materials.

Connectors will encourage you to stay in vibrational harmony with Source out of a sense of responsibility to the entire planet, and they regard this as a vital function to emulate. This isn't something they think about and discuss from a purely intellectual perspective; it's what they feel deeply within themselves and live passionately every day.

As you observe these connectors, you'll note that they don't dwell on illness and disease. They move through their life as if their body is in perfect health. They actually think and feel that any current disease pattern has never been present, and they believe that they're already healed. They believe that they attract the new outcome, because they know that there are many possible outcomes for any given condition, even for a condition that may seem to others to be impossible to overcome. They'll tell you that the possibilities for healing outcomes are here and now, and the course that an illness will take is a matter of their own perspective. Just as they believe that external turbulent systems become peaceful in the presence of our peace, they see this as a possibility for internal turbulence. Ask them about their healing capabilities and they'll say, *I'm already healed, and I think and feel from only this perspective.*

You'll often see your illnesses and physical complaints disappear when you're in the presence of exceptionally high-energy connectors. Why? Because their high spiritual energy nullifies and eradicates the lower energies of illness. Just as being in the presence of connectors makes you feel better because they exude and radiate joyful appreciative energy, so too will your body heal by being in this kind of energy field.

Connectors are aware of the need to avoid low energy. They'll quietly retreat from loud, bellicose, opinionated people, sending them a silent blessing and unobtrusively moving along. They don't spend time watching violent TV shows or reading accounts of atrocities and war statistics. They might appear docile or uninteresting to people who wallow in the horrors being discussed and broadcast. Since connectors have no need to win, to be right, or to dominate others, their power is the fact that they uplift others with their presence. They communicate their views by being in harmony with the creative energy of the Source. They're never offended, because their ego isn't involved in their opinions.

273

Connectors live their lives matched up vibrationally to the field of intention. To them, everything is energy. They know that being hostile, hateful, or even angry toward people who believe in and support low-energy activities, which involve violence in any form, will only contribute to that kind of debilitating activity in the world.

The connectors live through higher/faster energy that allows them to access their intuitive powers readily. They have an inner knowing about what's coming. If you ask them about it, they'll tell you, *I can't explain it, but I just know it because I feel it inside.* Consequently, they're seldom confounded when the events they anticipate and intend to create . . . manifest. Rather than being surprised, they actually expect things to work out. By staying so connected to Source energy, they're able to activate their intuition and have insight into what is possible and how to go about achieving it. Their inner knowing allows them to be infinitely patient, and they're never dissatisfied with the speed or the manner in which their intentions are manifesting.

Connectors frequently mirror the seven faces of intention written about throughout the pages of this book. You'll see people who are extraordinarily creative, who have no need to fit in or to do things the way others expect them to. They apply their unique individuality to tasks, and they'll tell you that they can create anything that they place their attention and imagination on.

Connectors are exceptionally kind and loving people. They know that harmonizing with Source energy is replicating the kindness from which they originated. Yet it's not an effort for connectors to be kind. They're always grateful for what comes to them, and they know that kindness toward all of life and our planet is how to display gratitude. By being kind, others want to return the favor and become allies in helping them achieve their intentions. They associate with an unlimited number of people, all of whom are full of love, kindness, and generosity—assisting each other in fulfilling their desires.

You'll also notice how connectors see the beauty in our world. They always find something to appreciate. They can get lost in the beauty of a starry night or a frog on a lily pad. They see beauty in children, and they find a natural radiance and splendor in the aged. They have no desire to judge anyone in low-energy negative terms, and they know that the all-creating Source brings only beauty into material form and so it is always available.

Connectors never know enough! They're inquisitive about life, and they're attracted to every manner of activity. They find something to enjoy in all fields of human and creative endeavors, and are always expanding their own horizons. This openness to everything and all possibilities, and this quality of always expanding, characterizes their proficiency at manifesting their desires. They never say *no* to the universe. Whatever life sends them, they say, *Thank you. What can I learn, and how can I grow from what I'm receiving?* They refuse to judge anyone or anything that the Source offers them, and this always-expanding attitude is what ultimately matches them up with Source energy and opens up their life to receiving all that the Source is willing to provide. They're an open door that's never closed to possibilities. This makes them totally receptive to the abundance that's always ceaselessly flowing.

These attitudes that you see in connector people are precisely the reason that these folks seem so lucky in life. When you're around them, you feel energized, purposeful, inspired, and unified. You're seeing people whom you want to hang around with because they energize you, and this brings you a feeling of empowerment. When you feel empowered and energized, you step into the flow of abundant Source energy yourself, and you inadvertently invite others to do the same. The connection isn't just to Source energy, it's to everyone else and everything in the universe. Connectors are aligned with the entire cosmos and every particle within the cosmos. This connection makes the infinite power of intention possible and available.

These highly realized people think *from the end,* experiencing what they wish to intend before it shows up in material form. They use their feelings as a gauge to determine if they're synchronized with the power of intention. If they feel good, they know that they're in vibrational harmony with Source. If they feel bad, they use this indicator to adjust to higher energy levels. And finally, they act on these thoughts of intention and good feelings as if all that they desired were already here. If you ask them what you can do to make your desires come true, they'll unhesitatingly advise you to *change the way you look at things, and the things you look at will change.*

I urge you to replicate their inner world, and rejoice in the infinitely magnificent power of intention.

It works—I guarantee it!

❋❋❋❋❋

Acknowledgments

I would like to acknowledge Joanna Pyle, who has been my personal editor for two decades. You, Joanna, make my ideas and my disjointed stream-of-consciousness writing into a cogent format called a book. I couldn't do it without you, and I'm deeply grateful for your loving presence in my life.

To my personal manager, Maya Labos, for almost a quarter of a century you've been there for me, and you've never once said, "That's not my job." Other writers and speakers have 25 assistants every year; I've had only *one* for 25 years. Thank you, thank you, thank you!

For my publisher and my close personal friend, Reid Tracy, at Hay House, you've believed in this project from the very beginning, and you were willing to do what it took to make it all happen. Thanks, friend. I love and respect you and your courage.

I'd also like to recognize the teachings of Abraham, as brought to us through Esther and Jerry Hicks.

And finally, to Ellen Beth Goldhar, your loving inspiration guided me throughout the writing of this book. Thank you for your spirited suggestions and critical analysis of these ideas on intention as a synonym for the loving Source from which we all emanate and to which we all aspire to reconnect.

About the Author

Dr. Wayne W. Dyer is an internationally renowned author and speaker in the field of self-development. He's the author of more than 30 books, has created many audio programs and videos, and has appeared on thousands of television and radio shows. His books *Manifest Your Destiny*, *Wisdom of the Ages*, *There's a Spiritual Solution to Every Problem*, and *The New York Times* bestsellers *10 Secrets for Success and Inner Peace*, *The Power of Intention*, *Inspiration*, *Change Your Thoughts— Change Your Life*, and *Excuses Begone!* have all been featured as National Public Television specials.

Wayne holds a doctorate in educational counseling from Wayne State University and was an associate professor at St. John's University in New York.

Website: **www.DrWayneDyer.com**

✸✸✸✸✸

Hay House Titles of Related Interest

Notes

Notes

Notes

Notes

Notes

Notes

Notes

Notes

Notes

Notes

Notes

Notes

Notes

Notes

Notes

Notes

We hope you enjoyed this Hay House Lifestyles book. If you'd like to receive our online catalog featuring additional information on Hay House books and products, or if you'd like to find out more about the Hay Foundation, please contact:

Hay House, Inc.
P.O. Box 5100
Carlsbad, CA 92018-5100

(760) 431-7695 or (800) 654-5126
(760) 431-6948 (fax) or (800) 650-5115 (fax)
www.hayhouse.com® • www.hayfoundation.org

✦ ✦ ✦

Published and distributed in Australia by:
Hay House Australia Pty. Ltd., 18/36 Ralph St., Alexandria NSW 2015
Phone: 612-9669-4299 • *Fax:* 612-9669-4144 • www.hayhouse.com.au

Published and distributed in the United Kingdom by:
Hay House UK, Ltd., 292B Kensal Rd., London W10 5BE
Phone: 44-20-8962-1230 • *Fax:* 44-20-8962-1239 • www.hayhouse.co.uk

Published and distributed in the Republic of South Africa by:
Hay House SA (Pty), Ltd., P.O. Box 990, Witkoppen 2068 • *Phone/Fax:*
27-11-467-8904 • info@hayhouse.co.za • www.hayhouse.co.za

Published in India by:
Hay House Publishers India, Muskaan Complex, Plot No. 3, B-2,
Vasant Kunj, New Delhi 110 070 • *Phone:* 91-11-4176-1620
Fax: 91-11-4176-1630 • www.hayhouse.co.in

Distributed in Canada by:
Raincoast, 9050 Shaughnessy St., Vancouver, B.C. V6P 6E5
Phone: (604) 323-7100 • *Fax:* (604) 323-2600 • www.raincoast.com

✦ ✦ ✦

Take Your Soul on a Vacation

Visit **www.HealYourLife.com**® to regroup, recharge, and reconnect with your own magnificence. Featuring blogs, mind-body-spirit news, and life-changing wisdom from Louise Hay and friends.

Visit **www.HealYourLife.com** today!